# A Java™ Programming Introductory and Intermediate Training Course

# A Java™ Programming Introductory and Intermediate Training Course

By

**Dr. Stephen Blaha**
**Janus Associates Inc.**

# ABOUT THE COURSE

This course provides a detailed introduction to the Java language together with numerous intermediate Java topics. The course has been given to thousands of students at some of the largest software and hardware companies in the World. It was adopted as the standard Java course by seven U. S. government agencies as well as being taught at Wall Street firms and state government agencies. It has been refined to provide a clear, practical introduction to Java. It contains numerous examples and hands-on exercises. The course was given in five-day sessions and typically cost several thousand dollars per student to attend.

# CONTENTS

# Course Description

## SUMMARY OF COURSE

Java programming is an exciting new approach to creating multi-media Web pages for the Internet. Java enables you to create World Wide Web pages with color graphics, audio playback, and eventually video presentations.

This course provides a comprehensive introduction to Java programming designed for both the novice and experienced programmer. It is a completely self-contained course covering the following topics: basic Internet features and World Wide Web pages; elementary Java features; Java classes and objects; methods; compiling and running Java programs; creating Java applets; running Java applets in HTML documents (Web pages); object-oriented design; subclasses (inheritance); interfaces; packages; throwing and catching exceptions; multithreading; class libraries; file and terminal input and output; building pages with graphical (GUI) features such as panels, scrollbars, canvases, menus, buttons, lists and textfields; double buffering for fast graphics display; running audio playback on Web pages; and TCP/IP networking in Java.

This course is a fast-paced course with many hands-on lab exercises to test your progress.

## COURSE OBJECTIVES

After completing this course you will be able to:

- Understand Java programming and its capabilities to create multi-media World Wide Web pages.

- Use all the features of the Java language.

- Write Java applets which can be used in Web Pages.

- Run Java applets in WWW browsers.

- Create standalone Java programs.

# HOW TO GO THROUGH THIS COURSE

Each reader has a different background. This course can be profitably read by a wide range of programmers ranging from beginning programmers to experienced programmers. The best way to read the material is to go through it page by page starting from the beginning.

Skim read as long as the material is easy and familiar from your background. When it starts to get challenging then slow down and go through it carefuly at your pace. It is very helpful to do the lab exercises. Compare your work to the solutions that are provided.

# SOFTWARE REQUIREMENTS

To understand Java you must compile and run the examples in the text and you must do the lab exercises. Doing these exercises will help you understand this language better and will also help you remember the material.

A zip file containing all the example programs in the text and solutions for the exercises is available for free download at the 1stBooks.com website at http:// www.1stBooks.com. Search book authors for "Blaha" and select *A Java Programming Introductory and Intermediate Training Course: JavaExamples.* Register at the site before you download.

To do the compiles and execute the programs you can obtain the Java Development Kit (JDK or SDK) from **java.sun.com** for free. This software is all you need for this course. You can also use Integrated Development Environments (IDE) from a variety of vendors. Visual Café and the Borland Java IDE are popular as is the Sun Java Workbench and IBM's Visual Age IDE.

.

# 1. *The Internet & World Wide Web*

## OBJECTIVES

At the end of this module you should be able to:

- Understand the overall structure of the Internet and World Wide Web.

- Understand some Browser basics.

- Describe the nature of HTML hypertext Web Pages.

- Describe the advantages of Mosaic browsers.

- Describe the features and benefits of browsers supporting Java applets.

# WHAT IS THE INTERNET?

- A worldwide network of computers linked together by telephone lines and other kinds of cabling. Each computer in the Internet is called a **node**.

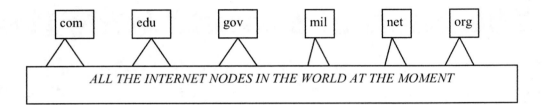

| com | edu | gov | mil | net | org |

*ALL THE INTERNET NODES IN THE WORLD AT THE MOMENT*

- The nodes were arranged in six hierarchies shown above. Many more hierarchies are in the process of being implemented. The base of each hierarchy is called a **domain**.

**Internet Domains**

| | |
|---|---|
| com | commercial sites |
| edu | educational sites |
| gov | governmental sites |
| mil | military sites |
| net | network services |
| org | other organizations |
| etc. | |

- Computers in principle communicate with each other along the hierarchy although shortcuts are often taken.

# INTERNET ADDRESSES

**Dotted Decimal Form** - Used in the specification of a node in a network or the Internet.

Example:  123.45.97.83

**Dotted English-like Names** - used to specify a node in one of the Internet hierarchies.

Example:  mars.ibm.com

- English-like addresses specify a node by its location in the hierarchy with the domain name specified last and the node name specified first.  The path through the hierarchy is specified in right to left format.

- Easier to remember than dotted decimal addresses.

- English-like names are translated to Internet addresses, telephone numbers, etc. by domain name servers.

# THE WORLD WIDE WEB (WWW)

- Initial development in 1990 by Tim Berners-Lee at European Center for Nuclear Research.

- Built around a hypertext language for computers communicating over the Internet. **Hypertext** is text with highlighted words or phrases. If a highlighted area is selected, then another document opens up explaining or giving more detail on the word or phrase. The connection between documents is called a **hyperlink**.

- WWW documents can be formatted and support hyperlinks unlike previous Internet text transfer.

- WWW hypertext documents are written in a markup language called HyperText Markup Language or HTML.

- HTML files consist of text and HTML codes.

# EXAMPLE OF AN HTML SPECIFICATION FILE

<H1>Principal Cities of the United States</H1>

Among the principal cities of Massachusetts are
<A HREF="http://cit.gov/mass/cities/wor.html">Worcester</A> and
<A HREF="http://cit.gov/mass/cities/bost.html">Boston</A>.

## Output WWW Page

Principal Cities of the United States

Among the principal cities of Massachusetts are
<u>Worcester</u> and <u>Boston</u>.

- Note the hyperlinks for Worcester and Boston.

- Titles and other text formatting features can be specified with HTML codes.

- HTML codes are words, acronyms, characters, and phrases placed in < > brackets.

- Hyperlinks are usually selected with a mouse.

- HTML filename specifications usually begin with http:// followed by the English-like name of the computer and the path to the file (directory paths always use / separators).

- HTML filenames often have a .html (or .htm) extension.

# HYPERTEXT TRANSFER PROTOCOL (HTTP)
# and

# UNIFORM RESOURCE LOCATOR (URL)

- HTML files are transferred over the Internet using the HyperText Transfer Protocol (HTTP).

- An HTML filename specification is called a Uniform Resource Locator (URL).

- A URL often specifies a filename. Usually, a filename is specified in the same way as a filename hypertext link in an HTML document. For example, the modelZ.html file in the year1916 subdirectory of models on the cars node under the duryea node which is part of the com domain is specified with:

  http://cars.duryea.com/models/year1916/modelZ.html

- The original WWW hypertext standard consisted of an early version of HTML and HTTP. It supported character-based formatted text without graphics.

# MOSAIC BROWSERS

A browser is a software program that fetches HTML documents over the Internet.

The first browsers were character-based.

In 1992 the Mosaic browser was developed by Marc Andreeson (later of Netscape). It is an HTML browser program

- with full-color graphics.

- with a wide variety of fonts.

- mouse driven.

- windows-based.

- supports hypertext with both underlined items as well as highlighted text in color.

Mosaic made the Internet popular with ordinary individuals.

Mosaic-like browsers download data from a server. Some data such as graphics or audio data must then be presented using other programs on the client computer.

# BROWSERS SUPPORTING JAVA

All major browsers support the Java programming language to create highly interactive multi-media Web pages.

Java-supporting browser features usually include:

- Full HTML support.

- Color graphics.

- Runs multi-media Java programs within browser.

- Supports interaction with user.

- Supports Java programs with such features as file handling, mathematics, and the other features expected in a program created with a modern programming language.

- Multi-threaded Java programs provide faster and better multi-media applications.

- Strong security safeguards to prevent Trojan horses and viruses.

Browsers supporting Java are being created by many major vendors including:

- Netscape - Windows xxx, Windows NT
- Internet Explorer (IE)
- IBM - OS/2 and AIX
- Apple Macintosh
- HPUX
- Other UNIX operating systems

# SOME INTERNET SOURCES OF JAVA INFORMATION

Java Development Kit and other Java information:        http://java.sun.com

Electronic Magazine:        http://www.javaworld.com

Great Java applets:        http://www.gamelan.com

http://weber.u.washington.edu/~jgurney/java/

http://www.javasoft.com/applets/applets.html

# A SAMPLE JAVA APPLET

Generally easy and fun compared to other programming approaches.

**c1_1.html**
```
<applet code="c1_1.class" width = 300 height = 300></applet>
```

**c1_1.java**
```java
import java.awt.*;
import java.applet.*;

public class c1_1 extends Applet
{
        private int begin_x, begin_y;

        public boolean mouseDown(Event e, int x, int y)
        {
                begin_x = x;
                begin_y = y;
                return true;
        }
        public boolean mouseDrag(Event e, int x, int y)
        {
                Graphics g = getGraphics();
                g.drawLine(begin_x, begin_y, x, y);
                begin_x = x;
                begin_y = y;
                return true;
        }
}
```

Compiled Java program

Java applet class definition

Mouse Down Event Handler

Mouse Drag Event Handler

# 2. *Elementary Java Features*

## OBJECTIVES

At the end of this module you should be able to:

- Describe the Java programming environment.

- Describe the basic features of the Java language.

- Create simple Java programs using primitive variables.

- Compile and run Java standalone programs.

# JAVA PROGRAMMING ENVIRONMENT

**Components of the Java Language**

- Primitive data type variables and simple programming features.

    Similar to the C language

- Classes, objects, and methods and object-oriented programming.

    Similar to C++ language plus Smalltalk features

- Class libraries (packages) supporting specific capabilities: buttons, scrollbars, audio, graphics, networking, file handling, and so on.

    Excellent graphical libraries

**Java Development Kit (JDK, also called SDK) Tools**

Sources:     http://java.sun.com              - Sun Microsystems Version

Contents:

- Java compiler - javac

- Java standalone interpreter - java

- Java applet interpreter - "prototype" browser
    Most platforms:          appletviewer
    Earlier OS/2 version:   applet

- Java debugger - jdb

- Java documentation generator - javadoc

- Plus more

We will use the Sun JDK for lab work because it is the most efficient. Also some browser versions "still" have Java bugs.  IDE's such as Visual Café and J++ are also less efficient for  smaller applications such as we will develop. They also produce "weird" machine generated code in some instances that is hard to understand and debug. Also it is better to get your hands dirty and write all the code if you really want to learn the language.

## Course Strategy

Phase 1 – This module. Basic Java features.

Phase 2 – Modules 3 to 6. Object-oriented Java programming.

Phase 3 – Remainder of course. Creating Java programs and applets for Web pages using Class Libraries.

# SIMPLE STANDALONE PROGRAM STRUCTURE

- The simplest standalone program you can write in Java requires one class definition. Within the class definition appears a main method which contains Java code.

- To learn basic Java features in the most efficient way we will consider a "simple" one file Java program.

- Rule: *All Java program files must end in a .java extension.*

- C and C++ programmers beware! Basic Java features are different from corresponding C and C++ features.

**One form of a simple program - myfile.java**

```java
class myclass
{
        public static void main(String args[])
        {

                // We will learn to write code here in this module.


        }
}
```

- Since we haven't considered classes or methods yet we will take a "cookbook" approach and use the above program format in this module. Our focus will be on the code which we can place within the braces { } of the main method.

- Note: the stem of the program filename, the class name myclass, and the name args can be changed to other names. The other parts of the superstructure are required except for comments. The main() function must return void.

- The remainder of this module describes the basic features of Java using examples of code which can be placed inside the main method.

# COMPILING AND RUNNING PROGRAMS

The basic process begins with creating a program like the one on the previous page in a word processor such as notepad or edit on a PC or vi in a UNIX (LINUX) environment. Then you must compile the program to produce a file that contains your program translated to a form that the java interpreter can understand. This type of file has the extension **.class**. You then run the translated program with the java interpreter. When you run the program it runs as a "Standalone" program – meaning that it runs on your computer and does not need to use a browser or Internet access. Many individuals and companies use Java as a standalone programming language – as an alternative to C++, C or Visual Basic programming.

The commands needed to produce a Java standalone program are:

<u>**MS-DOS Prompt Window**</u>
C:\WORK> notepad  myprog.java
C:\WORK> javac  myprog.java
C:\WORK> java  myclass

<u>**UNIX Window**</u>
$ vi  myprog.java
$ javac  myprog.java
$ java  myclass

## Compile Procedure
Use the java compiler, javac, to compile the .java file.

```
javac xxxxxxx.java
```

The compiler generates a file with a name of the form:   **classname.class**

The stem of the compiler output file is the name of the class in the file.

Style rule:  The stem of the program filename is often the same as the name of the class defined in the file. For <u>public</u> classes which we will see in a few modules this is a requirement.

Example:

```
javac c2_1.java
```

produces the file:   c2_1.class    because c2_1 is the name of the <u>class</u> inside the .java file.

## To Run the Program
The Java interpreter will be used to run the program at this stage of the course.  The format is:

```
java classname
```

Example:

```
java c2_1
```

**2.  Elementary Java Features**

We now will examine the basic features of the Java language - feature by feature. If you are familiar with the C language you will see many familiar features.

# COMMENTS

Placing descriptive comments in code is an important part of preogramming. Java has three forms of comments:

- One line comments beginning with // and extending to the end of the line - the preferred form.

- Multi-line comments enclosed in /* */. This form of comment is considered more dangerous than // comments since programmers often mistype the */ which marks the end of the comment. It is just like C language comments.

- Multi-line comments enclosed in /** */. This form of comment should appear above variable declarations. The contents of the comment are placed in HTML documents generated from javadoc - the java documentation tool. This form of commenting enables you to easily generate html help documents for the documentation of code.

Examples:

```
// comment

a = b + c;      //  comment

a = /* comment */ c;

/* comments
   comments
*/

/**  Documenting comments */
int j;
```

# IDENTIFIERS AND UNICODE

Variables and other items in Java code have names called identifiers. Identifiers must satisfy a number of rules:

- Identifiers are created from letters (Unicode contains foreign language letters), underscores, $ signs, and digits. Identifiers can also contain Unicode escape sequences of the form \unnnn (described later). Other escape sequences cannot be present in an identifier.

- An identifier can contain any number of characters.

- An identifier cannot begin with a digit.

- The case of each character in an identifier is significant. Java is a case sensitive language.

- A Java keyword cannot be an identifier.

Unicode contains the standard keyboard characters with other characters in the ASCII character set, and foreign language characters such as é, Ï, Ë, and ç. Unicode is an extension of the ASCII character set.

Examples of valid identifiers:

```
my_var$1      _new_time     $money      éte      Ïnter      çopier
```

**Style Rule: Avoid the use of the underscore character. If an identifier consists of several words run together, then capitalize the first character of the second, third, ... word within the identifier.**

Example:

```
net_present_value      // not preferred.

netPresentValue        // preferred form.
```

**Style Rule: Capitalize the names of classes.**

Example:

```
MyClass
```

Java keywords cannot be used as the names of variables. Here is a list of Java keywords. We will encounter most of them as the course progresses.

## Java Keywords

| | | | | |
|---|---|---|---|---|
| abstract | continue | for | new | switch |
| boolean | default | goto* | null | synchronized |
| break | do | if | package | this |
| byte | double | implements | private | throw |
| byvalue* | else | import | protected | transient |
| case | extends | instanceof | public | true |
| catch | false | int | return | try |
| char | final | interface | short | void |
| class | finally | long | static | while |
| const* | float | native | super | |

\* Java keywords reserved for future use.

# PRIMITIVE VARIABLES AND DATA TYPES

Java primitive variables have a name (identifier) and a value. Variables take up space – a certain number of bytes – in computer memory. The values of variables can be integers or floating point numbers or characters or booleans (true and false are values). The types of primitive data are listed below. Long integers can have extremely large values ranging from –9 times ten to the 18th power to +9 times ten to the 18th power.

Java variables are either primitive variables or objects. Objects are not called primitive variables.

### Java Primitive Data Types

```
        Type          Size (bytes)        Range of Values

Integer Data Types:
        byte              1           -128        to    +127
        short             2           -32768      to    +32767
        int               4           -2147483648 to    +2147483647
        long              8           -9.22 e+18  to    +9.22 e+18


Floating Point Data Types:
        float             4                      1.4 e-45   to    3.40 e+38
        double            8                      4.9 e-324  to    1.8 e+308


Character Data Type:
        char              2                      0 to 0xFFFF (the Unicode characters)
                                                 The only unsigned Java data type.

Boolean Data Type:
        boolean                                  true  and false
```

## Primitive Variable Declarations and Initialization

*All Java variables __must__ be declared before they can be used.*

Variable declaration statements have the form:

**datatype variableName1, variableName2, ... ;**

Some examples of variable declarations are:

```
byte b1, b2;

short s1;

int j, k;

long m, n;

float x, y;

double z;

char c;

boolean t;
```

Variables can also be initialized or assigned values in the declaration statement:

```
int j = 10, k = 99;

boolean b = true;

double d = 77.3, e = 45.1;

short n;

n = 12;
```

Note:
- Every Java variable should normally be explicitly initialized or assigned a value before it is used as a matter of good style.

- Note all statements end in a semicolon and several comma-separated variables can appear in a declaration.

# LITERALS (CONSTANTS)

Java programs often contain constants. Constants are called literals in Java. Literals have data types just like variables: integer, long, float, double, char, and boolean.

## Integer Literals

Integer literals can be written in three ways in Java statements: decimal - base 10, octal - base 8, or hexadecimal - base 16. Luckily we use simple base 10 numbers most of the time. Some Java statements containing int literals are:

```
j = 65;          // decimal 10 literal

j = 0101;        //  octal literal - octal literals always begin with a zero.

j = 0x41;        // hexadecimal literal - hexadecimal literals always begin
                 // with a zero followed by an X or an x.
```

## Long Literals

Long integer literals have the same representation in code as integers except that an upper or lower case L is added to the end of the value. Upper case L is preferred to avoid confusion between one and lower case L: l vs. 1.

```
j = 65L;         // decimal 10 long literal

j = 0101L;       //  octal long literal - octal literals always begin with a zero.

j = 0x41L;       // hexadecimal long literal - hexadecimal literals always begin
                 // with a zero followed by an X or an x.
```

## Double Literals

Double literals can be represented in fixed decimal point format or in exponential scientific format. Some examples are:

```
4.6    5.92e6        9.345e+12     6.3E+4        4.226E7        6.2e-3
```

Double literals can also have a D or d added to the end of the value to indicate they are double data type. For example,

```
4.6d   5.92e6D       9.345e+12D    6.3E+4d       4.226E7D       6.2e-3d
```

## Float Literals

Float literals are similar to double literals except they add an f or an F to the end of the value. Some examples are:

```
4.6F   5.92e6F       9.345e+12f    6.3E+4f       4.226E7F       6.2e-3f
```

## Char Literals

Char literals can be represented in a variety of ways in Java code. Their values are Unicode characters which include the ASCII character set. The easiest way to represent a char literal is to place it in single quotes:

```
ch1 = 'Z';
ch2 = ' ';
```

Another way to represent char literals is with what are called escape sequences. They start with a \ within the single quotes. The kinds of escape sequences are:

```
'\m'    where m is an octal digit between 0 and 7.
        Example:    '\7'  is the bell character.

'\mm'   where each m is an octal digit between 0 and 7.
        For example '\62' is the digit character 2.

'\pmm'  where p is 0, 1, 2, or 3 and the next two digits are between 0 and 7.
        Example:    '\141' is the letter a.

'\ummmm'        where the m's are hexadecimal digits representing the value
                of a Unicode character.  The u is typed literally.
                Example:  '\u0008' is the backspace character.
```

Java also has special escape sequence literals for certain commonly occurring characters:

```
'\b'    backspace
'\t'    tab
'\n'    newline: a carriage return and a line feed
'\f'    form feed
'\r'    carriage return
'\''    single quote - Note: '' are two single quotes, not a double quote
'\\'    backslash
'\"'    double quote
```

These literals are used in statements such as:

```
ch = '\n';

d = '\105';

a = '\f';
```

Most of the time we can use simple single-quoted characters such as 'A'.

## ASCII Character Set

The ASCII character set is an important subset of the Unicode character set. It assigns a number value to each American keyboard character as well as certain other characters. The numbers in the ASCII character table range from 0 to 127. The standard keyboard characters and their <u>octal</u> numeric values are:

### Some Characters in the ASCII Character Set and their Octal Values

| 040 [space] | 064 4 | 110 H | 134 \ | 160 p |
|---|---|---|---|---|
| 041 ! | 065 5 | 111 I | 135 ] | 161 q |
| 042 " | 066 6 | 112 J | 136 ^ | 162 r |
| 043 # | 067 7 | 113 K | 137 _ | 163 s |
| 044 $ | 070 8 | 114 L | 140 ` | 164 t |
| 045 % | 071 9 | 115 M | 141 a | 165 u |
| 046 & | 072 : | 116 N | 142 b | 166 v |
| 047 ' | 073 ; | 117 O | 143 c | 167 w |
| 050 ( | 074 < | 120 P | 144 d | 170 x |
| 051 ) | 075 = | 121 Q | 145 e | 171 y |
| 052 * | 076 > | 122 R | 146 f | 172 z |
| 053 + | 077 ? | 123 S | 147 g | 173 { |
| 054 , | 100 @ | 124 T | 150 h | 174 | |
| 055 - | 101 A | 125 U | 151 i | 175 } |
| 056 . | 102 B | 126 V | 152 j | 176 ~ |
| 057 / | 103 C | 127 W | 153 k | |
| 060 0 | 104 D | 130 X | 154 l | |
| 061 1 | 105 E | 131 Y | 155 m | |
| 062 2 | 106 F | 132 Z | 156 n | |
| 063 3 | 107 G | 133 [ | 157 o | |

### Some White Space ASCII Characters

```
010 [backspace]     011 [tab]     012 [newline]     015 [carriage return]
```

You can use the octal values listed above to create char literals. For example,

```
ch1 = '\101';    // ch1 = 'A';

ch2 = '\141';    // ch2 = 'a';
```

**2. Elementary Java Features**

## Boolean Literals

There are only two Boolean literals: true and false. They are the only allowed values of boolean variables. Unlike the C Language an integer does NOT map into a boolean value. Integers are integers. Booleans are booleans.

```
b1 = true;
b2 = false;
```

# STATEMENTS

- Java programs are mostly composed of statements.

- Java statements end in a semicolon.

- White space in statements is ignored. Statements can be spread across multiple lines. There are exceptions to this rule. For example strings cannot be divided and placed on separate lines without extra steps being performed (we will see later).

    Example:

    ```
    z =
        x +
            y;
    ```

- A set of statements enclosed in braces are called a **block of code** or a **compound statement**. The statements are normally indented one tab stop from the column containing the braces. For example,

    ```
    {
        x = y + z;
        v = 3 * w;
    }
    ```

    is a block of code.

- A variable can be declared at any point in a block of code. The variable can be used (referenced) in code following the declaration in the same code block. A variable cannot be used before its declaration in a block of code.

# OPERATORS

- Java has many operators for mathematics and other purposes.

- Operators have precedence levels and associativity. The Java Operator Precedence Table specifies the precedence and associativity of Java operators. The precedence of the operators in a statement determines the order in which they will execute when the statement is executed. High precedence operators execute first. The lowest precence operator executes last. The order of execution may be affected by parentheses appearing in the statement.

**Java Operator Precedence Table**

| Java Operator Precedence Table | |
|---|---|
| ++  --  +  -  ~  .  !  (datatype)  [] | unary - right to left |
| *    /    % | binary - left to right |
| +    -    + (for Strings) | binary - left to right |
| <<    >>    >>> | binary - left to right |
| <    >    <=    >=    instanceof | binary - left to right |
| ==    != | binary - left to right |
| & | binary left to right |
| ^ | binary - left to right |
| \| | binary - left to right |
| && | binary - left to right |
| \|\| | binary - left to right |
| ?: | ternary - right to left |
| =    +=    -=    *=    /=    %=    and so on | binary - right to left |

- Operators at the top of the table have the highest precedence. Operators at the bottom of the table have the lowest precedence.

- The *precedence* of an operator is used by the Java compiler to decide the order in which to execute the operators in statements containing several operators.

- Example:

```
z = a * b + c;
```

- There are three operators in the statement, =, * and +.

- Order of precedence is * followed by + followed by =.

# ASSOCIATIVITY OF OPERATORS

The Java Operator Precedence Table also specifies the associativity of Java operators. In the case a statement contains several operators of the same precedence – a tie – then associativity is used to break the tie and determine the order in which the operators execute.

Example 1:

$$a = b + c + d + e;$$

The add operator is Left to Right associative (see table on previous page) so the additions are executed in the statement from left to right. The assigment (= operator) executes last.

|  | $4^{th}$ |  | $1^{st}$ | $2^{nd}$ | $3^{rd}$ |
|---|---|---|---|---|---|
| a | = | b | + c | + d | + e; |

Example 2:

$$w = x = y = z;$$

The = operator is Right to Left associative (see table on previous page) so the = operators are executed in the statement from right to left.

|  | $3^{rd}$ | $2^{nd}$ | $1^{st}$ |
|---|---|---|---|
| w | = x | = y | = z; |

# SOME JAVA OPERATORS

## Math Operators

- Familiar operators from mathematics such as +, -, * and /.

## Remainder or Modulus Operator

- The remainder or modulus operator calculates the remainder resulting from integer division.

Example

```
j = 7 % 4;    // Result:  j = 3
```

## Pointer Operators

Java does not contain pointers so it does not have the & and * pointer operators.

Also Java does not have a sizeof operator.

## Assignment Operators

- The assignment operators such as +=, -=, and so on are a shorthand notation for resetting the value of a variable.

```
j += 910;
```

is the same as

```
j = j + 910;
```

- The statement

```
j *= 410;
```

is the same as

```
j = j * 410;
```

- Generally,

```
variable  op=   expression;
```

is equivalent to the "longhand" form:

```
variable  =  variable  op  (expression);
```

- The operator must be binary.

- If there is an expression on the right side it is evaluated first:

```
z /= a + b;
```

is equivalent to

```
z = z / (a + b);
```

**2. Elementary Java Features**

## Increment/Decrement Operators ++ and --

- Increase or decrease the value of a variable by one.

    Simplest formats:

    ```
    j++;    // increase j by one

    ++j;    // increase j by one

    j--;    // decrease j by one

    --j;    // decrease j by one
    ```

- The ++ and -- operators can be placed either before or after the variable name with the same result <u>in this case</u>.

- More complex statements: prefix or postfix produce different results.

    ```
    k = 7;
    j = ++k;
    ```

    Prefix causes j to be set equal to the new incremented value of k, namely 8.

- The value of any expression with the form

    ```
    ++variable
    ```

    is the new incremented value of the variable. Prefix ++ is called a *preincrement*.

- For postfix ++ the value of the expression is the old value of the variable before the increment. Example:

    ```
    k = 99;
    j = k++;
    ```

    causes j to receive the value 99, the old value of k before k is incremented to 100.

- Postfix ++ is called *postincrement* because the value of the expression is the old value of the variable. Think of the variable as being incremented after (post) the rest of the statement is executed. Postincrement expressions have the form

  ```
  variable++
  ```

- Decrement operator, --, has a *postdecrement* and *predecrement* format:

  ```
  variable--    //  postdecrement

  --variable    //  predecrement
  ```

- Postdecrement: similar to postincrement except that the value of the variable is decreased by one. Example:

  ```
  k = 88;
  j = k--;
  ```

  results in j receiving the old value of k. So k becomes 87 and j gets the value 88.

- Predecrement is similar to preincrement except that the value of the variable is decreased by one. For example

  ```
  k = 77;
  j = --k;
  ```

  results in j receiving the new value of k. So k becomes 76 and j gets the value 76.

# TYPE CASTING

Java is a strict type checking language.  The Java compiler generates error messages for certain mixed data type expressions.  Java has an operator, called a *typecast operator*, to change the data types of expressions to avoid compiler error messages.

Java allows you to explicitly change the data type of an expression by performing a typecast.  A typecast operator expression consists of a data type enclosed in parentheses.   An example of a typecast:

```
double x;
int j;

x = (double) j;    // Automatic type conversion also supported:   x = j; is ok
```

Possible problems:

```
double x;
float y;
int j;

j = (int) x;   // if x is too large j gets incorrect value.
               // Also the fractional part of x is lost.
y = (float) x;   // loss of precision
```

# TYPE CONVERSIONS IN OPERATOR EXPRESSIONS

- Statements often contain variables and literals with different data types.

- For statements with only primitive data types there are rules for combining expressions with different data types.

- These rules describe *automatic data type conversions* which are performed by the compiler. Automatic data type conversions are also called *implicit data type conversions*.

- Automatic data type conversions are applied in binary arithmetic operator expressions with operands of different data types, and in assignments where the left operand's data type is different from the right operand's data type.

  ```
  a + b
  ```

- *Assignments* are statements setting a variable equal to a value:

  ```
  a = b;
  ```

## Binary Arithmetic Operator Expressions

The rules for data type conversion of a <u>binary arithmetic operator expression</u> are:

- If either operand is a double, then the other operand is converted to a double.

- Otherwise, if either operand is a float, then the other operand is converted to a float.

- Otherwise, if either operand is a long, then the other operand is converted to a long.

- Otherwise, both operands are converted to int's.

Then the arithmetic is performed.

## Assignment Statements

If the left and right operand in an <u>assignment</u> statement have different primitive data types then the operand on the right side will be automatically data type converted to the data type of the left in certain cases and then the right side value copied over to the left side variable. There are two chains of automatic primitive data type conversions for the right side:

$$byte \rightarrow short \rightarrow int \rightarrow long \rightarrow float \rightarrow double$$

and

$$char \rightarrow int \rightarrow long \rightarrow float \rightarrow double$$

These chains indicate automatic data type conversions performed by Java. A right operand can be automatically data type converted to any type to the right of its data type in the above chains of data type conversions.

Example:

```
int j = 5;
double x = 99.3;

x = j;
```

causes the value of the j variable to be automatically type converted to a double value 5.0. As a result x gets the value 5.0.

- If the expression on the right side of the = sign is of a wider data type than the variable on the left side, then you must use an explicit data type conversion in most cases. For example,

```
double d = 5.0;
int j;

j = (int) d;    // explicit cast required
```

- A variable of a non-boolean cannot be set equal to a boolean data type expression.

When a data type conversion takes place the data type converted value can be different from the original value. We saw an example of this difference in the preceding example when the value of x = 99.3 produced the temporary int value 99.

Data type conversion can cause the decimal part of a floating point number to be lost and can also cause a loss of precision. If a double is converted to a float the number of significant figures in the value decreases from 15 to 7 resulting in a loss of precision.

There are two types of conversions: *widening conversions* which do not lose information (such as the decimal part); and *narrowing conversions* which may cause loss of information. The widening conversions supported by Java are:

- float to double
- long to float or double
- int to long, float, or double
- char to int, float, or double
- short to long, float, or double
- byte to short, int, long, float, or double

The narrowing conversions supported by Java are:

- double to byte, short, char, int, long, or float
- float to byte, short, char, int, or long
- long to byte, short, char, or int
- int to byte, short, or char
- short to byte or char
- char to byte or short

More information on data type conversions can be found in the Java Language Specification.

# CONTROL CONSTRUCTS

*Control constructs* are features of the Java language which control the execution of statements.

- if construct,

- switch construct,

- while loops,

- do-while loops,

- for loops.

# IF-ELSE CONSTRUCTS

## And and OR Operators

The && and || operators perform logical AND and OR operations just like the C language. They combine conditions to produce a compound condition which is true or false.

And Operator &&

| Condition1 | && | Condition2 | Truth Value of Compound Condition |
|------------|-----|------------|-----------------------------------|
| True | | True | True |
| True | | False | False |
| False | | True | False |
| False | | False | False |

Example:

| I will go home | && | I will watch TV | |
|----------------|-----|-----------------|---|
| True | | True | means the combined compound statement is true. |

Or Operator || (vertical line on keyboard on the \ key normally)

| Condition1 | || | Condition2 | Truth Value of Compound Condition |
|------------|-----|------------|-----------------------------------|
| True | | True | True |
| True | | False | True |
| False | | True | True |
| False | | False | False |

Example:

| I will go home | || | I will watch TV | |
|----------------|-----|-----------------|---|
| True | | True | True |
| True | | False | True |
| False | | True | True |

All the three above sets of conditions mean the combined compound statement is true.

Simplest form of if:

```
if( condition )   // conditions MUST be boolean valued.
     statement
```

Equivalent to:

> If the condition is true execute the statement. If the condition is false do not execute the statement.

Example:

```
if( x > y )
     a = b + c;
```

---

## Inequality Operators

```
>  greater than
<  less than
>= greater than or equal
<= less than or equal
== equality test
!= not equal
```

The inequality operators are used in if constructs, while constructs, do-while constructs, and for loops.

## Compound Logical Expressions

And operator    &&

Or operator      | |

Examples:

```
if( a < b && c > d)  // if both conditions are true execute statement.
     z = x - y;

if( a >= d || c == b)   // if either condition is true execute statement.
     w = x * z;

if( a < b && c > d && e >= f )// if all 3 conditions are true execute statement.
     z = x +y;

if( (a > b || c < d) && j != k )
     x = z * y;
```

## Compound Statements

Compound statement = Block of code in braces {   }

Two popular formats:

```
if( condition ) {
       // code
}
```

or

```
if( condition )
{
       // code
}
```

If the condition is true all the code in the block is executed. If the condition is false then none of the code in the block executes.

## else Block

```
if( condition )
{
       // code
}
else
{
       // code
}
```

## Braces Optional

- If the code in any block contains only one statement, then the braces can be omitted.

```
if( a > b )
      z = x + y;
else
      z = x - y;
```

## if - else if Construct

The block following the first true condition in the "if – else if" construct executes. If none of the conditions is true then the else block executes if there is an else block. (The else block is optional.)

```
if( condition1 )
{
        // code1
}
else if( condition2 )
{
        // code2
}
else if(condition3 )
{
        // code3
}
// ...
else
{
        // code
}
```

Example:
```
if( x < y)
        z = x + y;
else if( x == y )
{
        z = w;
        w = x;
}
else if( x > 2 * y )
        z = x;
else
{
        z = y;
        w = 2 * x;
}
```

Notice no semicolon at the end of the if, else, or else if lines.

# SWITCH CONSTRUCT

- The switch construct enables the programmer to compare the value of an integer expression against a set of constant values.

- The values can be constants or constant expressions.

- The values cannot be variable expressions.

- The switch construct is often used to test a value such as a menu selection letter or number against a set of possible values. The code associated with the matching value is executed.

The form of the switch construct is:

```
switch(expression)    // Note: no semicolon on this line.
{
        case value1:
                    // code
        case value2:
                    // code
        case value3:
                    // code
        // ...
        default:
                    // code
}
```

- Each value, value1, value2, … can be a constant or a constant expression of data type int, short, byte or char.

- The expression in the switch parentheses must be of type int, short, byte or char.

- This expression and the case values are converted to int and then compared. The expression is matched against the values. The first exact numeric match wins and the code following the case executes. If there is no match then the code following **default:** executes (if there is a default).

- The default case matches all values of the expression. No matter where it appears in the list of cases the default code is only executed if no case matches. The default code can also execute if a preceding case matches it and no "break" statement breaks out of the switch. ("break" discussed next).

- The break statement causes a program to stop executing statements in a switch and to start executing statements after the } brace ending the switch.

Example:

```
switch(j)
{
    case 1:
        a = b + c;
    case 2:
        d = e - f;
    case 3:
        g = h - i;
    default:
        r = s - t;
}
```

If j equals 1, then all four assignment statements will execute. If j equals 2, then the last three assignment statements will execute.

## Effect of break statement

The break statement "breaks" the program out of the switch construct. The code following the swich() block starts to execute.

```
switch(j)
{
    case 1:
        a = b + c;
        break;
    case 2:
        d = e - f;
        break;
    case 3:
        g = h - i;
        break;
    default:
        r = s - t;
        break;
}
```

In this switch if the value of j is 1 or 2 or 3, only the assignment statement following the case statement executes. A break statement ends the switch and the next statement following the } of the switch executes.

Stacked case example:

```
switch(c)
{
        case 'a':       // the cases are stacked up.
        case 'e':
        case 'i':
        case 'o':
        case 'u':
                numvowels++;
                break;
        default:
                numcons++;
                break;
}
```

The next switch and the previous switch do the same thing. The location of the default case doesn't matter in this situation.

```
switch(c)
{
        default:
                numcons++;
                break;
        case 'a':
        case 'e':
        case 'i':
        case 'o':
        case 'u':
                numvowels++;
                break;
}
```

**2. Elementary Java Features**

# WHILE LOOPS

while loops repeatedly execute a block of code as long as a condition remains true.

Examples:

```
while( c >= d)
        c--;


while( a < b )
{
        b--;
        sum += b;
}
```

If the condition starts out false then the block of the while loop never executes.

Notice: no ; at end of while line.

# DO-WHILE LOOPS

do-while loops are similar to while loops except the block of the do-while always executes at least once.

Examples:

```
do
        a += b;
while( a < d);


do
{
        c *= d;
        e -= f;
} while( c < e );
```

Notice the semicolon at the end of the while line.

# FOR LOOPS

for loops cycle through a block of code repeatedly until a condition becomes false. A for loop often has a "counter" variable which is like a "do loop" variable in other programming languages.

Examples:

```
for( j = 1;  j < 10;  j++)
      sum += j;
```

General format:

```
for( initialization; condition; increment)
{
      // code
}
```

- Order of Execution:

        initialization
        test condition
        true - do block of code
        increment
        test condition
        true - do block of code
        increment
        test condition
        ...

- Program goes to next stage when condition becomes false.

- If condition starts out false, then block never executes.

- No ; at end of for line.

- Any or all three parts of for may be omitted but two ;'s cannot be omitted.
    Result:
        omit initialization - no initialization
        omit condition - loop runs forever (unless break statement executes)
        omit increment - no increment

Most minimal loop:

```
for(;;)          // an infinite loop
{
       // code
}
```

How do we get out of an infinite for loop?  With a break statement.  For example,

```
for( j = 1; ; j++)
{
       sum1 += j;
       if ( j == 99 )
              break;
       sum2++;
}

a = b + c;
```

Break statements can be used in for loops, while loops, do while loops, and switch statements.

Another kind of statement which is used with loops:  the *continue statement*.  For example,

```
for( ; j < 77; j++)
{
       sum1 += j;
       if ( j == 33 )
              continue;
       sum2++;
}

a = b + c;
```

The continue statement takes the program to the } and then the loop continues by doing the increment.  The continue statement can be used in for loops, while loops, and do while loops. It is a "go to the end of the block" statement.

More complex for loops are possible using comma separated statements in a for loop.  For example,

```
for( j = 1, k = 3; k < 66; k += 5, m++ ) //  no , separated expressions are allowed
                                         //  in the condition part.
{
       // code
}
```

# SIMPLE STANDALONE JAVA PROGRAMS

We now have all the pices needed for simple standalone programming. We will now look at the simplest form of Java program to pull together the basic features described in this module.  The simplest format is:

```
class myclass
{
        public static void main(String args[])
        {


                // Code

        }
}
```

Example 1:

```
class c2_1                              // File: c2_1.java
{
        public static void main(String args[])
        {
                int j;

                j = 7799;

                System.out.println(j);   // print j on screen.
        }
}
```

Note:
  System = class name
  out = variable name
  println = method

The println method prints a variable of any data type.  It can also print a string of  characters enclosed in double quotes such as "abc".  We will see more about println statements later.

# COMPILING AND RUNNING STANDALONE PROGRAMS

**MS-DOS Prompt Window**
C:\WORK> notepad myprog.java
C:\WORK> javac myprog.java
C:\WORK> java myclass

**UNIX Window**
$ vi myprog.java
$ javac myprog.java
$ java myclass

## Compile Procedure

Use the java compiler, javac, to compile the .java file.

```
javac xxxxxxx.java
```

The output of the compiler is a file with a name of the form:

> classname.class

The stem of the compiler output file is the name of the class in the file.

Style rule: The stem of the program filename is often the same as the name of the class defined in the file.

Example:

```
javac c2_1.java
```

produces the file: c2_1.class   because c2_1 is the name of the <u>class</u> inside the .java file.

## To Run the Program

The Java interpreter will be used to run the program at this stage of the course. The format is:

```
java classname
```

Example:

```
java c2_1
```

# MORE EXAMPLES OF PROGRAMS

Example 2:  A program to sum the integers between 1 and 99:

**File: c2_2.java**
```
class c2_2                        // File:  c2_2.java
{
        public static void main(String args[])
        {
                int sum = 0;

                for(int j = 1; j < 100; j++)
                    sum += j;

                System.out.println("Answer: " + sum);
        }
}
```

Output:

                    Answer:  4950

Example 3:

**File: c2_3.java**
```
class c2_3                        // File:  c2_3.java
{
        public static void main(String args[])
        {
                int sum = 0;

                for(int j = 1; j < 100; j++)
                {
                        switch(j)
                        {
                                case 20:
                                        sum += 120;
                                        break;
                                default:
                                        sum += j;
                                        break;
                        }
                }

                System.out.println("Answer: " + sum);
        }
}
```

Output:

                    Answer:  5050

**Note:  The + in println() usually performs string concatenation — not arithmetic.**

---

# USING THE CLASS AND SOLUTION FILES

The zip file that is available for this course contains the code for the examples in this course so you don't have to waste time typing them. It also contains suggested solutions for the lab exercises at the end of each module. The names of the files are based on the module number.

<u>Example Files</u>
All files shown in this document are in the CLASS subdirectory in the zip file. They are named according to the following convention:

CmoduleNumber_ExampleNumber.java

with a few exceptions. The file names of the exceptions are shown in the text. An example of the naming convention is the file named:

C5_12.java

This file has the code of example 12 in module 5.

<u>Exercise Solutions</u>
All exercise solution files are in the SOL (for solution) subdirectory in the zip file. They are named according to the following convention:

EmoduleNumber_ExerciseNumber.java

Wihere E stands for exercise. An example of the naming convention is the file named:

E6_4.java

This file has the code of exercise 4 in module 6.

**2. Elementary Java Features**

# SUMMARY

This module has introduced the basic features of Java programs: primitive variables, operators and control constructs. We have seen how to create simple standalone programs and compile and run them.

# EXERCISES

1. Write a simple Java program which declares three int variables named a, b and answer. Give a the value 3 and b the value 4. Set answer equal to a plus b. Display answer on screen.

2. Write a Java program which defines two int variables j and k. Set j = 4 and k = 5. Then code an if construct which displays the sum of j and k if j is greater than k, and displays the difference j - k otherwise.

3. Write a Java program which sums the integers from 1 through 30 and displays the sum.

# 3. *Java Methods*

## OBJECTIVES

At the end of this module you should be able to:

- Describe Java methods.

- Use Java methods in programs.

- Describe and use method overloading.

# WHAT IS A METHOD?

A block of code with a name that

- Performs an activity or calculates a value.

- Specifies part of the behavior of an entity such as a window, button, financial account, etc.

- Is implemented as a function in languages such as C, C++ which are similar to Java.

Methods are related to messages as we see when we discuss object-oriented Java programming.

# DEFINITION OF JAVA METHODS

## Definition of a Java Method

Java methods have a top line with their name and a list of input parameters specified together with their data types. The return data type appears before the name of the method. The return data type specifies the data type of the "answer" calculated by the method. Below the top line is a block of code in curly braces { }. One possible format for a Java method definition:

```
ReturnType   MethodName( parameter data type list)
{

    //  block of code

}
```

Example:

```
double weight(double density, double length, double width, double height)
{
    double volume;

    volume = length * width * height;

    return density * volume;
}
```

Parameters → (point to density, length, width, height)

double volume; ← Local Variable

return density * volume; ← Return Statement

## Program Features to Note

**Parameters:**

Parameters are the inputs to the method. Notice they are declared with their data types in a comma-separated list within the parentheses.

**Local Variables:**

Variables can be defined at any point in a block.

**return Statement Returning a Value:**

Purpose: to give back the "answer" calculated by the method.
Format:

```
return value;
```

## Method "Calls"

One method can call another method (or cause another method to execute). The called method executes and can return a value – "an answer".

When a method is called values are placed inside the parentheses following the method name. These values are called the arguments. The arguments become the values of the parameters when the block of code of the method execute.

Example:

```
                        A r g u m e n t s
myweight = weight( 2.10, 1.08, x, 5.8);
```

Compare to the method definition's top line:

```
                        P a r a m e t e r s

double weight(double density, double length, double width, double height)
```

The arguments in the parentheses are the inputs for the method.  Each parameter of the method definition is set equal to the corresponding argument value:  density = 2.10,  length = 1.08, etc. and then the block of code of the method executes to calculate the "answer" which is returned by the return statement.  The variable myweight is set equal to the "answer".

## Void Methods

Some methods only perform an action and do not return a value. These methods are called void methods. They are declared as void.

Example:

```
void my_print(int x)
{
        // code to perform some printing chore

        return;    // Causes method to end returning execution to the call point.
}
```

## Forms of return Statement

If a method returns a value then any return statement in its block must have the form:

```
return value;
```

If a method is declared void, then any return statement in its block must have the form:

```
return;
```

# SAMPLE PROGRAM WITH METHODS

An example of a program which contains methods is:

Example:

**File: c3_1.java**

```
class c3_1                        // File: c3_1.java
{
        public static void main(String args[])
        {
                double lengthBox = 2.5;
                double widthBox = 4.0;
                double heightBox = 3.0;
                double densityBox = 1.0;
                double weightBox, sizeBox;

                weightBox = weight(densityBox, widthBox, lengthBox,
                                                heightBox);
                sizeBox = shipLength(widthBox, lengthBox, heightBox);

                System.out.println("Shipping Size: " + sizeBox);
                System.out.println("\nWeight: " + weightBox);
        }
        static double weight(double density, double width,
                                        double length, double height)
        {
                return density * width * length * height;
        }
        static double shipLength(double width, double length,
                                        double height)
        {
                return width + length + height;
        }
}
```

Output:

```
        Shipping Size: 9.5

        Weight: 30
```

The methods appearing in class c3_1 in addition to the main method are weight() and shipLength(). These methods have to be declared static in order to be called from main() because main() is declared static. The static declaration will be described in detail later. For the moment we will follow a "cookbook" approach.

# METHOD OVERLOADING

- There are often several methods in the Java environment which perform a similar task but differ in details. Java style guidelines encourage programmers to give each of these methods the same name rather than different names to avoid burdening the programmer's memory.

- Java allows methods to have the same name. A set of methods with the same name is called an *overloaded set of methods*. Each method in an overloaded set is a member of a different class and/or has a different parameter data type list.

- Overloaded methods in the same class must have a different number of parameters and/or the ordered list of parameter data types must be different.

Example containing an overloaded set of methods:

**File: c3_2.java**

```
class c3_2                              // File: c3_2.java
{
        public static void main(String args[])
        {
                double x = 1.5;
                int j = 3;
                float y = 4.4F;

                print(x);
                print(y);
                print(y, j);
        }

        static void print(double d)
        {
                System.out.println("Double: " + d);
        }

        static void print(float f, int m)
        {
                System.out.println("Float and int: " + f + m); // not addition!
        }                       // + with strings implements concatenation.

        static void print(float f)
        {
                System.out.println("Float: " + f);
        }
}
```

Output:
```
Double: 1.5
Float: 4.4
Float and int: 4.43
```

**3. Java Methods**

# SUMMARY

This module described the nature and features of methods. It showed how to define and use a method. Method overloading was also described.

# EXERCISES

1.  Add a method to c3_1.java which calculates the volume of the box (length * width * height) and use this method in the weight() method instead of the corresponding multiplications.

2.  Create a program which defines two overloaded methods named display. One method has two int parameters and returns their sum. The other display() method has three int parameters and returns their product. Print the return values of display(3, 5) and display( 2, 4, 6) on the terminal screen with println().

**3. Java Methods**

# 4. Classes and Objects

## OBJECTIVES

At the end of this module you should be able to:

- Describe object-oriented Java programming concepts.

- Write Java programs containing multiple classes.

- Describe Java features such as automatic garbage collection, constructors, finalizers, static variables, static methods, and the this keyword.

# WHY DO OBJECT-ORIENTED PROGRAMMING?

- Java programming deals with complex entities such as windows, screens, buttons, scrollbars, other GUI objects, files, audio, and other multimedia entities.

- To handle these complex entities, and the actions and events related to them, we can either engage in object-oriented programming OR nitty-gritty low level programming which is laborious, time consuming, and difficult to enhance and maintain.

- In object-oriented programming we can create objects corresponding to these entities and manipulate them in programs with methods which specify, describe and govern their behavior and evolution.

- Benefits of object-oriented programming:

    - Easier coding to manage complex situations and events.

    - More readable code.

    - More efficient code maintenance.

    - Easier to enhance code.

# WHAT ARE CLASSES AND OBJECTS?

## Objects

Objects are entities (things) which:

- are complex.

- have a well-defined behavior.

- have a well-defined set of state variables.

- have a well-defined boundary.

Examples of objects:

- Windows

- Buttons

- Scrollbars

- Graphics Displays

Java programming is a form of object-oriented programming because Java deals with these kinds of complex objects.

## Classes

A class is a specification for a kind of object. A class definition specifies variables which define the state of an object. It also specifies the behavior of an object with methods.

Example:

Audio Player Class:

> state:
> > "on-line" or "off-line".
> > volume
> > bass
> > treble
> > other internal characteristics of the audio player.
>
> Behavior:
> > Play.
> > Fast forward.
> > Rewind.

# JAVA PROGRAMMING

## Class Definition

Classes are defined with a block of code containing methods specifying the behavior of objects and instance variables specifying the state of objects.

One possible format:

```
class classname
{
        // variable declarations

        // method definitions or declarations

}
```

- The class keyword may be preceded by keywords specifying access rights and other class features. More on this topic later.

- All variables and methods must be part of a class.

- Member variables have two forms: **instance** variables and **static** variables (discussed later).

- Member variable and method definitions can begin with keywords which specify when a method can be used.

- The order of the methods and variables in a class definition are irrelevant.

Example of a class definition:

```
class Dog
{
        private double height;
        private double weight;

        void setDog(double inHeight, double inWeight)
        {
                height = inHeight;
                weight = inWeight;
        }
        void eat(double amount)
        {
            weight += amount;
            height += .01 * amount;
        }
        void run(double runtime)
        {
            weight -= .03 * runtime;
        }
        void showDog()
        {
                System.out.println("Height: " + height);
                System.out.println("Weight: " + weight);
                System.out.println("What a dog!");
        }
}
```

## Definition of Objects

- Objects are instances (variables) of some class data type.

- Objects have a different nature from C++ objects.

- Objects can be viewed as being created in two steps although they are often created with one line of code.

> Step 1: Declare an object reference (name).

> Step 2: Allocate storage for the object.

Example:

```
Dog d;          // declares reference variable (a name without storage)
d = new Dog();  // allocates storage and "pins" reference to storage
```

- The first statement declares the data type of d – a reference variable.

- The new operator allocates storage in the program's memory for a Dog object.

- The assignment part of the statement  "d = "  pins the name d on the new object.

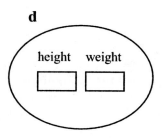

# JAVA OBJECTS AND DYNAMIC REFERENCES

- A Java object has a **dynamic reference** variable (or reference variable for short) pinned to storage for an object in memory. A dynamic reference variable is a type of variable that has a name only. It does not have storage in itself. The name can be attached to allocated storage. When the name is attached to allocated storage then the storage can be referenced by the program. Data at the storage location can be fetched or changed using the reference variable. Reference variables are used in a way similar to pointers in other progrtamming languages.

- We allocate storage for an object and pin (attach) the reference (name) to the allocated storage.

- Because of its "movability", a Java reference variable is described as **dynamic**.

- An object name can be pinned to different storage at different points in a program. For example,

  ```
  myClass m;

  m = new myClass(…);

  // code

  m = new myClass(…);   // m now refers to different allocated storage.
  ```

- When allocated storage loses its name, the storage is marked for deallocation by the garbage collection thread (described later). The first allocated object in the above code becomes non-referencable and is marked for deallocation when the variable m is assigned to another object in the last code statement above.

  ```
  m = null;
  ```

- Any reference variable can be set equal to **null**. A null value specifies a reference is not pinned (attached) to any allocated storage. null cannot be represented as zero. Null is not zero. A primitive data type variable cannot be set equal to null (with or without a typecast).

# DATA ENCAPSULATION

- *All variables and methods must be defined inside a class in Java.* Java strictly enforces this form of encapsulation in object-oriented design.

- Object-oriented design rules specify a stricter form of data encapsulation. Member variables in a class should only be accessed and manipulated by member methods of the same class. These methods set, change and use the values of the member variables. This rule can be strictly enforced by making all member variables **private** (next page). See the Dog class where the methods manage the data variables.

- Many earlier Java programming efforts including the built-in libraries (packages) have not followed the private variables rule. Many variables are public. Programmer convenience seems to have been the guiding principle. Recently there has been a tendency to more strictly observe the private variable rule. This can be seen in the newer Java packages (class libraries).

**4. Classes and Objects**

# FIRST LOOK AT PACKAGES

A Java program normally consists of several (sometimes many) classes which use variables and methods in class libraries which are called packages in Java.

*A package is a set of classes which have been grouped together because they have some common purpose or functionality.* A package is analogous to a library in other programming language environments. The procedure for creating a package will be described in module 6.

When the java compiler javac compiles your program the compiler creates a *default package* consisting of all the classes comprising your program which are not part of an existing package.

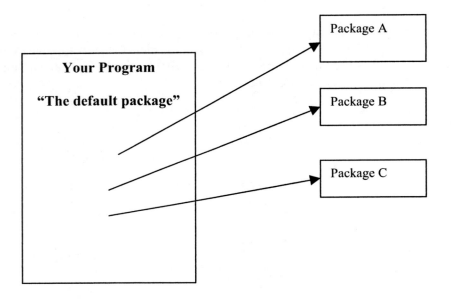

Figure. A program constitutes a default package. The code in the program can reference methods and variables in classes in other packages.

# "PACKAGE" VS. PRIVATE VARIABLES AND METHODS

A member variable or member method in a Java class can be private, package, protected or public. Each category specifies a different level of accessibility (or scope). We will consider package and private variables and methods now (and other categories later).

Variables

A *private variable* can only be referenced by the methods in its own class. Methods in other classes cannot reference the variable. Private variables are declared using the private keyword. For example,

```
private double height;
```

In other object-oriented languages variables are normally declared private to obtain a higher level of data encapsulation. In Java variables are often not private.

Variables are *package variables* by default in Java. If you do not specify a different category with a keyword then a member variable is in the package category. For example,

```
double height;
```

specifies a package variable.

Package variables can be accessed by all methods in all classes in the same package. In this module we will be building one file programs which contain several classes. Package variables can be referenced by any method in any class in the file since all these classes are placed in the same default package.

Methods

A *private method* can only be called (invoked) by the methods in its own class. Methods in other classes cannot call a private method in another class. Private methods are declared using the private keyword. For example,

```
private double calculateHeight()
{    ...   }
```

Methods are *package methods* by default in Java. If you do not specify a different category with a keyword then a member method is in the package category. For example,

```
double calculateHeight()
{    ...   }
```

specifies a package method. Package methods can be accessed by all methods in all classes in the same package. In this module we will be building one file programs which contain several classes. Package methods can be called by any method in any class in the file since all these classes are placed in the same default package.

**4. Classes and Objects**

# SENDING MESSAGES TO OBJECTS

The methods in a class definition specify the behavior of class objects. After we create an object we can send messages to an object telling it to perform a specific behavior. The message consists of one of the methods in its class. For example, we send messages to Dog object d with

```
d.setDog(9.3, 19.5);  // initializes the Dog d.

d.run(15.4);   // Tells the dog d to run 15.4 seconds.

d.eat(1.2);  // Tells the dog d to eat 1.2 pounds of food.
```

The object receiving the message is called the **recipient object**. The object d is the recipient object in the preceding example. A method fetches and/or sets variable values in the recipient object.

# PROGRAMS WITH MULTIPLE CLASSES

A Java program can contain several classes.  For example,

**File: c4_1.java**

```
class c4_1            // File: c4_1.java
{
        public static void main(String args[])
        {
                Dog d = new Dog();
                d.setDog(19.5, 15.5);
                d.run(12.4);
                d.eat(1.2);
                d.showDog();
        }
}

class Dog
{
        private double height;
        private double weight;

        void setDog(double inHeight, double inWeight)
        {
                height = inHeight;
                weight = inWeight;
        }

        void eat(double amount)
        {
                weight += amount;
                height += .01 * amount;
        }

        void run(double runtime)
        {
                weight -= .03 * runtime;
        }

        void showDog()
        {
                System.out.println("Height: " + height);
                System.out.println("Weight: " + weight);
                System.out.println("What a dog!");
        }
}
```

Output:
Height: 19.512
Weight: 16.328
What a dog!

# CREATING AND COMPILING

# STANDALONE JAVA PROGRAMS

- Java program files can be created with one or more class definitions in them.

- The best procedure is to name the program classname.java using the name of the class containing the main() method which "runs" the program.

- Compile and Run Procedure:

      notepad xxxxx.java

      javac xxxxx.java

      java nameOfClassContainingMain

The Java interpreter command must have the classname of the class containing the main() method on the command line.

# AUTOMATIC GARBAGE COLLECTION

- Java has a feature called automatic garbage collection. The Java runtime environment detects when allocated storage can no longer be referenced (not usable) and automatically deallocates it.

- A running Java program executes on a thread of execution - a linear step-by-step execution of the program steps.

- The Java environment also runs another thread of execution which performs automatic garbage collection.

- The garbage collection thread monitors the running program looking for storage which is no longer being used and deallocates it.

- Threads will be discussed in more detail in module 8.

- The program can allocate storage for objects with the new operator. Only the garbage collector can deallocate storage.

- You can request the garbage collection thread to run with the gc() method of the System class:

```
System.gc();
```

# CONSTRUCTORS

- Constructors are methods which automatically initialize objects. When an object has storage allocated for it a constructor runs if an appropriate matching constructor is defined in the class of the object. An example is :

```
Dog d = new Dog(3.4, 5.6);
```

The above statement allocates storage for a Dog object because of the new operator. Then the constructor in class Dog that has exactly two double parameters executes to initialize the Dog object. Lastly the name d is placed on the object. The matching Dog constructor must have a top line similar to:

```
Dog(double p1, double p2)
{
          ...
}
```

where p1 and p2 are parameter names.

- Constructors always have the same name as their class.

- Constructors never return a value. A return value should not be specified on the top line of a constructor. If a return value is specified the method becomes an ordinary method that will only run if explicitly called. It is no longer a constructor.

- Constructors can contain the return statement:

```
return;
```

- If a constructor is not provided in a class, then a default constructor executes which provides a default initialization. The default constructor is automatically placed in the class defi nition when the class is compiled. It has the form:

```
Classname() {    }
```

For example if class Dog has no constructor placed in it by the programmer, then the compiler inserts the code

```
Dog()  {  }
```

- Instance variables can also be explicitly initialized by setting them equal to a value in the class definition. For example,

```
class Cat
{
        double weight = 16.4;
        double height;

        //  code

}
```

- A class can have several constructors - an overloaded set of constructors. Each constructor has a parameter list which differs from the parameter lists of the other constructors.

- When an object is created with a new expression or otherwise, the constructor which has an exactly matching number of input arguments and matching argument data types runs. If there is no exact match, the compiler will perform automatic data type conversions on the arguments to obtain a match on a provided constructor. If no match is found a compiler error message is generated.

**Example:**

**File: c4_2.java**

```
class c4_2              // File: c4_2.java
{
        public static void main(String args[])
        {
                box b = new box(1, 2, 3);  // constructor initialization
                double weightBox, sizeBox;

                weightBox = b.shipWeight();
                sizeBox = b.shipLength();
                System.out.println("Shipping Size: " + sizeBox);
                System.out.println("Weight: " + weightBox);

                b = new box(4, 5, 6);    // New object. Old object - garbage.

                System.gc();                     // Request garbage collection.

                weightBox = b.shipWeight();
                sizeBox = b.shipLength();
                System.out.println("\nShipping Size: " + sizeBox);
                System.out.println("Weight: " + weightBox);
        }
}

class box
{
        private double length = 2.5;
        private double width = 4.0;
        private double height = 3.0;
        private double density = 1.0;

        box(double l, double w, double h) // a constructor
        {
                length = l;            // some default initial values overrridden.
                width = w;
                height = h;
        }
        double shipWeight()
        {
                return density * width * length * height;
        }
        double shipLength()
        {
                return width + length + height;
        }
}
```

**Output:**
Shipping Size: 6.0
Weight: 6.0

Shipping Size: 15.0
Weight: 120.0

**4.  Classes and Objects**

## Another example of a class containing a constructor

**File: c4_3.java**

```
class Dog1                          // File: c4_3.java
{
        private double height;
        private double weight;

        Dog1(double inHeight, double inWeight)
        {
                height = inHeight;
                weight = inWeight;
        }
        void eat(double amount)
        {
            weight += amount;
            height += .01 * amount;
        }
        void run(double runtime)
        {
                weight -= .03 * runtime;
        }
        void showDog()
        {
                System.out.println("Height: " + height);
                System.out.println("Weight: " + weight);
                System.out.println("What a dog!");
        }
}

class c4_3
{
        public static void main(String args[])
        {
                Dog1 d = new Dog1(19.5, 15.5);   // Constructor automatically
                                                 // executes.
                d.run(12.4);
                d.eat(1.2);
                d.showDog();
        }
}
```

The Dog constructor automatically executes with specified arguments producing:

### Dog1 Object d

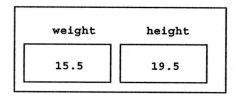

**4.  Classes and Objects**

# FINALIZERS

- A finalizer is a method which is executed automatically when an object comes to the end of its lifetime just before it is deallocated by the garbage collector.

- Objects will usually not be garbage-collected immediately after they become unusable (cannot be referenced). Their storage usually remains allocated for some time afterwards.

- *Finalizers are rarely used* because the programmer cannot know when they will execute since they depend on the garbage collector. They may not execute at all if the program is short.

- Finalizers can close files, reset variables, resurrect objects and perform other kinds of cleanup for an object. They perform cleanup.

- The finalizer of a class always has the form:

```
protected void finalize()
{

        // code

}
```

- A finalizer must always be declared as void, cannot be static, and has no parameters.

- A finalizer should be declared protected because class Object has a protected finalizer and all classes ultimately subclass from class Object. This will be described in more detail later.

- Some other finalizer rules:

    1. After an object has had a finalizer run for it, the automatic storage management mechanism checks to determine whether the object can again be referenced (has acquired a name). A finalizer can revive an object by assigning a reference (object name) to it.

    2. A finalizer can be applied only once to an object so an object can be revived only once at most.

**Finalizer Example:**

```java
class Dog2
{
        private double height;
        private double weight;

        Dog2(double inHeight, double inWeight)
        {
                height = inHeight;
                weight = inWeight;
        }

        void eat(double amount)
        {
                weight += amount;
                height += .01 * amount;
        }

        void run(double runtime)
        {
                weight -= .03 * runtime;
        }

        void showDog()
        {
                System.out.println("Height: " + height);
                System.out.println("Weight: " + weight);
                System.out.println("What a dog!");
        }

        protected void finalize()
        {
                System.out.println("Deallocating …");
        }
}
```

# this KEYWORD

- The "this" keyword is used to reference the recipient object when messages are sent to objects.

- "this" is a duplicate reference (name) given to the recipient object when a message is sent to it (a method runs on it). It gives us a handle on the recipient object inside the block of a member method.

- "this" can only be used in the block of code of a member method to reference the recipient object in a "method call".

- Sometimes the use of the word "this" is the only way to reference the recipient object. Sometimes the use of "this" is optional. An example of an often required use of "this" is in method calls such as:

```
prepareImage(myImage, this);
```

We will see this method in module 9.

Example using "this"in a constructor and other methods:

**Dog Object**

this

height    weight

**Constructor Parameters**

height    weight

**File: c4_4.java**

```
class Dog2                  // c4_4.java
{
        private double height;
        private double weight;

        Dog2(double height, double weight)
        { // local parameter names always shadow (override) external names.
                this.height = height;   // "this" used to override local
                this.weight = weight;   // parameters. Values set in object.
                                        // Required in this situation.
        }
        void eat(double amount)
        {
                this.weight += amount;        // "this" optional.
                this.height += .01 * amount;  // "this" optional.
        }
        void run(double runtime)
        {
                weight -= .03 * runtime; // "this" optional. Omitted.
        }
        void showDog()
        {                           // "this" optional. Omitted in the method.
                System.out.println("Height: " + height);
                System.out.println("Weight: " + weight);
                System.out.println("What a dog!");
        }
        protected void finalize()
        {
                System.out.println("finalize: Dog expired.");
        }
}

class c4_4
{
        public static void main(String args[])
        {
                Dog2 d = new Dog2(19.5, 15.5); // Constructor runs.
                d.run(12.4);
                d.eat(1.2);
                d.showDog();
                d = new Dog2(10.4, 7.5);
                System.gc();              // Request garbage collection.
                for(int j=0; j < 100000; j +=2)  // Kills time so
                        j--;                     // garbage collection
        }                                        // can take place.
}
```

**Output:**
Height: 19.512
Weight: 16.328
What a dog!
finalize: Dog expired.

Comments:

- The "this" keyword is used in the Dog constructor to override the parameter variable names so the instance variables can be set.

- The System.gc() method of class System requests the garbage collector to deallocate the nameless object.

- The for() loop causes the program to run a few more seconds to give the garbage collection thread a chance to execute a cleanup.

# STATIC VARIABLES

- Static variables (also called *class* variables) are member variables which have the same value in all objects of a class.

- Their purpose is to hold a common data value. Sometimes a static variable is a constant like PI = 3.14. Sometimes a static variable holds the value of a common property of all the objects such as the number of instantiated objects of the class.

- A static variable has its storage allocated and is given an initial value at the beginning (load point) of a Java program. Any object of its class which is created includes this memory location with its value. So all objects of the class share the same memory location for a static variable.

- Static variables are initialized to zero in the absence of explicit initialization.

Example:

```
class circle
{
        static double PI = 3.14159;
        private double radius;
        private static int numCircles;

        circle(double r)
        {
                radius = r;
                numCircles++;
        }
        // other method definitions
 }

// code

circle c1 = new circle(1.5);
circle c2 = new circle(3.7);

// code
```

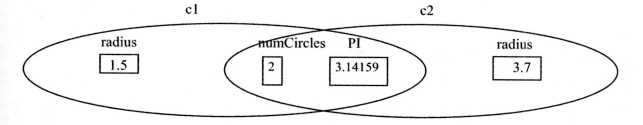

---

## Referencing Static Variables

- Static variables should normally be referenced without using an object:

<code>classname.statVariable</code>

This method of referencing shows they are static – self-documenting the code. For example,

```
circle.PI
circle.numCircles
```

They can also be referenced in the form:

```
object.PI
```

For example:

```
c1.PI
```

This format is not preferred because it suggests the PI value is specific to the recipient object.

## Initializing Static Variables

- Java supports exotic initializations for static variables using "static blocks". For example,

```
class Strange
{
        static int j = 99;
        static long k;
        static
        {
                j--;
        }
        static int m = 77;
        static Font f = new font();
        static
        {
                k = 66L;
        }
}
```

The order of initialization of the static variables in class Strange is:

1. j is set equal to 99.
2. The first static initializer executes decreasing j to 98.
3. Then m is set equal to 77.
4. A font object f is allocated.
5. The second static initializer sets k equal to 66.

- Static variable initializations cannot have a forward reference. For example,

```
class Stranger
{
        static int j = k + 10;     //   ERROR: forward reference
        static int k = 66;
}
```

- The initialization of static variables cannot contain references to instance variables or non-static methods of the class.

- Static variable initializations can contain calls to static methods and can use methods of classes already loaded. However, any circularity generates runtime error messages.

# STATIC METHODS

- Static methods are methods which perform some kind of generic task.

- For example, System.gc() performs a generic task by requesting the garbage collector to deallocate storage for all objects marked for deallocation.  The Math class contains many static methods which perform generic calculations such as Math.sqrt().

- There are many applications for static methods. A programmer might define a static method to open a file from which the objects of the class can fetch data.  Or a programmer might define a static method which sets the value of one or more static variables.

## Static Method Rules

- Static methods cannot reference instance variables or non-static methods in their class.

- Static methods can reference static variables and static methods in their own class.

- Static methods can reference any accessible methods and variables of other classes.

- Static methods cannot reference the keyword "this".

## Static Method Style Rule

- Static methods can and should be referenced by class name without using a recipient object:

```
classname.methodName( ... )
```

## Preferred Format for Static Method Calls

The preferred way to call static methods is using its class name.   For example,

```
x = Math.sqrt(25.0);
```

```
System.gc();
```

Static Method example:

```
class circle
{
     static double PI = 3.14159;
      private double radius;
     private static int numCircles;

     circle(double r)
     {
          radius = r;
          numCircles++;
     }

     static void setPI(double p)   // Change value of PI static variable.
     {
          PI = p;
     }

      // other method definitions
 }

// code

circle c1 = new circle(1.5);
circle c2 = new circle(3.7);

// code

circle.setPI(3.59);
```

# PASS BY REFERENCE VS. PASS BY VALUE

- When a call to a Java method occurs the arguments inside the method call are passed to the definition of the method as the values of the parameters. There are two ways to give argument values to a parameter in Java: pass by value and pass by reference.

- Primitive data type parameters (int, byte, float, double, ...) always are Pass by Value. Parameters that have the data type of a class are always Pass by Reference. These language rules are not changeable.

- **Pass by Value - Primitive data type parameters** in a method definition get the values of arguments through pass by value. Only the numeric or character value of the argument is given to the parameter. If the input argument is a variable it cannot be changed by the execution of the block of the method. The variable's value before and after the method call is the same.

- **Pass by Reference** - Parameters of a class type - **object parameters** - get their values through a form of pass by reference. The parameter name (which is a reference) is pinned to the input object argument. Therefore the execution of the block of the method can change the object argument.

Example:

```
int x = 3;
double y = 4;

// code

obj1.myMethod(   3.5,    x,    obj2,    y,    obj3);

// code
```

```
...  myMethod(double d, double z, myClass m, double w, yourClass yc)
{

// code

}
```

The primitive data arguments x and y can't be changed by the method call. Their values are passed to z and w using Pass by Value.

The object arguments obj2 and obj3 can be different after the method call. The names m and yc are placed on obj2 and obj3 and the objects are directly accessible. - Pass by Reference.

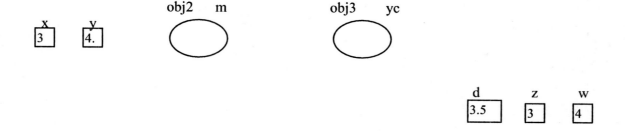

**4. Classes and Objects**

# SUMMARY

This module has introduced the basic concepts of classes and objects. Topics covered include:

- class definitions
- objects
- instance variables
- static variables
- methods
- static methods
- messages
- constructors
- finalizers
- "this" keyword

# EXERCISES

1. Add a sleep() method to class Dog in c4_1.java. This method should reduce a Dog object's weight by .05 for every hour it sleeps. The method should have a double parameter specifying the number of hours slept. The method should return void. Run the sleep method in the main() method with the dog sleeping 8 hours. Print the new weight of the Dog object with showDog().

2. Add another Dog1 constructor to class Dog1 in c4_3.java. This constructor should have one double parameter which sets the Dog1 object's weight. The height of the Dog1 object should be set to 14 in this constructor. Create another Dog1 object <u>with a different name</u> in main() with a weight of 20 which uses the new constructor. Run showDog() on the new object.

3. Add a static int variable called dogColor to the Dog1 class in the solution to exercise 2 which has int values corresponding to various dog colors (which are not specified).

    i. Modify the Dog1(double inHeight, double inWeight) constructor to set dogColor to 5.

    ii. Modify the Dog1(double inWeight) constructor to set dogColor to 10.

    iii. Modify the showDog() method to print "Dog Color" and its value on the screen. Notice the effect of static on the output. (Both dogs have the same dogColor value by running showDog() on both Dog1 objects.) <u>Run showDog() on both objects and note they have the same dogColor value - the effect of the static keyword.</u>

4. Add a finalizer to the solution of the last exercise which prints "Dog buried." on the monitor screen. Then modify the main() method in the following way:

    i. Set d equal to a new Dog1 object with weight 25 after the d.showDog() line.

    ii. Place the statement "`System.gc();`" after the line creating the new Dog1 in step i. This statement forces the garbage collector to run.

    iii. At the end of the main() method place three for() loops that causes the program to run a bit longer to give the garbage collector time to execute. Place a System.gc() after each for() loop. Each for() loop should iterate 100,000 times using a counter variable j which does j++ 100,000 times.

# 5. Class Interrelationships

## OBJECTIVES

At the end of this module you should be able to:

- Describe and create classes with subobjects.

- Describe implementing inheritance through subclassing.

- Implement and use classes with subclasses.

- Describe the types of classes: abstract, final, and public.

- Describe and create interfaces.

- Define and use packages.

# CLASS INTERRELATIONSHIPS

Java supports many forms of interrelationships between classes. Some types of class interrelationships are:

- **Subobjects** - objects which are instance variables or static variables in classes.

- **Subclassing** - one class inherits the variables and methods of another class.

- **Interfaces** - a class-like construct that is used to constrain the methods in a set of classes to have a common interface and for other purposes as well.

- **Packages** - sets of classes which are grouped together usually because they support a common function such as graphics or communications, etc.

# SUBOBJECTS

- A subobject is a variable inside a class which is an object of another class. It must have storage allocated by new to obtain storage for its own data variables.

- A subobject implements the "HASA" relationship of object-oriented design.
  Example: A frame **has a** button.

- The methods in the class of the subobject can often be used to manipulate the subobject.

```java
class c5_1                 // File: c5_1.java
{
        private static box1 b = new box1(1, 2, 3, 4);   // subobject

        public static void main(String args[])
        {
                double weightBox, sizeBox;

                weightBox = b.shipWeight();
                sizeBox = b.shipLength();
                System.out.println("Shipping Size: " + sizeBox);
                System.out.println("\nWeight: " + weightBox);
        }
}

class box1
{
        private double length = 2.5;
        private double width = 4.0;
        private double height = 3.0;
        private double density = 1.0;
        box1(double len, double wid, double heigt, double dens)
        {
                length = len;
                width = wid;
                height = heigt;
                density = dens;
        }
        double shipWeight()
        {
                return density * width * length * height;
        }
        double shipLength()
        {
                return width + length + height;
        }
}
```

Output:
```
Shipping Size:  6

Weight:  24
```

- Private variables and methods in the subobject's class cannot be referenced in methods in the class containing the subobject. **Private variables and methods can only be referenced by methods in their own class.**

- All other kinds (package, protected, and public) of variables and methods in the subobject's class can be referenced in methods in the class containing the subobject if the subobject's class is in the same package.

Example of the above rules:

```java
class c5_2              // File: c5_2.java  THIS FILE WILL NOT COMPILE SUCCESSFULLY
{
        private static box2 b = new box2(1, 2, 3, 4);

        public static void main(String args[])
        {
                double weightBox, sizeBox;

                weightBox = b.shipWeight();
                sizeBox = b.shipLength(); // ERROR: shipLength() private

                System.out.println("Shipping Size: " + sizeBox);
                System.out.println("\nWeight: " + weightBox);
        }
}

class box2
{
        private double length = 2.5;
        private double width = 4.0;
        private double height = 3.0;
        private double density = 1.0;
        public box2(double len, double wid, double heigt, double dens)
        {
                length = len;
                width = wid;
                height = heigt;
                density = dens;
        }
        protected double shipWeight()
        {
                return density * width * length * height;
        }
        private double shipLength()    // Source of error.
        {
                return width + length + height;
        }
}
```

Note: b is a static object to allow it to be referenced in static main().

---

## Subobject Initialization

Subobjects are initialized by allocating an object of the subobject class type with appropriate initialization values. The subobject name is a reference for an object. The subobject storage is usually allocated in the containing class' constructor.

Example:

**File: c5_3.java**

```java
class fangs        // File: c5_3.java
{
        private double venom;

        fangs(double v)
        {
                venom = v;
        }
        double displayVenom()
        {
                return venom;
        }
}

class cobra
{
        private fangs f;

        cobra(double v)
        {
                f = new fangs(v); // allocate and initialize subobject.
        }
        double display()
        {
                return f.displayVenom();
        }
}

class c5_3
{
        public static void main(String args[])
        {
                cobra c = new cobra(5.0);
                System.out.println("Cobra venom amount: " + c.display());
        }
}
```

Output:

```
Cobra venom amount:   5
```

# SUBCLASSING (INHERITANCE)

- Classes can be related to each other through inheritance.

- Inheritance is an object-oriented design concept that creates a new class by inheriting all the variables and methods of an existing class, and then adding more variables and methods.

- The purpose and major benefit of inheritance is to reuse the code of a class within another class without duplicating code. The result is more compact code which is easier to understand and maintain.

- In Java inheritance is called **subclassing**. The bequeathing class is called the **superclass**. The inheriting class is called the **subclass**. Inheritance relationships are diagrammed with inheritance hierarchies such as:

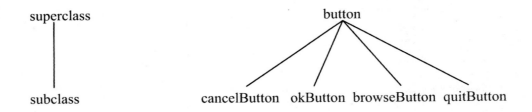

- Inheritance and subclass relationships are indicated by the "**ISA**" relationship of object-oriented design.

> Example:
>> A cancelButton is a button.

It states a class called cancelButton is a kind of button. The cancelButton class will be subclassed from the button class.

- Rule: *A subclass can only have one superclass. No multiple inheritance.*

- *If a class is not explicitly subclassed, then it is automatically subclassed from a class called Object* (described later).

Object
|
myClass

## Subclass Coding

A subclass relationship is specified with the **extends** keyword.

**File: c5_4.java**

```java
class animal          // File: c5_4.java
{
        private double weight;
        animal(double w)
        {
                weight = w;
        }
        double displayWeight()
        {
                return weight;
        }
}

class cobra extends animal          // makes animal a superclass
{
        private double strikingDistance; //
        cobra(double w, double s)        //
        {                                //
                super(w);                //
                strikingDistance = s;    //
        }                                //
        double strike()                  //
        {                                //
                return strikingDistance;
        }
}

class c5_4
{
        public static void main(String args[])
        {
                cobra c = new cobra(5.0, 6.0);
                System.out.println("Cobra weight: " + c.displayWeight());
                System.out.println("Strike Zone: " + c.strike());
        }
}
```

**Cobra Object**

Class cobra inherits all the variables and methods of class animal. A cobra object can receive any message from class cobra or class animal: displayWeight() or strike(). A cobra object contains an animal part.

Note: The super() call invokes the animal constructor to initialize the animal part – the weight variable. **You cannot use animal(w) in place of super(w) in the above code.**

Note: the displayWeight() and strike() methods are both called for the cobra object.

The rules and details of subclass constructors and methods are described on the next pages.

## Subclasses and Constructors

A subclass constructor has certain rules because the superclass part of a subclass object must be initialized. There are several possible initialization procedures which you can specify within a subclass constructor.

- The subclass constructor can have a **first** statement of the form:

```
super( args);
```

  The matching superclass constructor is executed to initialize the superclass part of the new subclass object. **You cannot invoke the superclass constructor using the superclass name.**

- OR the subclass constructor can have a **first** statement of the form:

```
this( args );
```

  This statement executes the matching constructor (matching on the argument data types) in the same subclass.

  Matching is done on the argument list. A subclass constructor can call another subclass constructor with this(...).

- The **first** statement in the subclass constructor can be ordinary code (not a super(...) or a this(...)). In this case the superclass constructor with no parameters runs by default.

- Additional rules:

  1. An explicit constructor call cannot contain arguments which are instance variables of the object being created.

  2. After an explicit superclass constructor call runs, the instance variables of the subclass are given default zero or null values, or their explicitly specified initialization value.

## Example Illustrating the Rules

**File: c5_5.java**

```
class animal2          // File: c5_5.java
{
        private double weight;
        animal2()              // No argument constructor required for cobra(double)
        {                      // and cobra() constructors
                weight = 1.0;
        }
        animal2(double w)
        {
                weight = w;
        }
        double displayWeight()
        {
                return weight;
        }
}

class cobra extends animal2
{
        private double strikingDistance;
        cobra()
        {
                this(2.0);     // cobra(double s) then runs.
        }
        cobra(double s)
        {                              // animal2() runs first
                strikingDistance = s;
        }
        cobra(double w, double s)
        {
                super(w);      // animal2(double) runs.
                strikingDistance = s;
        }
        double strike()
        {
                return strikingDistance;
        }
}
```

```
class c5_5
{
        public static void main(String args[])
        {
                cobra c = new cobra(5.0, 6.0);
                System.out.println("Cobra weight: " + c.displayWeight());
                System.out.println("Strike Zone: " + c.strike());

                c = new cobra(7.0);                    // cobra(double) runs.
                                                       // Garbage collect old object.
                System.out.println("\nCobra weight: " + c.displayWeight());
                System.out.println("Strike Zone: " + c.strike());

                c = new cobra();  // cobra() runs.  Garbage collect old object.
                System.out.println("\nCobra weight: " + c.displayWeight());
                System.out.println("Strike Zone: " + c.strike());
        }
}
```

Trace the code steps and see if you can understand the below output of the program.

Output:

```
Cobra weight: 5
Strike Zone: 6

Cobra weight: 1
Strike Zone: 7

Cobra weight: 1
Strike Zone: 2
```

## Summary: Allocation of Storage for Objects

When storage for an object is allocated the following events take place:

      1.  Storage is allocated by new for the object.

      2.  The constructor runs for the object.  If the class of the object is a subclass, then the superclass constructor runs before the rest of the object is initialized.

      3.  A reference is returned to which the object reference is set equal.

## Finalizers and Subclass Objects

- In Java when an object is at the point of being garbage collected the finalizer in its class executes if one is present.

- If the object's class is subclassed from another class, then the superclass finalize() will only execute if it is explicitly called from the subclass finalize() with the statement `super.finalize();`.

```
protected void finalize()
{
        // ...
        super.finalize();
        // ...
}
```

- If the subclass finalize() does not explicitly call the superclass finalize(), then the superclass finalize() will not execute for a subclass object.  Java does not automatically chain finalizers (unlike C++ destructors).

## Accessing Member Variables and Methods

A member variable or method of a class can have one of the following access categories:

private datatype variable;      // private variable:  can only be referenced by methods in its
      // own class.

private datatype methodName(...) { ...}    // private method: can only be referenced by methods
    // in its own class.

datatype variable;      // package variable:  can be referenced by methods in its own
      // class or in any class in the same package.

datatype methodName(...) { ...}    // package method: can be referenced by methods in its
    // own class or in any class in the same package.

protected datatype variable;    // protected variable:  can be referenced in any method in the
    // same package or in any method in a subclass whether the subclass is in the package or not.

protected datatype methodName(...) { ...} // protected method:  can be referenced in any method
// in the same package, or in a subclass whether the subclass is in the package or not.

public datatype variable;      // public variable:  can be referenced in any method.

public datatype methodName(...) { ...}    // public method: can be referenced in any method.

The distinctions between private, public, protected, and package will be discussed in more detail later in this module. The above categories and rules apply to individual methods and varaibles. The access to a method or variable also depends on its class: public classes allow access to their variables and methods. Package type classes have restricted access to their methods and variables. More on this topic later.

## Examples of Accessing Superclass Variables and Methods

Note the super.whatever notation below allows us to access superclass variables and methods – even if they have the same name as methods and variables in the subclass.

**File: c5_6.java**

```
class animal3        // File: c5_6.java
{
        protected double length = 3.0;
        private double weight;
        animal3()
        {
                weight = 1.0;
        }
        animal3(double w)
        {
                weight = w;
        }
        public double displayWeight()
        {
                return weight;
        }
        protected void finalize()   // protected required because finalize()
        {                           // is protected in class Object.
                System.out.println("Animal finalize.");
        }
}

class cobra extends animal3
{
        private double strikingDistance;
        private double length = 99.0;

        cobra(double s)
        {
                strikingDistance = s;
        }
        cobra(double w, double s)
        {
                super(w);
                strikingDistance = s;
        }
        double strike()
        {
                return strikingDistance;
        }
        public double displayWeight() // must be public because superclass
        {                             // displayWeight() is public.
                return super.displayWeight();    // super. notation
        }
```

```
        double displayLength()
        {
                return super.length;            // super. Notation.
//              return ((animal3)this).length; // an equivalent return statement.
        }
        double displaySum()
        {
                return length + super.displayWeight();  // super. notation
        }
        protected void finalize()    // protected required because finalize()
        {                            // is protected in class animal3
                System.out.println("Cobra finalize.");
        }
}

class c5_6
{
        public static void main(String args[])
        {
                cobra c = new cobra(4.0, 5.0);

                System.out.println("Cobra weight: " + c.displayWeight());

                System.out.println("Cobra length: " + c.displayLength());

                System.out.println("Cobra sum: " + c.displaySum());

                System.out.println("Strike Zone: " + c.strike());
        }
}
```

Output:

```
Cobra weight: 4.0
Cobra length: 3.0
Cobra sum: 103.0
Strike Zone: 5.0
```

- Only private superclass variables and methods cannot be referenced in subclass methods.

## Method Overloading and Subclassing

- Methods with the same name can appear in a superclass and subclass.

- Subclass methods with the same name and parameter list as a superclass method can either have the same access or be more public as indicated by the progression of "publicness":

$$private \rightarrow package \rightarrow protected \rightarrow public$$

- If a call is made to an overloaded method, then the matching call in the class of the recipient object executes. If no match is found because of differing parameter data types (taking account of possible automatic data type conversions of the arguments that might lead to a match), then the matching method is run in the superclass of the recipient object's class (or the superclasses above it).

Example:

```
class animal4       // File: c5_7.java
{
        protected double weight;
        animal4()
        {
                weight = 1.0;
        }
        animal4(double w)
        {
                weight = w;
        }
        double displayWeight(double w)
        {
                System.out.println("dW animal double.");
                return weight + w;
        }
        double displayWeight()
        {
                System.out.println("dW animal.");
                return weight;
        }
        protected void finalize()    // protected required because finalize()
        {                            // is protected in class Object.
                System.out.println("Animal finalize.");
        }
}
```

```
class cobra extends animal4
{
        private double strikingDistance;

        cobra(double s)
        {
                strikingDistance = s;
        }
        cobra(double w, double s)
        {
                super(w);
                strikingDistance = s;
        }
        double strike()
        {
                return strikingDistance;
        }
        double displayWeight()
        {
                System.out.println("dW Cobra.");
                return super.displayWeight();
        }
        protected void finalize()      // protected required because finalize()
        {                              // is protected in class animal
                System.out.println("Cobra finalize.");
        }
}

class c5_7
{
        public static void main(String args[])
        {
                cobra c = new cobra(3.0, 5.0);
                System.out.println("Cobra weight: " + c.displayWeight());
                System.out.println("Strike Zone: " + c.strike() + "\n");

                c = new cobra(7.0);
                System.out.println("Cobra weight: " + c.displayWeight(14.5));
                System.out.println("Strike Zone: " + c.strike());
        }
}
```

Output:

```
dW Cobra.
dW animal.
Cobra weight: 3
Strike Zone: 5

dW animal double.
Cobra weight: 15.5
Strike Zone: 7
```

calls class animal4 overload

- The displayWeight() method call executes the cobra displayWeight() method. The displayWeight(14.5) method call executes the animal4 displayWeight(double) method.

## Method Overloading Summary

- If methods of the same name appear in both the superclass and subclass, then a call to the method is resolved by matching the argument list of the method call with the parameter lists of the overloaded methods. The matching method executes.

- If the superclass and subclass have methods with the same name, return data type, and parameter list, then the subclass method overrides the superclass method in method calls in methods of other classes.

- Private methods and variables can only be referenced in methods in their own class.

- Protected methods and variables can only be referenced in methods in their own package or in methods in a subclass of their class (any package).

- Package methods and variables can be accessed in any method within a class in the same package.

- As seen earlier super can be used to override a method in a subclass to specify a method in a superclass.

# JAVA POLYMORPHISM

- Polymorphic means "the recipient object selects the message"

- Polymorphism is implemented in C++ with virtual functions.

- All Java methods are automatically polymorphic.

- Polymorphism in Java is based on these concepts:

  1. At compile time the Java compiler verifies that the class (or interface) type of the reference variable "before the ." contains a match for the method call "following the period" either within the definition of its data type or through inheritance.  For example,

       `c.getWeight();`

will generate a compiler error message if the class of the reference variable c (not the class of the object in memory) does not contain a match for getWeight() either directly or by inheritance.

  2. At runtime the Java runtime environment determines the data type of the object (the data type after the operator new when the object was created) in memory specified by the reference and then executes the method in the class of the object in memory.

  3. The class of the reference variable may not be the same as the class of the allocated object in memory. For example a superclass reference variable can be pinned on a subclass object. See example below.

Example:

**File: polymorph.java**
```
class organic
{
        double weight;

        organic(double weight)
        {
                this.weight = weight;
        }
        double getWeight()
        {
                return 99.0;
        }
}
```

```java
class myAnimal extends organic
{
        myAnimal(double w)
        {
                super(w);
        }
}

class myCobra extends myAnimal
{
        private double strikingDistance;
        private double wetWeight;

        myCobra(double w, double s)
        {
                super(w);
                wetWeight = 1.1 * w;
                strikingDistance = s;
        }
        double getWeight()
        {
                return wetWeight;
        }
        double getOrganicWeight()
        {
                return weight;
        }
}

class polymorph
{
        public static void main(String args[])
        {
                myCobra c = new myCobra(3.0, 5.0);
                System.out.println("Cobra wetWeight using c: "
                                                + c.getWeight());
                System.out.println("Cobra weight: " +
                                                c.getOrganicWeight());

                myAnimal an = c;
// Next line: Compiler requires getWeight() in myAnimal (or superclass).
// Runtime executes getWeight() in myCobra - polymorphism.
                System.out.println("\nCobra wetWeight using an: "
                                                + an.getWeight());
//              System.out.println("Cobra weight: "
//                              + an.getOrganicWeight()); COMPILER ERROR

                organic or = c;
// Next line:  Compiler requires getWeight() in organic.
// Runtime executes getWeight() in myCobra - polymorphism.
                System.out.println("\nCobra wetWeight using or: "
                                                + or.getWeight());
```

```
//              System.out.println("Cobra weight: "
//                       + or.getOrganicWeight()); COMPILER ERROR
          }
}
```

Output:
```
Cobra wetWeight using c: 3.3
Cobra weight: 3.0

Cobra wetWeight using an: 3.3

Cobra wetWeight using or: 3.3
```

Polymorphism has some important roles in programming. It can be used to process vectors and lists of objects in ways similar to other languages such as C++. See books on programming for examples.

# CLASS ACCESS TYPES

There are two types of Java classes from the point of view of access:

**package** - The contents (variables and methods) of a package class can be accessed by methods in other classes in its package. The package keyword is not used to specify a package class. Package classes are the default. A class is package class if it is not a public class.

**public** - The contents of a public class can be accessed by methods in other classes - regardless of which package they are in. Public classes must be defined in a file with the same filename stem as the class name. For example, public class myClass must be in the file myClass.java. (These filenames are required to have the same case letter by letter as the class name.)

# PUBLIC CLASS

- A public class is a class which is declared public with the public keyword. Its contents can be accessed by methods in other classes in its package or in other packages.

- A public class must be defined in a file className.java with the same class name as the public class. The cases of the letters in the class name and filename must match.

Format:

```
public class className
{

    // code

}
```

# SPECIAL KINDS OF CLASSES

**abstract** - An abstract class is a class which can only be used for subclassing. Abstract class objects cannot be instantiated with objects.

**final** - A final class cannot be subclassed.

## STATIC FINAL VARIABLES

- Static final variables can be viewed as the equivalent of #define symbolic constants in C. Their value cannot be changed once it is set during the course of a Java program. Since the java compiler is able to calculate the initial value of a static final variable at compile time, then this value can be used to calculate other compile-time constants.

- A final variable can have its value set by initialization or by an assignment statement. Any succeeding attempt to set a value for a final variable generates a compiler error message.

- *final variable = readonly variable*

## FINAL CLASS

A final class is a class which cannot be subclassed. It can be a subclass of a superclass.

Format:

```
final class className
{

    // code

}
```

## FINAL METHOD

A final method is a method which does not allow a method with the same name and same parameter data type list to appear in any subclass of its class. *Static methods are final by default.*

```
class super1
{
    // ...
    final double f(int x)
    {
        // ...
    }
}

class sub1 extends super1
{
    double f(int x)    //  Error message.
    {
        // ...
    }
}
```

**5. Class Interrelationships**

# ABSTRACT CLASSES AND METHODS

- An abstract class is a class which cannot be instantiated. Its only role is to be subclassed.

- Purpose: to implement the ISA relationship without the possibility of instantiation, and often to provide a uniform set of constraints on methods defined in subclasses.

- An abstract class can contain "normal" methods and abstract methods.

- An *abstract method* is a method which is declared as abstract in a class. No definition of the method is provided. The declaration specifies the data types of the method's parameters and the data type of the return value.

- Abstract methods can only be declared in abstract classes (and interfaces - described later).

- Every class subclassed from an abstract class must provide a true definition of each abstract method in the superclass - or the subclass will also be forced to be abstract.

- Abstract classes cannot contain abstract static methods.

Abstract Class Example:

**File: animal5.java**

```
public abstract class animal5    // File: animal5.java
{
        protected double weight = 0.0;
        private double height;
        public double width;
        double girth;
        static double number;

        public abstract void eat(double food);
                                    // parameter name required.
//        abstract static void f();
        abstract void g();
        protected abstract void h();
        abstract void m();

        public double display() { return weight; }
        static void n() {}
        protected void p() {}
        private void q() {}
        void r() {}
}
```

**File: cat.java**

```
public class cat extends animal5
{
        public void eat(double food)   // required by superclass
                        // constrained by superclass declaration of eat()
        {
            weight += food;
        }

        void g() {return;} // required by superclass

        protected void h() { }// required by superclass

        void m() { }// required by superclass

        // code
}
```

# THE INTERFACE CONCEPT

The following example illustrates the primary purpose of an interface: to specify a set of constraints on programmers defining the methods of a class.

Example:

Goal: to define a set of classes for various kinds of tapes and tape-like things:

> audioTape
> videoTape
> cdRom

Requirement: Certain common methods in these classes should have the same programming interface: same parameter data types and the same return value.

Reason: to make life easier for the programmers writing applications using the above class definitions.

Solution: force the developers of the audioTape, videoTape, and cdRom classes to implement the following method formats:

> void rewind()
> void play(int time)
> void fastForward(int time)
> void stop()
> int nextSelection()

Approach 1 - subclassing with tape being an abstract class containing the above abstract methods. An audioTape ISA tape.

Approach 2 - define an interface called tapeable containing the above abstract methods which each class will implement.

Approach 2 is the preferred choice in most cases because Java allows only one superclass but allows a class to implement any number of interfaces. Interfaces are cheaper from a programming point of view. Subclassing is precious and should be reserved for important purposes either currently or in a future version.

# INTERFACES

- An interface usually provides a set of abstract method specifications which declare the parameter data types and return value of each method in the interface.

- The set of method specifications structure the methods declared in classes implementing the interface.

- An interface can be implemented in several classes forcing a common interface on these classes.

- A class can implement several interfaces. A subclass can only specify one superclass. This difference is the primary difference between an interface and an abstract class.

- There are also technical differences in the kinds of variables and methods which are allowed to appear in an abstract superclass vs. an interface.

- Interface rules:

    - Interface variables can be package or public.

    - All allowed interface variables are final (readonly) and they must have an explicit initialization value. Interface variables cannot be assigned new values in methods in classes implementing the interface. The values of the variables can be fetched and used in methods of implementing the interface.

    - Interface variables are always static. They are declared static or are static by default.

    - Interface variables cannot be private or protected.

    - Interface methods are always public.

    - All interface methods are abstract whether or not they are explicitly declared abstract. Therefore no interface method is allowed to have a block of code.

    - Interface methods cannot be native, static, synchronized, final, private, or protected.

Example:

**File: social.java**

```
public interface social
{
        int grace = 1;
        public int dignity = 1;
//        protected int poise = 1;
//        private int calmness = 1;
        static int stature = 1;
        final int accent = 1;

        public abstract void b(double x);    // parameter name required
//        abstract static void f();            No static methods.
//        private abstract void g();           No private methods.
//        protected abstract void h();         No protected methods.
//        final abstract void j();             No final methods.
        abstract void m();                   // public by default.

// Abstract by default:
        public double display();
//        static void n();                   No static methods.
//        protected void p();                No protected methods.
//        private void q();                  No private methods.
//        final void r();                    No final methods.

//   No blocks allowed for methods:
//        public double display() { return weight; }
//        static void n() {}
//        protected void p() {}
//        private void q() {}
}


physical.java
public interface physical
{
        int strength = 1;
        public int size = 6;
        static int weight = 150;
        final int width = 31;

        public abstract int getSize();
        abstract int getWeight(); // public by default.
        public int getWidth();  // abstract by default.
}
```

**File: person.java**

```
public class person implements social, physical  // implements interfaces
{
        public void b(double x)
        {
                System.out.println(grace);
        }
        public void m()
        {
        }
        public double display()
        {
                return (double) dignity;
        }
        public int getSize()
        {
                return size;
        }
        public int getWeight()
        {
                return weight;
        }
        public int getWidth()
        {
                return width;
        }
}
```

# SUPER-INTERFACES AND SUB-INTERFACES

- Interfaces can be subclassed from other interfaces in the same way that classes are subclassed from classes.

- An interface has the extra feature that it can be subclassed from more than one interface.

Example:

```
public interface newPerson extends social, physical
{
      // code
}

public class doctor implements newPerson
{
      // code
}
```

# USING CLASSES AND PACKAGES

The CLASSPATH variable is a environmental shell variable in UNIX and LINUX, and a variable on Windows XX and Windows NT platforms. It specifies a list of directories and zip files that contain compiled class definitions. These files and directories are searched for needed class definitions when your program is compiled and when it executes. CLASSPATH specifies a search path for classes.

Browsers have automatic settings for the CLASSPATH and so you don't have to set the variable if you are simply using a browser to display Java applets. (If your Java applet uses a package that is not built into the browser then you might have to add an entry to the built-in CLASSPATH used by the browser. This process is browser dependent. See your browser documentation.)

If you are using the Java Development Kit (JDK or SDK) then you may have to set the CLASSPATH yourself. You may have to set the CLASSPATH if you are using a Java IDE (Integrated Development Environment).

The CLASSPATH is used slightly differently in Java 1.0 and 1.1 versions from Java 1.2 and Java 1.3 versions. Upward Java compatibility is maintained however.

## JDK 1.0 and 1.1 Versions Use of CLASSPATH

The CLASSPATH played a more important role in Java 1.0 and Java 1.1 versions. The Java compiler (javac) and the Java interpreters (java and appletviewer) do not have a default CLASSPATH. These versions of Java require you to specify a CLASSPATH to use the JDK.

The most minimal CLASSPATH specifies two items: the current directory (very important), and the zip file containing the built-in packages (class libraries). In PC environments it contains a semicolon separated list of directories. In UNIX and LINUX the directory list is colon separated.

A CLASSPATH will normally contain . (a period) in each environment to allow compiling in any directory. "." represents the current directory.

Minimal CLASSPATH
PC Windows XX (command normally placed in autoexec.bat):

```
set CLASSPATH=.;c:\jdk1.1.7b\lib\classes.zip;
```

PC Windows NT (entered on the Environmental Variables page):

```
.;c:\jdk1.1.7b\lib\classes.zip;
```

UNIX (LINUX) Korn or Bourne Shell (commands normally placed in .profile file) assuming Java is installed in the /opt directory:

```
CLASSPATH=.:/opt/java/lib/classes.zip:/java/classes:/java/myclasses
export CLASSPATH
```

UNIX (LINUX) C Shell (command normally placed in.cshrc file) assuming Java is installed in the /opt directory:

```
setenv CLASSPATH  .:/opt/java/lib/classes.zip:/java/classes:/java/myclasses
```

### General CLASSPATH

In general the CLASSPATH adds directories and zip files to the minimal CLASSPATH. An example adding one directory and one zip file is:

PC Windows XX (command normally placed in autoexec.bat):

```
set CLASSPATH=.;c:\jdk1.1.7b\lib\classes.zip;c:\myjava\classes;c:\myjava\myclass.zip;
```

PC Windows NT (entered on the Environmental Variables page):

```
.;c:\jdk1.1.7b\lib\classes.zip;c:\myjava\classes;c:\myjava\myclass.zip;
```

UNIX (LINUX) Korn or Bourne Shell (commands normally placed in .profile file) assuming Java is installed in the /opt directory:

```
CLASSPATH=.:/opt/java/lib/classes.zip:/myjava/classes:/myjava/myclass.zip
export CLASSPATH
```

UNIX (LINUX) C Shell (command normally placed in .cshrc file) assuming Java is installed in the /opt directory:

```
setenv CLASSPATH  .:/opt/java/lib/classes.zip:/myjava/classes:/myjava/myclass.zip
```

## JDK 1.2 and 1.3 Versions Use of CLASSPATH

The CLASSPATH played a slightly less important role in Java 1.2 and Java 1.3 versions. The Java compiler (javac) and the Java interpreters (java and appletviewer) effectively have a default CLASSPATH. You can specify a CLASSPATH to supplement the built-in CLASSPATH.

In PC environments it contains a semicolon separated list of directories. <u>In UNIX and LINUX the directory list is colon separated</u>.

For example to add one directory and one zip file use the CLASSPATH:

PC Windows XX (command normally placed in autoexec.bat):

```
set CLASSPATH=.;c:\myjava\classes;c:\myjava\myclass.zip;
```

PC Windows NT (entered on the Environmental Variables page):

```
.;c:\myjava\classes;c:\myjava\myclass.zip;
```

UNIX (LINUX) Korn or Bourne Shell (commands normally placed in .profile file) assuming Java is installed in the /opt directory:

```
CLASSPATH=.:/opt/java/lib/classes.zip:/myjava/classes:/myjava/myclass.zip
export CLASSPATH
```

UNIX (LINUX) C Shell (command normally placed in .cshrc file) assuming Java is installed in the /opt directory:

```
setenv CLASSPATH   .:/myjava/classes:/myjava/myclass.zip
```

- In Java 1.2 and 1.3 the CLASSPATH does not have to include the library of built-in packages. It is automatically specified when the JDK is installed.

- Java 1.2 and 1.3 allows you to install a jar file by placing it in the \jdk1.3\jre\lib\ext directory without uwse of the CLASSPATH.

- Classes not contained in a jar file can be added simply by placing them in the \jdk1.3\jre\classes directory. By default, the classes directory does not exist.

- The class search path procedure is:

    1. The first place searched is the boot classpath. This can be specified with the -Xbootclasspath option, and can be fetched with System.getProperty("sun.boot.class.path").

    2. The second place searched is the directories jre/lib/ext and jre\classes. The list of directories can be fetched with System.getProperty("java.ext.dirs").

    3.The last place searched is the application classpath set by -classpath or CLASSPATH. The value of this path can be fetched with System.getProperty("java.class.path").

# IMPORTING A JAVA PACKAGE

Java uses "import" statements to shorten the names used to refer to classes.

Methods and variables in Java classes can be specified in programs using fully qualified names such as

```
… java.awt.BorderLayout.CENTER   …
```

which specifies the CENTER variable in the BorderLayout class in the built-in awt package. Notice periods are used to separate parts of a fully qualified name.

OR variables and methods can be specified in an abbreviated form using import statements:

```
import java.awt.*;
```

…

```
… BorderLayout.CENTER …
```

The abbreviated form is usually preferred since the code is more compact, less cluttered, and more readable.

The import statement above tells the compiler to search the awt package for needed classes. The reference to BorderLayout.CENTER in the code causes the compiler to search for the needed BorderLayout class and then to fetch the CENTER variable from within that class.

When searching for a needed class the compiler will select the first one it finds on the search path. In some cases where two classes of the same name appear in different packages it may be necessary to use fully qualified names. For example if the class MyClass appears in the packages MyPackage and YourPackage then we must use fully qualified names in general:

MyPackage.MyClass.var1     or     YourPackage.MyClass.var2

to avoid potential ambiguities.

## Types of import Statements

You can import in either of two ways:

- To import one class only place a statement of the form:

  ```
  import java.package.classname;
  ```

  at the top of your file. For example,

  ```
  import java.awt.Color;
  ```

- To import all the classes in a package place a statement of the form:

  ```
  import java.package.*;
  ```

  at the top of your file. For example,

  ```
  import java.awt.*;
  ```

An imported class or package of classes can be referenced in abbreviated form. A fully qualified name need not be used.

## Important Notes:

- If a package has a sub-package then you must specify the sub-package explicitly to import its classes into your program. For example,

  ```
  import java.awt.peer.*;
  ```

  imports the classes in the peer sub-package of awt into your program.The "import java.awt.*;" statement does not import java.awt.peer into your program.

- Importing Java classes one at a time or using the .* approach results in Java code of the same size and efficiency.

## Using the CLASSPATH Variable and the import Statement

The following cases illustrate the role of the CLASSPATH variable.

### Importing an Individual Class Not in a Package

A class can be imported into a file with the import statement.  If the imported class file specifies no package, then it is placed in a default package together with the application classes.

If the CLASSPATH variable is not set, then the imported class .class file must be in the same directory as the source code being compiled or in \jdk1.x\lib (Java 1.1.x) or in \jdk1.3\jre\classes (Java 1.3) in PC environments.

If the CLASSPATH variable is set, then the imported class .class file must be in one of the directories listed in the CLASSPATH variable or in \jdk1.3\jre\classes (1.2 and 1.3 Java only).  The importing class .class file must also be in a directory listed in the CLASSPATH.

Example:

**File: c5_8.java**

```
import box3;        // imports class box3 from box3.class file

class c5_8            // File: c5_8.java      needs box3.class
{
        private static box3 b = new box3(1, 2, 3, 4);

        public static void main(String args[])
        {
                double weightBox, sizeBox;

                weightBox = b.shipWeight();
                sizeBox = b.shipLength();

                System.out.println("Shipping Size: " + sizeBox);
                System.out.println("\nWeight: " + weightBox);
        }
}
```

**File: box3.java**

```
class box3        // File: box3.java
{
        private double length = 2.5;
        private double width = 4.0;
        private double height = 3.0;
        private double density = 1.0;

        public box3(double len, double wid, double heigt, double dens)
        {
                length = len;
                width = wid;
                height = heigt;
                density = dens;
        }
        protected double shipWeight()  // protected or public allowed.
        {
                return density * width * length * height;
        }
        protected double shipLength()  // protected or public allowed.
        {
                return width + length + height;
        }
}
```

## Importing a Class in a Package

The imported class must have a package statement making it part of the package.

**File: c5_9.java**

```
import packbox4.box4;

class c5_9            // needs box4.class in packbox4 package
{
        private static box4 b = new box4(1, 2, 3, 4);

        public static void main(String args[])
        {
                double weightBox, sizeBox;

                weightBox = b.shipWeight();
                sizeBox = b.shipLength();
                System.out.println("Shipping Size: " + sizeBox);
                System.out.println("\nWeight: " + weightBox);
        }
}
```

- The above file must be in a directory listed in CLASSPATH.

- The compiled version of the below file must be in the packbox4 subdirectory of a directory listed in the CLASSPATH (or in a zip file in the relative path subdirectory packbox4).

**File: packbox4\box4.java**

```
package packbox4;
public class box4
{
        private double length = 2.5;
        private double width = 4.0;
        private double height = 3.0;
        private double density = 1.0;

        public box4(double len, double wid, double heigt, double dens)
        {
                length = len;
                width = wid;
                height = heigt;
                density = dens;
        }
        public double shipWeight()
        {
                return density * width * length * height;
        }
        public double shipLength()
        {
                return width + length + height;
        }
}
```

**Picture of the Directory Layout for the Preceding Example**

- Public subobject methods in a public class of another package can be accessed in methods of a class containing the subobject. The access to the methods MUST be public in this case since the public class is in a different package. The below <u>top</u> row of directories, dir1 and dir2, are listed in the CLASSPATH list:

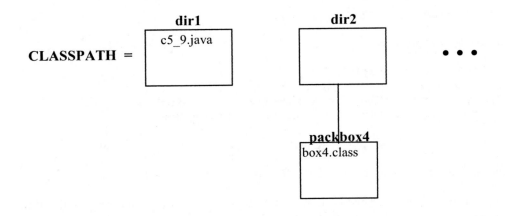

# BUILT-IN PACKAGES

Java has a number of built-in packages zipped into a file called classes.zip in \jdk1.1.x\lib or in a library file in \jdk1.3\lib on PC platforms. The Java compiler can read these files directly. Some of the currently available Java built-in packages are:

**java.io** - contains classes related to file input and output.

**java.lang** - Java language related classes including Math, Number, Integer, Float, String, Object, Thread, Exception, System, Runtime, Process, etc. *The java.lang package is automatically imported in every javac compile.*

**java.applet** - Java classes and interfaces which are used within applets: Applet, AudioClip, AppletStub, and AppletContext.

**java.awt** - A set of Java classes related to windowing including Button, CheckBox, Component, Choice, Graphics, Panel, Menu, TextField and TextArea.

**java.util** - A set of useful Java classes including Vector, Stack, Enumeration, Date, and Dictionary.

**java.net** - A set of network and Internet related classes including Socket, URL, DatagramSocket, DatagramPacket and ServerSocket.

**java.rmi** - Classes supporting remote method invocation for remote Java objects.

**java.security** - Classes supporting security features.

**java.sql** - Classes supporting SQL database access through jdbc.

**java.text** - Classes supporting international date and time formats.

**java.beans** - Classes supporting Java beans manipulation.

**java.math** - Classes supporting infinite precision mathematics.

# CREATING AND USING YOUR OWN PACKAGES

You can <u>define</u> your own package of classes.  One procedure is:

1.  Create a directory below one of the directories in the directory list in the CLASSPATH variable. The directory should have the name of the package.

2.  Create a file for each class in the package with the name of the class it contains with a .java extension added.  Classes can be public or package classes. Place the statement "`package packagename;`" at the top of each classfile.  Compile each class file. You can use the command

> **javac   *.java**

in the package directory.

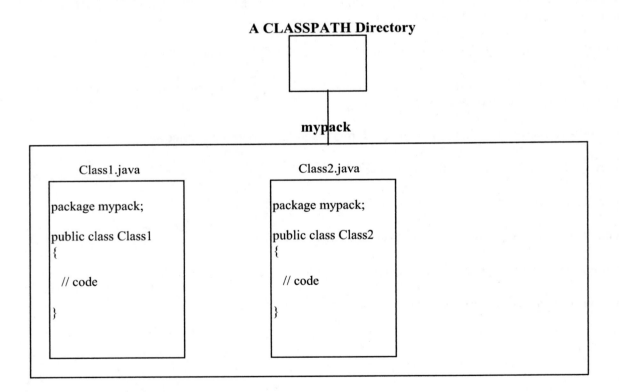

The .class files in a package may be zipped to create a package zip file with the jar command.

**jar –cf mypack.zip *.class**

The zip file for the above package should expand to a directory called mypack in the "current" directory containing the .class files. The CLASSPATH should have the complete path to the zip file specified:

```
CLASSPATH = …;c:\mydir\mypack.zip
```

if the zip file is placed in c:\mydir and given the name mypack.zip.

## import Statements for mypack

Import statements for your package can have the form:

```
import  mypack.*;     // imports all the classes in the package.
```

or

```
import mypack.classname;// imports only the specified class in package.
```

at the top of your program file.

# SUMMARY

This module has examined interrelationships between classes: subobjects, and subclassing.

The access rules for private, public, package and protected variables and methods were described.

The features of the various kinds of classes, package, abstract, final and public, were explored.

The definition and use of interfaces was examined.

The definition and use of packages was described. The Java environment built-in packages were identified.

The role of the CLASSPATH variable was described.

# EXERCISES

1. Add another subobject b1 to class c5_1 of c5_1.java and initialize its length, width, height and density to 5, 6, 7 and 8 respectively. Print its shipping weight and length.

2. Starting from c5_3.java add a fangs() constructor to class fangs setting venom = 3.0. Then add a cobra() constructor to class cobra which creates a fangs subobject using the new fangs constructor. Lastly, create a cobra object in main() which uses the new constructors and then display the venom value of this new object.

3. Modify the cobra(double s) constructor of c5_5.java to explicitly call the animal2(double w) constructor with the value w = 3.5. What effect does this change have on the displayed cobra weights?

4. What happens if you change the eat() method in class cat (in the cat.java file) to return int? (Remember to place a return statement in the method's block of code.) Compile ONLY and view any error messages. Compare to class animal5 (animal5.java file) from which cat is subclassed.

5. What happens if you change the display() method in class person (person.java file) to return int? Compare the modified method to the corresponding abstract method in interface social. Compile ONLY and view any error messages.

6. What CLASSPATH will enable c5_9.java to be successfully compiled? Try it. (Note: the packbox4 directory is in the box subdirectory of the class directory.)

# 6. Arrays and Lang Package Classes

## OBJECTIVES

At the end of this module you should be able to:

- Describe and use Java arrays.

- Describe and use the features of the String, numeric, mathematics and other classes.

- Use Command line arguments (parameters) in a Java program.

# OBJECT CLASS

- The Object class is the superclass, either directly or indirectly, for all other Java classes.

- A class which is not explicitly a subclass is automatically a subclass of class Object.

- Class Object methods can be used with objects of any class.

- Some useful methods are:

**Object clone()**

This method creates a true bitwise copy of an object. For example,

```
myClass obj2 = (myClass) obj1.clone();
```

effectively creates a new object obj2 with data variable values identical to obj1. The clone() method makes a deep (complete) copy of an array of primitive data or an array of objects. To make a duplicate of an array you can also use System.arraycopy() (described later).

**boolean equals(Object o)**

This method returns true if two Object objects are equal. For example,

```
if( obj1.equals(obj2) )
```

is true if obj1 equals obj2 in the sense they both contain identical data values. Many classes define equals() overloads for their objects.

Note: The == operator tests whether two variables are references to the same allocated object returning true in this case. Otherwise it returns false even if the objects have identical content.

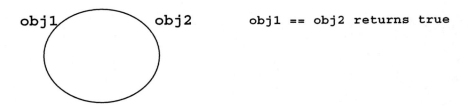

© Copyright 1996-2000 Dr. Stephen Blaha, Janus Associates Inc. All rights reserved. Copying prohibited

# ROLE OF CLASS OBJECT

Since Object is the ancestor of all classes an object of any class is type compatible with class Object. In other words any object can be treated as a class Object object. For example an Object reference variable can be pinned to any object in memory:

```
Object o = new MyClass(...);
```

A major role played by the Object class is to specify the return data type and/or parameter datatypes in general purpose methods (functions) that deal with a wide variety of Java objects.

Method Examples: In Module 9 we will create vectors of objects. A vector of objects is a set of objects that is index numbered starting from zero. Among the methods used to manipulate vectors that use class Object are:

**void addElement(Object obj)** - adds an object of any datatype to a vector.

**Object elementAt(int index)** – returns the object (of any data type) in the vector of the specified index number.

Sample code:

```
Vector v;
MyClass m = new MyClass(...);
YourClass y;
...

v.addElement(m);

...

y = (YourClass) v.elementAt(3);
```

# JAVA ARRAYS

- An array is an object in Java. It receives special handling from the Java compiler. An array is a linear set of components that are numbered with an index number starting from zero.

- Arrays can have any number of dimensions.

- There are three kinds of arrays:

  - Arrays of primitive data type components.

  - Arrays of component objects of some class type.

  - Arrays of components of an interface type (This type of array "contains" objects so it is similar to arrays of objects. The difference is the formal data type of the array of references just happens to be an interface. This array can contain an object of any class that implements the interface data type.)

- Array elements can be referenced using an index number ranging from zero to the number of components minus one. The index value must have an int, short, byte, or char data type. The index cannot be long.

index =   0   1   2

|   |   |   |   ... |   |

- If an array index value is out of the range of allowed array component index numbers, an exception *ArrayIndexOutofBoundsException* is thrown indicating an error. Java does array boundary checking. See module 7 for details.

# ARRAYS WITH PRIMITIVE DATA TYPE COMPONENTS

## One Dimensional Arrays

A one-dimensional array reference variable is declared with a statement such as:

```
int arr[];    // int [] arr; is an allowed alternative.
              // int arr[5]; is not allowed.
```

The size of the array is specified with a storage allocation statement such as

```
arr = new int[10];
```

This statement allocates storage for 10 int's. The declaration and storage allocation can be combined in a statement such as:

```
int arr[] = new int[10];
```

Array elements can be referenced using an index number ranging from zero to the number of components minus one.   The index must have an int, short, byte, or char data  type.  The index cannot be long.   For example, we can do math. with array components with statements such as

```
j = arr[0] * arr[9];
```

Arrays can be created and initialized with (started off with) a comma-separated list of values enclosed in braces.  For example,

```
int arr[] = { 44, 55, 66, 77};
```

Storage is allocated for  four int components which are given initial values 44, 55, 66, and 77..

Another example of  an array initialization is:

```
char carr[] = { 'a', 'b', 'c' };  // single quoted characters.
```

A char array is an ordinary set of characters.  No end of string character is needed (unlike C or C++).

Array components can be changed with assignment and other kinds of statements. For example,

```
carr[1] = 'x';
```

A primitive array is an object. Methods of class Object can be run on any array. For example,

```
char carr2[] = (char []) carr.clone();  // Type cast required since clone()
                                        // returns Object.
```

creates a duplicate of the carr array with the formal data type Object. The type cast is required so that we can place a name on the new array of data type char []. There is no automatic data type conversion from Object to char []. The result can be pictured as:

| carr | | carr2 | |
|------|--|-------|--|
|      |  |       |  |

## length Variable of Arrays

Every array object has a length member variable whose value equals the number of components in the array. The length value can never be changed. It is read-only. Some examples are:

```
System.out.println(carr.length);   // length = 3
System.out.println(arr.length);    // length = 4
```

## Two-Dimensional Arrays

- A two-dimensional Java array is an "array of one-dimensional arrays" in reality. We will not dwell on two-dimensional and higher dimensional arrays because they are not frequently used currently. When Java becomes a computational language after super-fast PC's appear then arrays will be more important.

- Two-dimensional arrays can be declared and defined in two ways:

  ```
  int tarr[][];

  // code

  tarr = new int[3][6];
  ```

  or in one statement

  ```
  int tarr[][] = new int[3][6];
  ```

- Array elements are referenced with two indices specified in braces. For example,

  ```
  j = tarr[1][3] + tarr[0][2];
  ```

- **All array indices begin with zero and range up to the number of components minus one.**

- Initialized arrays can also be defined with statements such as:

  ```
  int tarr[][] = {{1,2,3}, {4,5,6}};
  ```

  The braces indicate the array has two rows containing three columns each. The value of tarr[1][2] is 6.

  The length member can be used to specify the number of row and columns:

  `tarr.length` - the number of rows in tarr.

  `tarr[0].length` - the number of columns in row 0 of tarr.

## Multi-dimensional Arrays

- Arrays of any dimension can be defined in Java.

- Some ways of declaring and defining a three-dimensional array are:

```
int myarr[][][];

myarr = new int [3][4][10];
```

    or

```
 int myarr[][][] = new int [3][4][10];
```

    or

```
int myarr[][][] = new int[12][][];
```

- The last example illustrates a rule that some of the <u>rightmost</u> values may be omitted in a multidimensional array storage allocation. However int myarr[ ][ ][ ] = new int[ ][3][ ] is illegal.

- An initialized array can be defined with a statement such as:

```
int yourarr[][][] = {{{1,2,3},{4,5,6}}, {{7,8,9},{10,11,12}}};
```

    This array has two pages with two rows of three columns on each page.

- The memory layout of this array is:

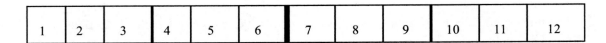

| 1 | 2 | 3 | 4 | 5 | 6 | 7 | 8 | 9 | 10 | 11 | 12 |

    The component yourarr[1][0][0] has the value 7.

- An example of a statement using a three-dimensional array is:

```
yourarr[1][1][0] = 99;
```

- Arrays of four or more dimensions can also be created.

## Example of a Program with Arrays

**File: c6_1.java**

```
class c6_1                    // File: c6_1.java
{
        public static void main(String args[])
        {
//              int badarr[5];

                int a[] = new int[5];
                a[0] = 11;
                System.out.println("a[0] = " + a[0]);

                int b[] = { 22, 33, 44};
                System.out.println("b[0] = " + b[0]);

                char carr[] = {'a', 'b', 'c'};
                System.out.println("carr[0] = " + carr[0]);
                System.out.println("carr = " + String.valueOf(carr));
                System.out.println("carr length = " + carr.length);

                int aa[][];
                aa = new int [3][6];
                aa[0][0] = 888;
                System.out.println("aa[0][0] = " + aa[0][0]);
                System.out.println("Number aa rows = " + aa.length);
                System.out.println("Number aa columns = " + aa[0].length);

                int bb[][] = {{1,2,3},{4,5,6}};
                System.out.println("bb[1][2] = " + bb[1][2]);

                int aaa[][][] = new int[10][2][3];
                aaa[1][1][2] = 99;
                System.out.println("aaa[1][1][2] = " + aaa[1][1][2]);

                aaa = new int[4][2][3];   // new storage allocated.
                aaa[3][1][2] = 66;
                System.out.println("aaa[3][1][2] = " + aaa[3][1][2]);
        }
}
```

Output:

```
a[0] = 11
b[0] = 22
carr[0] = a
carr = abc
carr length = 3
aa[0][0] = 888
Number aa rows = 3
Number aa columns = 6
bb[1][2] = 6
aaa[1][1][2] = 99
aaa[3][1][2] = 66
```

# ARRAYS WITH OBJECT COMPONENTS

Arrays with objects as components have a similar notation to arrays of primitive data type components.

```
myClass arrobj[];    //  or myClass [] arrobj;

arrobj = new myClass[10];
```

or in one statement

```
myClass arrobj[] = new myClass[10];
```

The above storage allocation allocates an array of names or references (not objects):

      `arrobj[0]`      `arrobj[1]`      `arrobj[2]`    …    `arrobj[9]`

with no storage allocated for the actual objects.


To allocate storage for objects individual assignment statements can be used:

```
arrobj[0] = new myClass( … );      // new required.
arrobj[1] = new myClass( … );
…
```

The result can be pictured as:

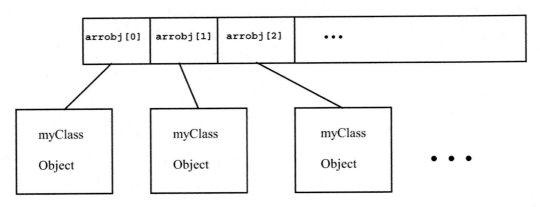

**arrobj**

# INITIALIZATION OF AN ARRAY OF OBJECTS

- An array of objects can be created and initialized with a list of initializers in braces. For example,

```
myClass arrobj[] = { new myClass(…), new myClass(…), new myClass(…), … };
```

- Each allocated object must be specified with a "new" allocation expression. The argument list in each parentheses must match a myClass constructor.

- A procedure to enlarge an array of objects at a later point in the program: an array identifier can be attached to a new larger set of references with statements such as

```
myClass tmp[] = arrobj;  // adds tmp as a name to the array.

arrobj = new myClass[20];

for(int j = 0; j < 10; j++)
        arrobj[j] = tmp[j];  // "copies" objects to new array

tmp = null;   // old array of names marked for garbage collection.
```

Effectively, the arrobj array now can reference 20 objects. It is "enlarged". The previous allocated storage, to which the array name was tied, is marked for garbage collection.

### Example of a Program with Arrays of Objects

**File: c6_2.java**

```
class c6_2              // File: c6_2.java
{
        public static void main(String args[])
        {
                mouse m[];
                m = new mouse[5];
                m[1] = new mouse(11);
                System.out.println("m[1] = " + m[1].display());
                m[1].set(111);
                System.out.println("m[1] = " + m[1].display());
//              System.out.println("m[2] = " + m[2].display());
// Runtime error: no object allocated for m[2].
                System.out.println("Number of elements: " + m.length);

                mouse marr[] = { new mouse(1), new mouse(), new mouse(2),
                               new mouse(), new mouse(3) };
                System.out.println("\nmarr[0] = " + marr[0].display());
                System.out.println("marr[1] = " + marr[1].display());
                System.out.println("marr[2] = " + marr[2].display());
                System.out.println("marr[3] = " + marr[3].display());
                System.out.println("marr[4] = " + marr[4].display());

                mouse fam[][];
                fam = new mouse [3][4];
                fam[1][3] = new mouse();
                System.out.println("\nfam[1][3] = " + fam[1][3].display());
                fam[1][3].set(999);
                System.out.println("fam[1][3] = " + fam[1][3].display());
                System.out.println("Number of rows: " + fam.length);
                System.out.println("Number of columns: " + fam[0].length);
        }
}
```

**File: mouse.java**

```
public class mouse        // File: mouse.java
{
        private int squeak;
        public mouse()
        {
                squeak = 99;
        }
        public mouse(int s)
        {
                squeak = s;
        }
        public void set(int s)
        {
                squeak = s;
        }
        public int display()
        {
                return squeak;
        }
}
```

The program's output is:

```
m[1] = 11
m[1] = 111
Number of elements: 5

marr[0] = 1
marr[1] = 99
marr[2] = 2
marr[3] = 99
marr[4] = 3

fam[1][3] = 99
fam[1][3] = 999
Number of rows: 3
Number of columns: 4
```

# MAKING COPIES OF ARRAYS

- Arrays of primitives or objects can be copied with the System.arraycopy() static method. The format of this method is

```
System.arraycopy(Object srcArr, int indexSrc,
                 Object destArr, int indexDest, int length)
```

- For arrays of primitives, the destination array destArr must have storage previously allocated for the components receiving values.

- For arrays of objects, the storage for the array of references must be allocated previously.

- Java programs can also use the clone() method to make a copy of an array of primitive data or an array of objects.

Example:

```
class c6_3                 // File: c6_3.java
{
        public static void main(String args[])
        {
                char carr[] = {'a', 'b', 'c'};
                char carr1[] = new char[3];


                System.arraycopy(carr, 0, carr1, 0, 3);


                System.out.println("carr1[0] = " + carr1[0]);
                System.out.println("carr1[2] = " + carr1[2]);


                char carr2[] = (char []) carr.clone();


                System.out.println("\ncarr2[0] = " + carr2[0]);
                System.out.println("carr2[1] = " + carr2[1]);


                mouse marr[] = { new mouse(1), new mouse(2), new mouse(3)};


                mouse marr2[] = (mouse []) marr.clone();


                System.out.println("\nmarr2[0] = " + marr2[0].display());
                System.out.println("marr2[1] = " + marr2[1].display());
        }
}
```

Output:

```
carr1[0] = a
carr1[2] = c

carr2[0] = a
carr2[1] = b

marr2[0] = 1
marr2[1] = 2
```

# STRING CLASS

- The String class is designed to hold a data string of characters. The data string cannot be lengthened or otherwise changed after the object is created. A String object contains a char array which holds Unicode characters in the object (ASCII characters are part of Unicode). The char's in the array have index numbers like normal char arrays. However, you can't reference the array components directly.

String Object example:

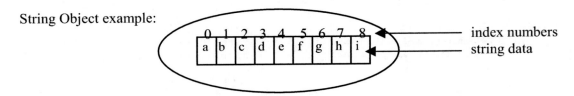

- String class objects are <u>unchangeable</u> after they are created. Characters can't be changed. Strings cannot be lengthened or shortened. See StringBuffer (later) for changeable dynamic strings.

- Every literal character string in a Java program is a String object. For example, "abc" is an object of class String.

String Example:

```
class c6_4               // File: c6_4.java
{
        public static void main(String args[])
        {
                String s1 = new String("xyz");   // not efficient.
                                                 // See s2 statement below.
                System.out.println(s1);

                String s2 = "uvw";        // s2 attached to "uvw" object. Good.
                System.out.println(s2);

                s2 = s1;          // "uvw" object marked for garbage collection.
                System.out.println(s2);

                char carr[] = {'a', 'b', 'c'};
                String s3 = new String(carr);
                System.out.println(s3);
        }
}
```

Output:

```
xyz
uvw
xyz
abc
```

allocated by compiler

( xyz )      s1 ( xyz )      s2 ( uvw )      s3 ( abc )

---

# OVERLOADED OPERATORS FOR STRING OBJECTS

- Java does not support operator overloading by programmers - extending the definition of operators.

- However, + and += are overloaded for String object operands or, in other words, have an additional definition for String object operands.

**File: c6_5.java**

```
class c6_5                      // File: c6_5.java
{
        public static void main(String args[])
        {
                String s1 = "abc";
                String s2 = "def";
                String s3;

                s3 = s1 + s2;        // new object created containing
                                     // concatenated strings

                System.out.println("Sum = " + s3); // + overload used here.

                s3 += s1;   // new object created containing appended string.

                System.out.println("Result of += is " + s3);
        }
}
```

Output:

```
Sum = abcdef
Result of += is abcdefabc
```

# ARRAYS OF STRING OBJECTS

Arrays of string objects are similar to arrays of other kinds of objects.

Example:

```
class c6_6                 // File: c6_6.java
{
        public static void main(String args[])
        {
                String dogs[] = {"fido", "shep", "lassie"};

                System.out.println("dogs[0] = " + dogs[0]);

                String cats[];
                cats = new String[3];

                cats[0] = "morris";
                cats[1] = "tom";
                cats[2] = "calvin hobbes";
                System.out.println("cats[2] = " + cats[2]);

                dogs[2] = "lightning"; // garbage collect old object
                System.out.println("dogs[2] = " + dogs[2]);
        }
}
```

Output:

```
dogs[0] = fido
cats[2] = calvin hobbes
dogs[2] = lightning
```

# STRING CLASS METHODS

The String class has numerous methods which you can see in the java.lang.String source file. Some of the more important methods are listed in this section.

**Some Constructors**

**String()**

**String(char carr[])**

**String(String s)**

**Some Important Methods**

**char charAt(int indexNumber)** - return the character at the specified index.

```
c = s.charAt(0);
```

**int length()** - return length of character string in String object.

```
len = s.length();
```

**boolean equals(Object o)** - returns true if equal

```
if(s1.equals(s2))
```

**int compareTo(String s)** - returns < 0 if s1 < s2 lexicographically;  0 if equal;  > 0 if s1 > s2

```
order = s1.compareTo(s2)
```

**boolean equalsIgnoreCase(Object o)** - case insensitive, returns true if equal.

```
if(s1.equalsIgnoreCase(s2))
```

**String substring(int begin, int end)** - end is index after last char of substring

```
s2 = s1.substring(3, 7); // 4 char's in s2
```

**String toLowerCase()**
```
s2 = s1.toLowerCase();
```

**String toUpperCase()**
```
s2 = s1.toUpperCase();
```

**char [] toCharArray()** - returns char array.

```
char carr[] = s.toCharArray();
```

**boolean regionMatches(boolean ignoreCase, int thisOffset, String s, int sOffset, int len)**

```
if(s1.regionMatches(true, 3, s2, 5, 4))
```

Example:

**File: c6_7.java**
```
class c6_7                 // File: c6_7.java
{
        public static void main(String args[])
        {
                String dogs[] = {"fido", "shep", "lassie"};

                System.out.println("dogs[0] = " + dogs[0]);

                dogs[1] = dogs[1].toUpperCase(); // new object containing SHEP

                char carr[];

                carr = dogs[1].toCharArray();

                System.out.println("carr = " + String.valueOf(carr));
                System.out.println("carr[1] = " + carr[1]);

                String s = dogs[1].substring(1, 4);
                System.out.println("Substring = " + s);

                if(dogs[1].regionMatches(true, 1, s, 0, 3))
                        System.out.println("Match");
        }
}
```

Output:

```
dogs[0] = fido
carr = SHEP
carr[1] = H
Substring = HEP
Match
```

## Some Other String Methods

**boolean startsWith(String prefixObject)** - returns true if prefixObject matches beginning of current String object.

**boolean startsWith(String prefixObject, int offset)** - As above but starting from offset.

**boolean endsWith(String suffixObject)** - returns true if suffix match.

**String replace(char oldchar, char newchar)** - replaces all instances of oldchar in object

**String trim()** - returns object with same char's but leading and trailing white space stripped.

**int indexOf(int searchchar, int fromIndex)** - returns index of search character.

**int lastIndexOf(int searchchar, fromIndex)** - returns index of last occurrence of search character.

**int indexOf(String s, fromIndex)** - returns index of occurrence of s after fromIndex.

**String valueOf(datatype d)** - The data type can be boolean, int, long, float, double, Object, and char[]. A String object containing the value is returned.

**String copyValueOf(char arr[], int offset, int count)** - returns String object containing count characters in array starting from offset.

# STRINGBUFFER CLASS

- The String class only allows fixed size data strings within objects. The strings within objects cannot be augmented.

- The StringBuffer class allows objects to grow by augmenting the strings within objects. They can also shrink.

- Three popular constructors in class StringBuffer are:

  **StringBuffer()**

  **StringBuffer(String s)** - initialize with String s.

  **StringBuffer(int length)** - initialize to length characters.

- Some ways of defining StringBuffer objects are:

```
StringBuffer sb1 = new StringBuffer();


StringBuffer sb2 = new StringBuffer(s);


StringBuffer sb3 = new StringBuffer(10);
```

**Some StringBuffer Methods**

**void setLength(int newLength)** - sets length of buffer.

**int length()** - current number of characters in the StringBuffer object.

**int capacity()** - current available number of characters of storage in the StringBuffer object. Initially, the number of characters placed in the object plus sixteen. Fills to capacity then allocates another chunk of storage. The amount of new storage allocated is Java version dependent. Early Java versions added 16 more characters of storage. More recent versions double the storage.

**char charAt(int index)** - fetches character in current object at location index.

**void setCharAt(int index, char c)** - sets character in object.

**void getChars(int srcStart, int srcFinish, char dest[], int destStart)** - copies characters from current StringBuffer object to char array. The int's array are index numbers.

**String toString()** - creates a String object which shares the internal character array in the StringBuffer object. If the StringBuffer object's internal array is modified the String object makes its own copy of the unmodified character array.

### StringBuffer Resizing Methods

**StringBuffer append( datatype d)** - The allowed data types are Object, String, int, long, float, double, char, char [], and boolean.

**StringBuffer append(char [] carr, int offset, int length)** - Append part of char array to a StringBuffer object.

**StringBuffer insert(int offset, datatype d)** - The allowed data types are Object, String, int, long, float, double, char, char [], and boolean.  The insertion begins at index number offset.

Example:

**File: c6_8.java**
```
class c6_8                    // File: c6_8.java
{
        public static void main(String args[])
        {
                StringBuffer s1 = new StringBuffer("string1");

                System.out.println("length = " + s1.length());
                System.out.println("capacity = " + s1.capacity());

                char carr[] = new char[10];
                s1.getChars(0, 5, carr, 1);  // place char's in array carr.
                System.out.println("carr[1] = " + carr[1]);
                System.out.println("carr[5] = " + carr[5]);

                s1.append("string2");
                s1.insert(1, 999);
                System.out.println("s1 = " + s1);

                System.out.println("length = " + s1.length());
                System.out.println("capacity = " + s1.capacity());

        }
}
```

Output:

```
length = 7
capacity = 23                 // 16 + 7
carr[1] = s
carr[5] = n
s1 = s999tring1string2
length = 17
capacity = 23
```

# COMMAND LINE ARGUMENTS

Java enables you to specify data values on the java command line which can be used inside a Java program. Similar to C and C++ command line handling.

args[0] = first argument on the command line after classname.

args[1] = second argument on the command line.

args[2] = third argument on the command line.

…

args.length = number of arguments.

Example:

**File: c6_9.java**

```
class c6_9                      // File: c6_9.java
{
        public static void main(String args[])
        {
                System.out.println("Number of arguments = "
                                                + args.length);

                System.out.println("args[0] = " + args[0]);
                System.out.println("args[1] = " + args[1]);
                System.out.println("args[2] = " + args[2]);
        }
}
```

Sample run:

```
C:> java c6_9 abc def ghi
Number of arguments = 3
args[0] = abc
args[1] = def
args[2] = ghi
```

# MATH CLASS

The Math class contains a number of methods which implement standard mathematics functions.

Objects of the Math class cannot be created since the Math constructor is private.

Some Math *static* methods are:

```
abs(datatype y)        datatype can be int, long, float, or double
acos(double)
asin(double)
atan(double)
atan2(double,double)
ceil(double)
cos(double)
exp(double)
floor(double)
log(double)
max(x,y)     // int, long, float, double
min(x,y)     // int, long, float, double
pow(double, double)
random()        // returns double
rint(double)
round(x)    // float, double
sqrt(double)
tan(double)
```

Math methods are always called with the format:

```
Math.methodname ( ... )
```

Example:

```
x = Math.sqrt(25.);
```

Two constants in the Math class are:

```
Math.E  = 2.718...   transcendental constant
Math.PI = 3.14...    pi
```

# INTEGER CLASS

Class Integer provides a wrapper for int values. It wraps a simple int value within an object.

The Integer constructor creates an Integer object from an int.

Example:

```
Integer i1 = new Integer(15);
```

Class Integer contains the static variables Integer.MIN_VALUE and Integer.MAX_VALUE.

## Integer methods

Note the static methods below are preceded by their class name. All the below methods either transform their argument or the object before the "." to the return data type. They implement data type conversions.

### Static Methods

```
String Integer.toString(int j)
```

```
int Integer.parseInt(String s)
```

```
Integer Integer.valueOf(String s)
```

### Instance Methods

```
int i1.intValue()
```

```
long i1.longValue()
```

```
float i1.floatValue()
```

```
double i1.doubleValue()
```

```
String i1.toString()
```

# LONG CLASS

Class Long provides a wrapper for long values.

The Long constructor creates a Long object from a long.

Example:

```
Long L1 = new Long(25L);
```

Class Long contains the static variables Long.MIN_VALUE and Long.MAX_VALUE.

## Long methods

Note the static methods below are preceded by their class name.  All the below methods either transform their argument or the object before the "." to the return data type.

### Static Methods

```
String Long.toString(long j)
```

```
long Long.parseLong(String s)
```

```
Long Long.valueOf(String s)
```

### Instance Methods

```
int L1.intValue()
```

```
long L1.longValue()
```

```
float L1.floatValue()
```

```
double L1.doubleValue()
```

```
String L1.toString()
```

# FLOAT CLASS

Class Float provides a wrapper for float values.

The Float constructor creates a Float object from a float.

Example:

```
Float f1 = new Float(25.F);
```

Class Float contains the static variables Float.MIN_VALUE, Float.MAX_VALUE, Float.POSITIVE_INFINITY, and Float.NEGATIVE_INFINITY. It also has the static variable Float.NaN which represents Not a Number.

## Float methods

Note the static methods below are preceded by their class name. All the below methods either transform their argument or the object before the "." to the return data type.

## Static Methods

```
String Float.toString(float x)
```

```
Float Float.valueOf(String s)
```

## Instance Methods

```
int f1.intValue()
```

```
long f1.longValue()
```

```
float f1.floatValue()
```

```
double f1.doubleValue()
```

```
String f1.toString()
```

# DOUBLE CLASS

Class Double provides a wrapper for double values.

The Double constructor creates a Double object from a double.

Example:

```
Double d1 = new Double(25.);
```

Class Double contains the static variables Double.MIN_VALUE, Double.MAX_VALUE, Double.POSITIVE_INFINITY, and Double.NEGATIVE_INFINITY. It also has the static variable Double.NaN which represents Not a Number.

## Double methods

Note the static methods below are preceded by their class name. All the below methods either transform their argument or the object before the "." to the return data type.

### Static Methods

```
String Double.toString(double j)
```

```
Double Double.valueOf(String s)
```

### Instance Methods

```
int d1.intValue()
```

```
long d1.longValue()
```

```
float d1.floatValue()
```

```
double d1.doubleValue()
```

```
String d1.toString()
```

# CHARACTER CLASS

Class Character provides a wrapper for char values.

The Character constructor creates a Character object from a char.

Example:

```
Character c1 = new Character('a');
```

## Character methods

Note the static methods below are preceded by their class name. Many of the below methods transform their argument or the object before the "." to the return data type. The "is" methods test the nature of the character. Similar to the ctype.h macros of the C language.

### Static Methods

```
char Character.toLowerCase(char c)

char Character.toUpperCase(char c)

boolean Character.isLowerCase(char c)

boolean Character.isUpperCase(char c)

boolean Character.isDigit(char c)

boolean Character.isSpace(char c)
```

### Instance Methods

```
char c1.charValue()

String c1.toString()
```

# BOOLEAN CLASS

Class Boolean provides a wrapper for boolean values.

The Boolean constructor creates a Boolean object from a boolean.

Example:

```
Boolean b1 = new Boolean(true);
```

Boolean static variables are Boolean.TRUE and Boolean.FALSE - both objects of type Boolean.

Boolean methods include:

```
boolean b1.booleanValue()
```

```
String b1.toString()
```

```
boolean b1.equals(Object o)
```

# SUMMARY

This module has described several important Java classes including Object, String, StringBuffer, Math, Integer, Float, Boolean, Double, and Character. Arrays were discussed in detail. Command line arguments were also described.

# EXERCISES

1.  Write a Java program with a 4 component int array setting the components individually equal to 22, 33, 44, and 55.  Then print the third component on screen.

2.  Redo exercise 1 with {} initialization.

3.  Starting from exercise 2 make a copy of the 4-component array called newarr using the arraycopy() method and then print newarr[0].

4.  Create a program with a String object containing "Tom".  Then add " Swift" using the += operator. Print the resulting object's characters.  Then make all the characters in the object upper case and print it.

5.  Change the program of exercise 4 to use a StringBuffer object and use the append() method to add " Swift" to the object.  Eliminate the part making the characters upper case.

# 7.  Exceptions

## OBJECTIVES

At the end of this module you should be able to:

- Describe an exception.

- Write code throwing and catching exceptions.

- Write code catching throws from builtin Java constructs.

# WHAT IS AN EXCEPTION?

- If a problem develops during the course of execution of a program, an object called an exception can be thrown signalling an error. The object is usually eventually caught and the problem corrected.

- The thrown exception object can be caught by another part of the code which can correct the problem and, perhaps, restart the program.

- Exceptions are objects of a class which is normally subclassed from class Exception in java.lang.

- Another important class is the Error class. The Exception class and the Error class are both subclassed from Throwable. Exception classes subclassed from Error usually are related to deep problems such as dynamic linkage problems or virtual machine problems such as running out of memory. Usually it is impossible for the program to recover from these types of problems.

- Normally the exception classes we create are subclassed from Exception. These exceptions are normally conditions from which a program can recover.

- Exceptions are caught by data type.

- Steps followed in a throw and catch are:

    1. Problem found.

    2. Exception thrown.

    3. Thrown exception "passed" back through method call chain leading to problem.

    4. Each method not catching exception
        a. executes any "finally" blocks within it.
        b. has its storage deallocated with finalize() running for all deallocated objects.

    5. The catching method has the block of the catch execute.

    6. A "finally" block then executes if there is one in the catching method.

    7. The program then proceeds to execute from that point "normally".

- The program does not automatically restart executing at the point of the problem.

- *If an exception is never caught - not even by the main() method - then the Java interpreter prints an error message, a stack trace, and then exits.*

Example of a throw and catch:

**File: c7_1.java**

```
class c7_1                     // File: c7_1.java
{
        public static void main(String args[])
        {
                System.out.println("Begin");
                try
                {
                        for(int j = 0; j < 10; j++)
1                               f(j);
                }
4               catch(Err e)
                {
                        System.out.println("Caught: Err containing " + e.m);
                        System.out.println(e.toString());// Displays e data type
                }
5               System.out.println("End");
        }
        static void f(int k) throws Err
        {
                if(k == 3)
2                       throw new Err(10);
                System.out.println("f(): " + k);
        }
}

class Err extends Exception
{
        int m;
3        Err(int n)
        {
                m = n;
        }
}
```

Output:

```
Begin
f(): 0
f(): 1
f(): 2
Caught: Err containing 10
Err
End
```

# HOW EXCEPTIONS ARE USED PRACTICALLY

- Practically we use exceptions that are built into the methods in the Java packages. Sometimes we will create our own application specific exception classes and use them in our development work.

- The remainder of the module shows how to define exception classes and use them.

- Most of the time we will take a method in a built-in Java class and write simple code to handle the exception.

For example the parseInt method of class Integer in the lang package will throw a NumberFormatException if its argument is not a String object containing only digit characters. So we write code like:

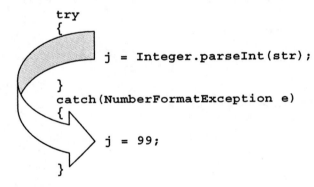

```
try
{

    j = Integer.parseInt(str);

}
catch(NumberFormatException e)
{

    j = 99;

}
```

- If the String object str only contains digit characters (0-9) within it then the digits are transformed into an int value which becomes the value of the j variable.

- If the String object str contains one or more non-digit characters within it then a NumberFormatException object is thrown. In the above example the thrown exception is caught by the catch following it. Then j is set equal to 99.

- The above example illustrates the common coding approach for exceptions.

# SOME BUILT-IN EXCEPTIONS

Java has many built-in exceptions within Java packages. Some of the more common built-in exceptions are:

*ArithmeticException* - usually result from integer divisions by zero.

*ArrayIndexOutofBoundsException* - results from an attempt to reference an array element with an index which is too large or negative.

*NegativeArraySizeException* - results from an arithmetic error when changing the size of an array.

*NullPointerException* - results from using a reference not attached to an object.

*IncompatibleClassChangeException* - results from an attempt to change a class which affects methods and/or references to that class in other classes when the other classes have not been compiled yet.

*ClassCastException* - results when you attempt to illegally typecast an object to another class type.

*OutOfMemoryException* - results if you fail to create an object with the new operator due to a lack of memory.

*NoClassDefFoundException* - results if you reference a class which cannot be found.

*IncompatibleTypeException* - results if you attempt to instantiate an interface.

*UnsatisfiedLinkException* - results if a native method cannot be linked in at run-time.

*InternalException* - results if "impossible" run-time events happen. This exception should never occur.

# DEFINING AN EXCEPTION

- An exception is defined as an object of a class which is subclassed from the Exception class (although objects of a class which is subclassed from Error or RuntimeException or Throwable are called exceptions as well).

- The Exception class is a subclass of the Throwable class which contains several useful methods. One method is toString() which displays the class name of the exception. Exception and Throwable are part of the java.lang package.

- The class of an exception can be an empty class. For example

```
class myException extends Exception
{   }
```

- The class of an exception can also contain variables and methods. An exception class can contain one or more constructors. For example,

```
class myException extends Exception
{
        int myerror;
        int yourerror;

        myException(int m)
        {
                super("Error 1 occurred.");
                myerror = m;
                yourerror = 0;
        }
        myException(int m, int y)
        {
                super("myException occurred.");
                myerror = m;
                yourerror = y;
        }
}
```

- The class, the variables in the class, and the methods in the class are defined as "package", public, protected or private depending on how you intend to use them. You must provide access required by the use of the exception.

- If you place a super(String s); statement at the beginning of your exception class constructor, then a message will be placed in the Throwable superclass. This message can be fetched with a statement such as

```
errorString = e.getMessage();
```

where e is the object caught in the catch() block.

# THROWING AN EXCEPTION

- Exceptions are thrown by throw statements. Throw statements have the form:

```
throw new classname( args );
```

- The arguments in the parentheses must match the parameter list of a constructor in the class of the exception. The arguments are used when the exception object is intialized.

When the throw statement executes:

> 1. An object of the specified class is allocated.
>
> 2. The matching constructor runs.

- The method containing a throw statement must declare the throw if the throw can emerge from the method <u>and if the thrown object's class is a subclass of Exception</u>. The format of a throws declaration is:

```
returnType methodName(parameterList) throws exception1, exception2, …
{
        // code
}
```

For example,

```
double method1(int x, double y) throws myException, yourException
{
        // code
}
```

- <u>Throws of objects whose classes are subclasses of Error or RuntimeException (such as ArrayIndexOutOfBoundsException ) do not have to de declared.</u> The programmer decides whether to declare these types of exception throws.

- A method which calls a method which performs a throw should also declare the throw unless it catches the throw.

- A method that overrides another method in a superclass can declare the same exceptions, or a subset of the same exceptions, and possibly declare more throws as long as the class of each new throw is a subclass of one of the throws specified for the superclass method. For example,

```
class mysuper
{
        // code
        int mymethod(int z) throws Err1, Err2
        {
                // code
        }
}

class mysub extends mysuper
{
        // code

        int mymethod(int z) throws Err1, Err2  // Cannot add more throws
        {
                // code
        }
}
```

Another example:

```
class mysuper
{
        // code
        int mymethod(int z) throws Exception
        {
                // code
        }
}

class mysub extends mysuper
{
        // code

        int mymethod(int z) throws Err1, Err2, Err3 // Any throw of an exception
                                                    // subclass object is ok.
        {
                // code
        }
}
```

# CATCHING AN EXCEPTION

- Exceptions can only be caught with catch expressions. Catch expressions can only appear after a try block. (More rules later.)

- The general format of a method containing a try construct is:

```
dataType methodName( parameterList)
{
        // code              1

        try
        {
                // code      2
        }
        catch(...)
        {
                // code      3
        }
        catch(...)
        {
                // code      4
        }

        // more catch blocks 5

        finally
        {
                // code      6
        }
        // code              7
}
```

- Zero or more catches can appear after a try block.

- The finally block is optional.

- The rules for catching in the different parts of the above method are:

  - Throws from the code of the try block, labeled 2, can be caught by the catches following the try block.

  - All other throws - from the code sections labeled 1, 3, 4, 5, 6 and 7 can only be caught by the method calling this method or by methods further back in the call chain.

# RULES FOR CATCHES

- Zero or more catch blocks can appear after a try block. Catch blocks cannot appear in any other context. If zero catch blocks appear after a try, then a finally block must be placed after the try block.

- Each catch must specify a class data type and a parameter name.

- An exception is caught by its data type. The data type matching rules are:

    - Exact match with the data type of the exception.

    - The class of the catch is a superclass of the thrown object's class.

    - The catch parameter is of an interface type and the class of the thrown object implements the interface.

- A try block can contain a try block and its accompanying set of catches. Throws not caught in the catches of the nested try block can be caught by the catches of the external try block.

- Catches are examined sequentially to find a match on a throw. The first matching catch has its block of code executed.

- A catch for a class Exception object catches any exception since each exception class is a subclass of class Exception. This catch is usually the last catch in the list of catches.

- An exception thrown from within a catch block must be caught further back in the call chain of methods (unless its from within a nested try block and the catches following the nested try can catch it). A new exception can be created and thrown from iside a catch block:

    **throw new myException(…);**

- To rethrow an exception object in a catch block you must throw it by its name:

    **throw obj;**

- A finally block is a block of code that usually does some kind of cleanup such as closing a file. The programmer places code in the finally block that the programmer wishes to have executed in all circumstances unless the program terminates with a System.exit() method.

- A finally block executes after the catch block code in all cases unless a System.exit() method executes. A finally block executes even if the catch block executes a return statement, or a throw statement. A finally block also executes if the try block executes normally (without doing a throw).

# EXAMPLE ILLUSTRATING CATCH RULES

It shows a multiple throws program and how a finally block executes.

**File: c7_2.java**

```
class c7_2                      // File: c7_2.java
{
    public static void main(String args[]) throws Err3
    {
        System.out.println("Begin");
        try
        {
            int j;
            if(args.length > 0)// tests for command line arguments
            {      // See sample command lines at end of program.
                try
                {
                    j = Integer.parseInt(args[0]);
                }    // parseInt() throws for a non-numeric
                catch(NumberFormatException e) // argument.
                { j = 99; }
            }
            else
                j = 0;
            f(j);
        }
        catch(Err1 e)
        {
            System.out.println("Caught: Err1 containing "
                                              + e.m);
            System.out.println(e.toString());
            System.exit(1);//finally block does not execute.
        }
        catch(Err2 e)
        {
            System.out.println("Caught: Err2 containing "
                                              + e.m);
            System.out.println(e.toString());
            return;  // finally block executes.
        }
        catch(Err3 e)
        {
            System.out.println("Caught: Err3 containing "
                                              + e.m);
            System.out.println(e.toString());
            throw e;                // finally block executes.
        }
        catch(Exception e)
        {
            System.out.println("Default: " + e.toString());
```

```
                                      // finally executes.
        }
        finally
        {
                System.out.println("finally ran.");
        }
        System.out.println("End");
    }

    static void f(int k) throws Err1, Err2, Err3, Err4
    {
        switch(k)
        {
                case 1:
                        throw new Err1(1);
                case 2:
                        throw new Err2(2);
                case 3:
                        throw new Err3(3);
                case 4:
                        throw new Err4(4);

        }
        System.out.println("f(): " + k);
    }
}

class Err1 extends Exception
{
        int m;
        Err1(int n)
        {
                m = n;
        }
}

class Err2 extends Exception
{
        int m;
        Err2(int n)
        {
                m = n;
        }
}

class Err3 extends Exception
{
        int m;
        Err3(int n)
        {
                m = n;
        }
}
```

**7. Exceptions**

```
class Err4 extends Exception
{
        int m;
        Err4(int n)
        {
                m = n;
        }
}
```

Sample command lines and their output:

Comment

\WORK> java c7_2 0                          No throw.
Begin
f(): 0
finally ran.
End

\WORK> java c7_2 1                          Throw Err1
Begin                                       caught then exit()
Caught: Err1 containing 1
Err1

\WORK> java c7_2 2                          Throw Err2
Begin                                       caught then return
Caught: Err2 containing 2
Err2
finally ran.

Comment

\WORK> java c7_2 3                          Throw Err3
Begin                                       caught
Caught: Err3 containing 3                   rethrown
Err3                                        uncaught exception error message
finally ran.
ERROR MESSAGE

\WORK> java c7_2 4                          Throw Err4
Begin                                       Caught by Exception default catch
Default: Err4
finally ran.
End

\WORK> java c7_2 5                          No throw.
Begin
f(): 5
finally ran.
End

# SUMMARY

This module has explored the features of exception handling in Java including throwing and catching exceptions, rules for catching exceptions, the finally block, the try block construct, and built-in Java exceptions.

# EXERCISES

1. Add a "finally" block to the program c7_1.java which prints "finally ran." on the screen. Then add a return; statement to the catch block and notice whether the "finally" block still executes. It should.

2. Change the method f(int k) of c7_2.java placing the switch() block and the following println() in a try block. The try block should be followed by a catch block which catches all exceptions and rethrows it. Then test the program with command lines similar to the command lines following c7_2.java in the module. Hint: the throws declaration declares the formal data types of thrown exceptions. The catch()'s catch by the actual data type of the caught object in memory.

# 8. *Multithreading*

## OBJECTIVES

At the end of this module you should be able to:

- Describe multithreading.

- Implement synchronized methods.

- Construct programs with multithreading.

- Write code managing multithreaded programs

- Implement synchronized access to objects.

# SINGLE THREADED JAVA PROGRAMS

- The Java programs which we have seen have been single threaded.

- A single threaded program executes program steps sequentially.

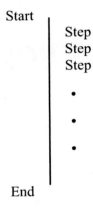

Start

Step
Step
Step

•

•

•

End

- Java single threaded programs have a second "hidden"thread which runs automatically called the garbage collection thread. This thread periodically examines the memory of an executing program looking for objects which have passed out of scope - no longer can be referenced since they have "lost their name". The garbage collection thread deallocates these objects.

- The garbage collection thread runs "silently in the background" so we normally do not worry about it.

- A Java browser will also be running on a separate thread although this is usually totally extraneous to the Java program. Several applets can run at the same time. Or you can move your mouse or scroll while a Java applet is running.

# MULTITHREADED JAVA PROGRAMS

- At times you may want several activities to take place simultaneously in a Java program or applet to take full advantage of the computer's capabilities.

- For example, you may wish a display to take place and also wish to perform a calculation or open another application process.

- Java allows you to set off several "simultaneous" threads of execution.

- Effectively, several parts of the Java program are run independently and "simultaneously".

**Java Program with Four Threads**

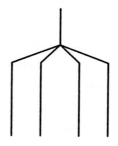

- Hardware implementation of threads:

    - Multiprocessor computer with each thread running on a separate processor. (Solaris and Win32 PC's) Uses native (built-in threads of the platform.)

    - A computer with time slicing giving time successively to each thread to execute.

- Java software approaches to multithreaded programs:

    - Subclassing from the Thread class.

    - Implementing the Runnable interface. PREFERRED because it allows another class to be a superclass (only one superclass allowed).

# MULTITHREADING BY SUBCLASSING FROM THREAD

The simplest way to implement multithreading is to define a threading class by subclassing from class Thread.

Steps to creating a threading class:

- Subclass from Thread.

- Provide a public void run() method specifying the actions the thread performs and gracefully ending the thread. The run() method can be viewed as the "main() method" of the thread.

- Create one or more objects of the new threading class. Each object corresponds to a thread. Execute the start() method on an object to start its thread.

Note: a useful method for managing a thread is the static sleep() method of class Thread. This method puts the thread executing it to sleep for the number of milliseconds specified by the argument. A thread can only put itself to sleep. This method cannot be used to put some other thread to sleep.

The next page provides an example of this approach to threading. It also contains code using the sleep() method. The sleep() method can throw an exception – an InterruptedException object – if the thread is interrupted by another thread. So we have to use a try – catch construct. (We will see more about interrupting a thread later.)

## Example of Thread subclass Approach to Threading

```
class c8_1                    // File: c8_1.java
{
        public static void main(String args[])
        {
                System.out.println("Begin");

                Thready td1 = new Thready("The first thread");
                Thready td2 = new Thready("The second thread");

                td1.start();  // start thread
                td2.start();  // start thread

                System.out.println("End");
        }
}

class Thready extends Thread
{
        private String s;

        public Thready(String s)
        {
                this.s = s;
        }
        public void run()
        {
                for(int j = 0; j < 5; j++)
                {
                        try
                        {
                                sleep(10);
                        }
                        catch(InterruptedException e)
                        {
                        }
                        System.out.println("Thread: " + s);
                }
        }
}
```

Output:

```
Begin
End
Thread: The first thread
Thread: The second thread
Thread: The second thread
Thread: The first thread
Thread: The second thread
Thread: The first thread
Thread: The second thread
Thread: The first thread
Thread: The second thread
Thread: The first thread
```

**8. Multithreading**

# MULTITHREADING BY IMPLEMENTING RUNNABLE

Multithreading can also be implemented by creating a threading class which implements the Runnable interface. This is the <u>preferred</u> approach since only one superclass is allowed and the superclass is often required to be a class such as Applet or Frame.

To create a threading class implementing Runnable:

- The class must be specified as implementing Runnable.

- The class must declare a Thread member variable (subobject).

- The constructor(s) must allocate storage for the Thread subobject invoking one of the Thread constructors that have a Runnable parameter.

- The class must contain a public void run() method specifying the code of the thread - the "main()" method of the thread.

The class constructor(s) can invoke the start() member of Thread on the Thread subobject. If the start() method is invoked in the constructor call then the thread starts running immediately after the object is created.

The thread created with this approach is managed using the Thread subobject. If the Thread subobject is private (good style – see next example) then you must create methods to manage the thread from other methods (see setName() in the next example).

```java
class c8_2                    // File: c8_2.java
{
        public static void main(String args[])
        {
                System.out.println("Begin");
                Runny r1 = new Runny("The first thread");
                Runny r2 = new Runny("The second thread");
        //    r1.setName("Great thread");
                System.out.println("End");
        }
}

class Runny implements Runnable
{
        private String s;
        private Thread myThread;
        public Runny(String s)
        {
                this.s = s;
                myThread = new Thread(this); // this is usually the argument of the
                        // constructor. It gives the suboject a reference to the Runny
                        // object being initialized enabling the Runny run() method to be
                        // invoked by the myThread.start() method call.
                myThread.start();
        }
        public void run()
        {
                for(int j = 0; j < 5; j++)
                {
                        try
                        {
                                Thread.sleep(10);// Thread must be specified
                        }          // since we are not subclassing from Thread.
                        catch(InterruptedException e)
                        { }

                        System.out.println("Thread: " + s);
                }
        }
        public void setName(String s)
        {       myThread.setName(s);    }
}
```

Output:
```
Begin
End
Thread: The first thread
Thread: The second thread
Thread: The first thread
Thread: The second thread
Thread: The first thread
Thread: The second thread
Thread: The first thread
Thread: The second thread
Thread: The first thread
Thread: The second thread
```

# MANAGING MULTITHREADED PROGRAMS

Java provides a variety of methods in class Thread to manage the execution of threads. Some of the more important methods are:

**Thread Constructors**

**public Thread()** - constructor for Thread object.

> Example:
> ```
> td1 = new Thread();
> ```

**public Thread(String name)** - constructor for Thread object which sets name of thread.

> Example:
> ```
> td1 = new Thread("mythread");
> ```

**public Thread(Runnable obj)** - constructor for Thread object which creates a Thread object from an object of a class implementing Runnable.

> Example:
> ```
> myThread = new Thread(this);
> ```

**public Thread(Runnable obj, String name)** - constructor for Thread object which creates a Thread object from an object of a class implementing Runnable and sets the name of the thread.

> Example:
> ```
> myThread = new Thread(this, "mythread1");
> ```

**public Thread(ThreadGroup t, String name)** - constructor for Thread object which specifies membership in ThreadGroup t and sets name of thread. ThreadGroups will be seen shortly.

> Example:
> ```
> td1 = new Thread(tg, "mythread");
> ```

**public Thread(ThreadGroup t, Runnable obj)** - constructor for Thread object which specifies membership in ThreadGroup t and specifies a Runnable object. Useful for classes implementing Runnable.

> Example:
> ```
> myThread = new Thread(tg, obj);
> ```

## General Thread Management

**public final void setName(String name)** - sets the name of a thread.

> Example:
> ```
> td1.setName("mythread");
> ```

**public final String getName()** - returns String containing name of a thread.

> Example:
> ```
> System.out.println(td1.getName());
> ```

**public final void suspend()** - suspends the execution of a thread. This method is deprecated (meaning it will eventually be phased out). However it serves a good purpose and you should be aware of it.

> Example:
> ```
> td1.suspend();
> ```

**public final void resume()** - resumes the execution of a suspended thread.

> Example:
> ```
> td1.resume();
> ```

**public static native void sleep(long millisecs)** - causes the current thread to sleep for a number of milliseconds. A sleep() causes the thread to yield the remainder of its time slice to the next thread waiting for a time slice.

> Example:
> ```
> Thread.sleep(100);   // sleep 100 milliseconds.
> ```

**public static native void yield()** - causes the current thread to yield the remainder of its time slice to the next thread waiting for a time slice.

> Example:
> ```
> Thread.yield();
> ```

**public final void stop()** - halts execution of a thread but does not destroy it. Thread cannot be restarted.

> Example:
> td1.stop();

**public void destroy()** - destroys a thread with no cleanup or removal of locks.  Last resort.

Example:
```
td1.destroy();
```

**public final native boolean isAlive()** - returns true if the current thread is active (alive means started but not stopped).

Example:
```
while(td1.isAlive())
```

**public static native Thread currentThread()** - returns a reference to the currently executing thread.

Example:
```
Thread t = Thread.currentThread();
```

**public String toString()** - creates a String containing the thread name, priority level and thread groupname.

Example:
```
System.out.println(currentThread().toString());
```

**void interrupt()** - sends an interrupt to a thread.  A method executing in the receiving thread which throws an InterruptedException will stop its activity and throw an InterruptedException in response to the interrupt(). The thread then enters the "interrupted" state. Methods that throw InterruptedException will not execute normally while the thread is in this state. The program simply goes to the next code statement. For example, the sleep() method will not sleep for the specified time while the thread is in an interrupted state. If the thread executes the interrupted() method (below) the thread goes back to the non-interrupted state.

Example:
```
td1.interrupt();
```

**static boolean interrupted()** - returns true if current thread is in the interrupted state. Puts the thread into the *non*-interrupted state.

Example:
```
if(Thread.interrupted())
```

**boolean isInterrupted()** - returns true if recipient object thread is in the interrupted state. Thread state remains unchanged.

Example:
```
if(td1.isInterrupted())
```

**void join()** - causes current thread to wait until recipient object's thread completes.  Waits forever if necessary.

Example:
```
td1.join();
```

**8. Multithreading**

**synchronized void join(long millis)** - causes current thread to wait until recipient object's thread completes. Waits up to millis milliseconds if necessary.

> Example:
> ```
> td1.join(100);
> ```

**void setDaemon(boolean state)** - this method makes a thread a daemon thread. The thread will continue to run as long as at least one non-daemon thread is running. setDaemon() must execute before the thread is started. When only daemon threads remain, the Java program ends. Daemon threads usually provide some service such as timing.

> Example:
> ```
> td1.setDaemon(true);
> td1.start();
> ```

## Thread Groups

There are numerous situations where a programmer wishes to manage sets of threads as a group. Groups of threads can be defined in Java. For example, all threads in a group can be stopped with one statement.

### Constructors for ThreadGroup Objects

**public ThreadGroup(String name) -** constructor.  The ThreadGroup name must be unique.

```
ThreadGroup tg = new ThreadGroup("myGroup");
```

**public ThreadGroup(ThreadGroup parent, String name) -** parent is the parent ThreadGroup object and the name is the name of the new ThreadGroup.

```
ThreadGroup tg = new ThreadGroup(tgp, "myGroup");
```

**public Thread(ThreadGroup t, String name)** - constructor for Thread object which specifies membership in ThreadGroup t and sets name of thread.

```
td1 = new Thread(tg, "mythread");
```

**public Thread(ThreadGroup t, Runnable obj)** - constructor for Thread object which specifies membership in ThreadGroup t and uses a Runnable object.  Useful for classes implementing Runnable.

Example:
```
myThread = new Thread(tg, obj);
```

### Methods Managing ThreadGroups

**public void suspend()** - suspends all threads in a ThreadGroup and its child ThreadGroups.

Example:
```
tg.suspend();
```

**public void resume()** - resumes all threads in a ThreadGroup and its child ThreadGroups.

Example:
```
tg.resume();
```

**public void stop()** - stops all threads in a ThreadGroup and its child ThreadGroups.

Example:
```
tg.stop();
```

**public int enumerate(Thread [] list)** - list becomes an array of references to the active threads in the ThreadGroup.

> Example:
> ```
> Thread [] threadList = new Thread[20];
> tg.enumerate(threadList);
> ```

**public int activeCount()** - returns an upper bound of the number of active threads in a ThreadGroup.

> Example:
> ```
> num = tg.activeCount();
> ```

**public ThreadGroup getParent()** - returns the parent ThreadGroup of a ThreadGroup object.

> Example:
> ```
> tgp = tg.getParent();
> ```

**public ThreadGroup getThreadGroup()** - returns the ThreadGroup of a Thread object.

> Example:
> ```
> tg = td1.getThreadGroup();
> ```

# THREAD PRIORITY LEVELS

- A thread can be assigned a priority level between 1 (lowest) and 10 (highest).

- The lowest priority is 1. The highest priority is 10. Normal priority is 5. Each of these values is the value of a public static variable in class Thread.

$$Thread.MAX\_PRIORITY = 10$$

$$Thread.NORM\_PRIORITY = 5$$

$$Thread.MIN\_PRIORITY = 1$$

Some Thread member methods for thread priorities are:

**public final void setPriority(int newprioritylevel)** - sets new priority level for current thread. Levels range from 1 through 10. Lowest priority is 1 with static variable name MIN_PRIORITY. Highest priority level is 10 with static variable name MAX_PRIORITY. Normal priority is 5 with static variable name NORM_PRIORITY.

Example:
```
td1.setPriority(Thread.MAX_PRIORITY);
```

**public final int getPriority()** - returns priority value of current thread.

Example:
```
System.out.println(td1.getPriority());
```

- The implementation of threads is operating system dependent.

- General procedure: In a multithreading program threads execute based on their priority. First all priority 10 threads execute – time slices are doled out to the level 10 threads in a round robin (rotating order) fashion. After all level 10 threads complete, the threads between priority levels 2 and 9 execute in a round robin fashion with higher priority threads receiving "proportionately" more time slices. After all these threads complete then the level 1 threads execute with round robin time slicing.

- Thread run() methods can contain yield() calls to give other threads a chance to execute.

# PROGRAM ILLUSTRATING THREAD MANAGEMENT

```java
class c8_3                              // File: c8_3.java
{
        public static void main(String args[])  // There is no logic to this program.
        {
                System.out.println("Begin");

                Thready td1 = new Thready("myThread1");
                Thready td2 = new Thready("myThread2");

                td1.start();
                td2.start();

                td1.suspend();
                td2.suspend();

                td1.setPriority(Thread.MAX_PRIORITY);
                td2.setPriority(Thread.MIN_PRIORITY);

                td2.resume();
                try
                {
                        Thread.sleep(200);
                }
                catch(InterruptedException e)
                {  }

                if(td1.isAlive())
                        System.out.println("Alive: " + td1.getName()
                        + "  Priority = " + td1.getPriority());

                td1.resume();
                try
                {
                        td1.join();
                        td2.join();
                }
                catch(InterruptedException e)
                {  }

                System.out.println("End");
        }
}

class Thready extends Thread
{
        private String s;

        public Thready(String s)
        {
                super(s);  // gives name to thread.
                this.s = s;
        }
```

```java
        public void run()
        {
                try
                {
                        sleep(2000);
                }
                catch(InterruptedException e)
                {  }

                for(int j = 0; j < 10; j++)
                {
                        try
                        {
                                sleep(100);
                        }
                        catch(InterruptedException e)
                        {
                        }
                        System.out.println("Current Thread = "
                                        + currentThread().toString());
                }           // outputs thread name, priority, parent thread
        }
}
```

Output:

```
Begin
Alive: myThread1   Priority = 10
Current Thread = Thread[myThread1,10,main]
Current Thread = Thread[myThread1,10,main]
Current Thread = Thread[myThread2,1,main]
Current Thread = Thread[myThread1,10,main]
Current Thread = Thread[myThread2,1,main]
Current Thread = Thread[myThread1,10,main]
Current Thread = Thread[myThread2,1,main]
Current Thread = Thread[myThread1,10,main]
Current Thread = Thread[myThread2,1,main]
Current Thread = Thread[myThread1,10,main]
Current Thread = Thread[myThread1,10,main]
Current Thread = Thread[myThread2,1,main]
Current Thread = Thread[myThread1,10,main]
Current Thread = Thread[myThread2,1,main]
Current Thread = Thread[myThread1,10,main]
Current Thread = Thread[myThread2,1,main]
Current Thread = Thread[myThread1,10,main]
Current Thread = Thread[myThread2,1,main]
Current Thread = Thread[myThread2,1,main]
Current Thread = Thread[myThread2,1,main]
End
```

# SYNCHRONIZED METHODS

A **monitor** is an object of a class containing one or more synchronized methods. The object can block or lock out synchronized methods giving one-at-a-time synchronized access to the object. This capability is important for database and other data processing operations.

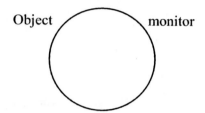

A monitor maintains a **locking capability** on its object allowing only one synchronized block of code at a time to access it. When synchronized code is accessing the object, the object is locked – no other synchronized method can access the object while it is locked. (Non-synchronized code can still access the object while it is locked.) When the synchronized code completes, the object is unlocked so other synchronized code can access it.

There are two ways to define synchronized code:

- A synchronized method - a method which is declared synchronized.

- A synchronized block - a block of code which is declared synchronized for a specific object.

## Synchronized Method

A synchronized method is declared with a header line such as

```
public synchronized datatype methodname( … )   // not necessarily public.
{                                               // { - locks recipient object.
        // code
}                                               // } - unlocked.
```

## Synchronized Block

A synchronized block of code is declared (within a method) with an expression such as:

```
synchronized (obj)
{                           // locks obj
        // code
}                           // unlocked obj
```

where object is an object name or an expression specifying an object such as *this*.

## Example of Synchronized Methods

Consider a object containing data that we wish to read and write. We want to place data in the object using one thread. We want to fetch the current data in the object with another thread. We want to synchronize the threads so data is not being read from the object while the other thread is placing data in the object. We also do not want data to be placed in the thread while the other thread is reading the data in the object. (No partial reads or writes.) We want to avoid data inconsistencies.

So we place a synchronized read method (get() method) and a synchronized write method (set() method) in the class of the data object. The below program implements this example.

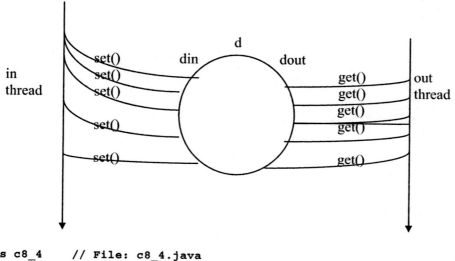

```
class c8_4      // File: c8_4.java
{
        public static void main(String args[])
        {
                Data d = new Data();
                inThread in = new inThread(d);
                outThread out = new outThread(d);
                in.start();
                out.start();
        }
}
```

```java
class Data
{
        private char arr[] = new char[5];
        public synchronized void set(char iarr[], int length)
        {
                for(int j = 0; j < length; j++)
                {
                        arr[j] = iarr[j];
                        try { Thread.sleep(500); } catch(Exception e) { }
                }
                System.out.println("arr = " + String.valueOf(arr));
        }
        public synchronized char [] get()
        {
                return arr;
        }
}

class inThread extends Thread
{
        private Data din;
        public inThread(Data d)
        {
                this.din = d;
        }
        public void run()
        {
                char in[] = {'a', 'b', 'c', 'd', 'e'};
                for(int j = 0; j < 5; j++)
                {
                        din.set(in, j+1);
                        try { Thread.sleep(100); } catch(Exception e) { }
                }
        }
}

class outThread extends Thread
{
        private Data dout;

        public outThread(Data d)
        {
                this.dout = d;
        }
        public void run()
        {
                for(int j = 0; j < 5; j++)
                {
                    try { Thread.sleep(300); } catch(Exception e) { }
                    System.out.println("Output: " + String.valueOf(dout.get()));
                }
        }
}
```

Output – The effect of the synchronization is to slow the output of lines since the println()'s must wait increasing amounts of time due to synchronization:

```
arr = a
Output: a
arr = ab
Output: ab
arr = abc
Output: abc
arr = abcd
Output: abcd
arr = abcde
Output: abcde
```

## Same as Previous Example But Without Synchronized Methods

```
class c8_5      // File: c8_5.java
{
        public static void main(String args[])
        {
                Data d = new Data();
                inThread in = new inThread(d);
                outThread out = new outThread(d);

                in.start();
                out.start();
        }
}

class Data
{
        private char arr[] = new char[5];

        public void set(char iarr[], int length)
        {
                for(int j = 0; j < length; j++)
                {
                        arr[j] = iarr[j];
                        try { Thread.sleep(500); } catch(Exception e) { }
                }

                System.out.println("arr = " + String.valueOf(arr));
        }
        public char [] get()
        {
                return arr;
        }
}

class inThread extends Thread
{
        private Data din;
        public inThread(Data d)
        {
                this.din = d;
        }
        public void run()
        {
                char in[] = {'a', 'b', 'c', 'd', 'e'};
                for(int j = 0; j < 5; j++)
                {
                        din.set(in, j+1);
                        try { Thread.sleep(100); } catch(Exception e) { }
                }
        }
}
```

```
class outThread extends Thread
{
        private Data dout;

        public outThread(Data d)
        {
                this.dout = d;
        }
        public void run()
        {
                for(int j = 0; j < 5; j++)
                {
                    try { Thread.sleep(300); } catch(Exception e) { }
                    System.out.println("Output: " + String.valueOf(dout.get()));
                }
        }
}
```

Output:
```
Output: a
arr = a
Output: a
Output: a
Output: ab
Output: ab
arr = ab
arr = abc
arr = abcd
arr = abcde
```

Note out of order execution due to lack of synchronization.

## Same Example Implemented with Synchronized Blocks

```java
class c8_6     // File: c8_6.java
{
        public static void main(String args[])
        {
                Data d = new Data();
                inThread in = new inThread(d);
                outThread out = new outThread(d);
                in.start();
                out.start();
        }
}

class Data
{
        private char arr[] = new char[5];
        public void set(char iarr[], int length)
        {
                synchronized (this)
                {
                        System.arraycopy(iarr, 0, arr, 0, length);
                        System.out.println("arr = " + String.valueOf(arr));
                }
        }
        public char [] get()
        {
                synchronized (this)
                {
                        return arr;
                }
        }
}

class inThread extends Thread
{
        private Data din;
        public inThread(Data d)
        {
                this.din = d;
        }
        public void run()
        {
                char in[] = {'a', 'b', 'c', 'd', 'e'};
                for(int j = 0; j < 5; j++)
                {
                        din.set(in, j+1);
                        try
                        {
                                Thread.sleep(100);
                        }
                        catch(Exception e)
                        {    }
                }
        }
}
```

```java
class outThread extends Thread
{
        private Data dout;

        public outThread(Data d)
        {
                this.dout = d;
        }
        public void run()
        {
                for(int j = 0; j < 5; j++)
                {
                    try
                    {
                            Thread.sleep(100);
                    }
                    catch(Exception e)
                    {     }
                    System.out.println("Output: " + String.valueOf(dout.get()));
                }
        }
}
```

Output:

```
arr = a
Output: a
arr = ab
Output: ab
arr = abc
Output: abc
arr = abcd
Output: abcd
arr = abcde
Output: abcde
```

## wait() and notify() Methods

Some methods in class Object which extend Java thread synchronization:

**void wait()** - A thread can call wait() inside a synchronized block to deactivate itself putting it in the waiting queue for access to an object. This allows another thread to perform some activity. The thread remains in the wait state until a notify() or notifyAll() executes in another thread's synchronized method. The waiting thread is then reactivated. Wait() throws an InterruptedException if the thread receives an interrupt.

Example:
```
try
{
        while(x < y)
                wait();
}
```

**void notify()** - The notify() method reactivates other threads waiting on an object locked by the current thread.

Example:
```
notify();
```

**void notifyAll()** - The notifyAll() method reactivates all threads waiting on any objects locked by any thread.

Example:
```
notifyAll();
```

Example: Consider a bank account object with on thread making deposits and another thread writing checks IF there is sufficient funds in the account. After each deposit we execute a notify() to release a wait() – thus allowing the sufficient funds condition to be tested. When the balance becomes large enough the check is written.

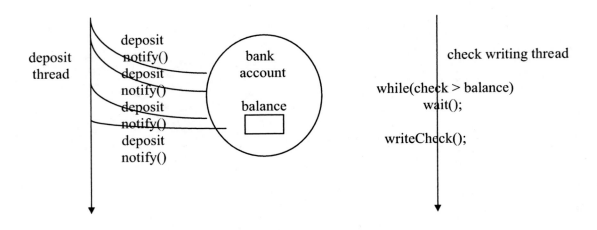

# SUMMARY

This module has examined single and multithreaded Java programs.

We have seen two ways to define classes for threads using subclassing from class Thread and by implementing the Runnable interface.

The methods which manage threads were described. Synchronization was described in detail.

# EXERCISES

1. Add a third thread to c8_1.java with the string "mythread" as the input.

2. Add a new Runnable class to c8_2.java called Runny2 whose run() method prints the name of the current thread 10 times using getName() with no time delays. Start the thread from main() with the input string "mine". Set the priority of the thread to MAX_PRIORITY.

3. Place a 400 millisecond time delay in the get() method of c8_4.java and make get() unsynchronized. Change the for loop in the outThread class to iterate 10 times. Run the program and note the resulting output.

4. Modify c8_4.java so that the get() method waits until the set method puts "abcde" in the Data object. Hint: set() must use notify().

# 9. Java Applets

## OBJECTIVES

At the end of this module you should be able to:

- Describe and create Java applets.

- Write simple HTML scripts calling Java applets.

- Set and use applet parameters.

- Use the appletviewer program

- Run Web pages in a Internet browser.

- Simple applet graphics.

- Applet mouse handling.

- Applet audio capabilities.

- Button implementation and handling.

- Perform some Delegation Event handling.

- Understand some Java-related security issues.

# STANDALONE JAVA PROGRAMS

Standalone programs begin with the execution of a main() method which calls other methods, …

```
class myClass
{
     public static void main(String args[])
     {
          // code
     }
}
```

# JAVA APPLETS

- A Java applet is defined in a .java file.

  ```
  public class myApplet extends Applet
  {
       // code
  }
  ```

- Java applets are executed from within an HTML document by a browser running the Java Virtual Machine (JVM). The browser plays the role of the main() method. It creates an applet object and runs certain applet methods to initialize the applet. The initial code the browser runs is roughly equivalent to (where init(), start() and paint() are applet methods described in the next few pages):

  ```
  myApplet m = new myApplet();
  m.init();
  m.start();
  m.paint(m.getGraphics());
  ```

**BROWSER**

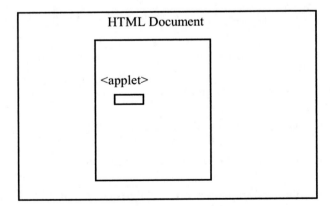

## A Simple Applet Definition

An applet is defined in a .java file that is then compiled. The compiled .java file is referenced in a html document that is displayed in a browser or in the appletviewer program. For example,

Java Program:

**File: c9_1.java**

```
import java.awt.Graphics;      //   File: c9_1.java
import java.applet.Applet;

public class c9_1 extends Applet
{
        public void paint(Graphics g)
        {
                g.drawString("myApplet String", 60, 60);
        }
}
```

HTML Document File:

**File: c9_1.html**

```
<applet code="c9_1.class" width = 200 height = 100>
</applet>
```

## Commands to Create and Display an Applet

edit c9_1.java

edit c9_1.html

javac c9_1.java

appletviewer c9_1.html

**Output:**

**9. Java Applets**

# SOME STANDARD APPLET METHODS

There are some standard methods that appear often in Java applets. Programmers define blocks of code for these methods to intialize an applet and to do cleanup when an applet ends execution. Some of these methods are automatically run by the browser when an applet is started and when an applet is ended.

**Methods that run <u>automatically</u> to initialize the Applet**

> **init()** - initializes the applet execution environment: initializes variables, ... If an init() method is not provided, then an inherited default init() executes performing no action. Runs once normally.

> **start()** - executed after init() to start graphics and text display, audio effects, animation, etc. If a start() method is not provided, then an inherited start() method runs performing no action. May be called many times during an applet's execution.

> **paint(Graphics g)** - executed to initially draw on the applet. Runs wnever the applet display needs to be refreshed. The inherited paint() usually draws a white background box if not overriden (version dependent).

**Methods that run <u>automatically</u> when the Applet ends**

> **stop()** - runs when the applet execution is stopped. Any executing threads started by the applet should be stopped in the block of this method. The inherited stop() method performs no action.

> **destroy()** - runs automatically after stop() and performs cleanup associated with the execution of the applet. destroy() should destroy any threads currently executing in its block of code by using the Thread destroy() method. The inherited destroy() method performs no action.

## Program Illustrating Standard Applet Methods

This program illustrates the fact that the applet environment runs some methods automatically.

**File: c9_2.html**
```
<applet code="c9_2.class" width = 200 height = 300>
</applet>
```

**File: c9_2.java**
```java
import java.awt.Graphics;
import java.applet.Applet;

public class c9_2 extends Applet        // File:  c9_2.java
{
        public void init()
        {
                System.out.println("init() ran");
        }
        public void start()
        {
                System.out.println("start() ran");
        }
        public void update(Graphics g)
        {
                g.drawString("update() ran", 60, 40);
                System.out.println("update() ran");
        }
        public void paint(Graphics g)
        {
                System.out.println("paint() ran");
                g.drawString("paint() ran", 60, 20);
        }
        public void stop()
        {
                System.out.println("stop() ran");
        }
        public void destroy()
        {
                System.out.println("destroy() ran");
        }
}
```

Note: that println() output is placed in the MS-DOS command window on PC's and in the command window in UNIX (LINUX) environments.

## MS-DOS PROMPT WINDOW

```
C:\WORK> edit c9_2.java
C:\WORK> edit c9_2.html
C:\WORK> javac c9_2.java
C:\WORK> appletviewer c9_2.html
init() ran
start() ran
paint() ran
stop() ran
destroy() ran
```

Note that g.drawString() places its output on the applet display. The Graphics object g is used to draw on the applet.

# SOME APPLETVIEWER MENU CHOICES

The appletviewer window has several menus: the coffee cup menu and the Applet menu. Applet menu choices causes certain methods within the applet to execute:

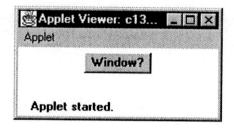

## Some Coffee Cup Menu Choices

Restore -        executes the paint() method.

Maximize -        executes the paint() method.

Close -        executes the stop() and destroy() methods.

## Some Applet Menu Choices

Restart - executes stop() followed by the init() and start() methods.

Reload - executes stop() followed by the destroy() method. Then a fresh copy of the applet is loaded from memory and restarted.

Quit - executes the destroy() method and ends the appletviewer session.

# FORMAT OF A JAVA APPLET

A Java applet class definition generally has a certain overall format:

```
//
//    Comments documenting the purpose, nature and special features of the applet
//                                    and
//    The author(s), telephone numbers, departments, etc.

//
//    import statements
//

public class myApplet extends Applet
{
        // declaration of variables

        // definition of applet methods (paint(), ...) and other methods.

}
```

# DEFINING HTML WEB PAGES

- This section describes general HTML features. The next section describes HTML applet features.

- HTML files contain literal text and formatting commands. HTML files contain only ASCII characters.

- HTML formatting commands begin with a keyword in < > braces and end with a keyword in braces with a slash: </ >.

- HTML keywords are called tags. Tags are usually upper case, but HTML also accepts upper case or lower case keywords.

General formats:

```
<tag>

<tag> text </tag>

<tag attribute=value> text </tag>
```

# SOME HTML COMMANDS

```
<HTML>

Contents of HTML page specification

</HTML>



<HEAD>
<TITLE>Title which will become the browser window title<\TITLE>
</HEAD>



<BODY>

Contents of the text part of the browser window.

</BODY>



<CENTER>

Centered Text

</CENTER>



<H1>Text Section Header - Type 1</H1>
<H2>Text Section Header - Type 2</H2>
...
<H6>Text Section Header - Type 6</H6>
```

**`<HR>`**   - Insert a horizontal rule.


**`<P>`**   - Start a new paragraph.


**`<BR>`**   - Insert a line break.


## Font Related Commands

The choice of font is limited by the browser environment.  However, you can choose various emphasized text font characteristics.  Some HTML commands supporting font feature selection are:


**`<H#>`** - Six levels of header choices.  Choice one is usually the large and bold. **`</H#>`**


**`<EM>`** **`text`** **`</EM>`**  - Emphasized print - this is usually italic.


**`<TT>`**   **`text`**   **`</TT>`** - Typewriter style fixed pitch font.


**`<B>`**   **`text`**   **`</B>`**  - bold type.


**`<I>`**   **`text`**   **`</I>`**   - italic type.

## Image Insertion Commands

`<IMG SRC="filename.gif">` - Insert a graphic image on the page. Can be centered.

`<IMG SRC="Filename.gif" ALT="String">` - Insert a graphic image. If the terminal does not support graphics the "String" is displayed instead.

## Hypertext Links

HTML has commands inserting hypertext links within a Web page.

`<A HREF="http://filename.html"> text </A>` - The text is inserted in the document (possibly with emphasis) and underlined or highlighted to indicate the hypertext link. If selected, the specified .html executes.

`<A HREF="file1.html"><IMG SRC="file2.gif" align=middle></A>` - Makes an image a hypertext link.

## URL Format

`ResourceType://host.domain:port/path/filename.html`

ResourceTypes:

        http
        file
        ftp
        gopher
        news
        telnet

## Lists

A list of items can be built using the following format:

```
<DL>
<DT>List Item text and/or hypertext link
<DD>An indented text passage for the list item.
<DT> …
<DD> …
…
</DL>
```

## Some HTML References

```
http://www.ncsa.uiuc.edu/General/Internet/WWW/HTMLPrimer.html
```

```
http://www.willamette.edu/html-composition/strict-html.html
```

```
http://www.ncsa.uiuc.edu/SDG/Software/Mosaic/Docs/fill-out-forms/overview.html
```

## Sample HTML Page

### HTML File

```
<HTML>
<HEAD>
<TITLE>Whatta Page!</TITLE>
</HEAD>
<BODY>
<CENTER>
<IMG SRC="myfile.gif">
<H1>Welcome to Our Page.</H1>
</CENTER>
<HR>
<HR>
<H2><I>Superstar Information</I></H2>
<P>
It's hard to be a superstar. Ask Bob
or Bill or Michael or even Peter Lynch.
<P>
<H2><I>Pick Your Star</I></H2>
<P>
Here's a list of your favorites:
<P>
<DL>
<DT><A HREF="bob.html"><B>Bob</B></A>
<DD>Check out Bob!
<DT><A HREF="bill.html"><B>Bill</B></A>
<DD>Here's Bill!
</DL>
</BODY>
</HTML>
```

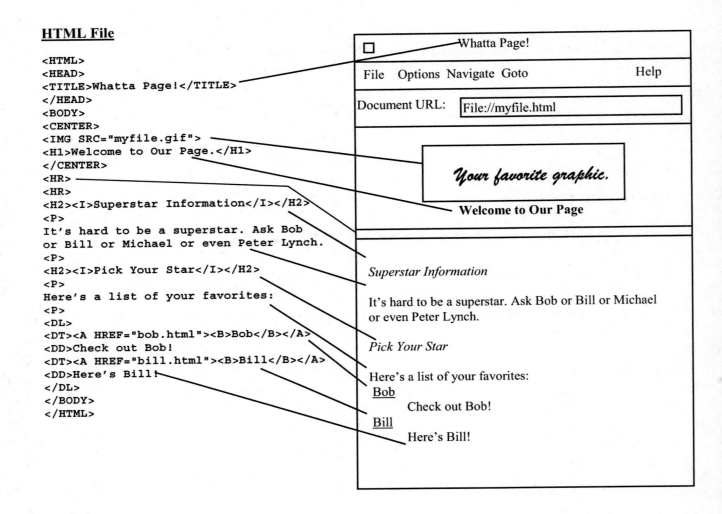

# APPLET PARAMETERS

- Applets can be inserted into HTML files using the applet command. In its simplest form it runs an applet class file with the width and height (in pixels) of the applet specified. For example,

```
<applet code="myClass.class" width = 200 height=300> </applet>
```

- Applet commands can also set parameter values which can be accessed within the applet code. For example,

```
<applet code="myClass.class" width=400 height=300>
<param name=var1   value=23>
<param name=str1    value="abc">
<param name=var2   value=45.67>
</applet>
```

- The names of parameters in HTML specifications are case insensitive. So your code can use either upper-case, lower-case or mixed-case names for parameters in the HTML document. Double quotes around strings are optional unless the string contains white space characters.

- Space is allowed around the = sign.

- The value is read into the Java applet using the getParameter method which returns a String object containing the character string value. The value can then be converted to other data types using methods of class Double, Integer, etc.

```
public String getParameter(String s)
```

getParameter() returns null if it can't find the parameter value in the HTML document.

getParameter() Example:

**File: c9_3.html**
```
<applet code="c9_3.class" width = 200 height = 200>
<param name=var1 value=23>
<param name= str1 value= "abc">
<param name=Var2   value=45.67>
</applet>
```

**File: c9_3.java**
```java
import java.awt.*;
import java.applet.Applet;

public class c9_3 extends Applet    // File: c9_3.java
{
        private int var1;
        private String str1;
        private double var2;
        private String s1, s2;

        public void start()
        {
                setBackground(Color.white);   // sets applet background color
                s1 = getParameter("var1");
                var1 = Integer.parseInt(s1);
                str1 = getParameter("str1");
                s2 = getParameter("var2");
                var2 = Double.valueOf(s2).doubleValue();
                System.out.println("var1 = " + var1);
                System.out.println("str1 = " + str1);
                System.out.println("var2 = " + var2);
        }
        public void paint(Graphics g)
        {
                g.drawString("var1 = " + s1, 60, 60);
                g.drawString("str1 = " + str1, 60, 80);
                g.drawString("var2 = " + s2, 60, 100);
        }
}
```

**Command Window Output:**
```
appletviewer c9_3.html
var1 = 23
str1 = abc
var2 = 45.67
```

**Output Applet Window:**

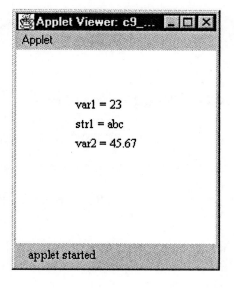

# BASIC APPLET GRAPHICS

This section introduces some basic graphics features of Java applets.

## Size and Position of Applet Window

- The size of the applet is specified by the width and height attributes.

- The placement of the applet is specified by the *align* attribute. For example,

```
<applet code="MC.class" width=100 height=100 align=left vspace=20 hspace=20>
```

- The align attribute values can be: left, right, top, texttop, middle, absmiddle, baseline, bottom, or absbottom.

- If align has the values left or right, the Web page text flows around the applet.

- The left and right values of align also allow vspace and hspace to be used to specify the amount of white space around the applet.

- The *setSize()* method can be used to set the size of an applet. It often appears in the init() method to guarantee a minimum size for an applet. It can override the height and width values for the applet specified in an HTML file. (These values set the size of the appletviewer window.)

```
public void setSize(int width, int height)
```

- Example:

```
public void init()
{
        setSize(300, 400);

        // code

}
```

## Drawing on Applets

- The preferred place to do drawing on an applet is the paint() method. This method runs automatically to refresh the applet display whenever needed - for example, when another window is placed in front of an applet and then removed.

- Java has a number of built-in drawing methods in its awt.Graphics class. These methods are run in the paint method with code of the form:

```
public void paint(Graphics g)
{
        g.drawXXXXX(…);
        …
}
```

- The drawing methods invoked in the paint() method execute when paint() runs to refresh the applet display.

- Later on we will see drawing done in other methods such as event handlers. When paint() runs to redraw the applet these methods do not run again automatically.

- If you wish automatic redrawing of drawings done in other methods, then a double buffer Image object should be used to store drawings. The stored drawings can be displayed by running drawImage() on the Image object in the paint() method. See Module 14 for details.

## Drawing Methods for Standard Graphic Shapes

Java has a number of methods for drawing standard graphic shapes. The recipient object is a Graphics object.

**void drawString(String s, int x, int y)**

**void drawChars(char [] chararr, int offset, int length, int x, int y)**

**void drawBytes(byte [] bytearr, int offset, int length, int x, int y)**

**void drawLine(int x1, int y1, int x2, int y2)**

**void drawRect(int x, int y, int width, int height)**

**void drawRoundRect(int x, int y, int width, int height, int arcWidth, int arcHeight)**

**void draw3DRect(int x, int y, int width, int height, boolean raised)**
            **// has differences in shading to simulate 3D.**
            **// 3D effect visible with gray shades.**

**void fillRect( int x, int y, int width, int height)**

**void clearRect( int x, int y, int width, int height)**

**void fillRoundRect( int x, int y, int width, int height, int arcWidth, int arcHeight)**

**void fill3DRect( int x, int y, int width, int height, boolean raised)**

**void drawOval( int x, int y, int width, int height)**

**void fillOval(int x, int y, int width, int height)**

**void drawArc( int x, int y, int width, int height, int startAngle, int arcAngle)**

**void fillArc( int x, int y, int width, int height, int startAngle, int arcAngle)**

**void drawPolygon( int [] xPoints, int [] yPoints, int numPoints)**

**void fillPolygon( int [] xPoints, int [] yPoints, int numPoints)**

**void copyArea(int xsrc, int ysrc, int width, int length, int xdest, int ydest)**

## Setting Colors

Colors can be set in Java methods using the setColor() method. Some of the standard built-in colors are red, white, blue, black, yellow, green, gray, lightGray, darkGray, pink, magenta, orange and cyan. The awt.Color.java file contains a list of builtin colors.

An example of code which selects and uses a color is:

```
import java.awt.Color;

// code

public void paint(Graphics g)
{
      g.setColor(Color.green);
      g.drawRect(15, 20, 10, 10);
}
```

**Example:**

**File: c9_4.html**
```
<applet code="c9_4.class" width = 300 height = 300>
</applet>
```

**File: c9_4.java**
```
import java.awt.*;
import java.awt.Color;
import java.applet.Applet;

public class c9_4 extends Applet
{
      public void start()
      {
             setBackground(Color.white);   // sets applet background color
      }
      public void paint(Graphics g)
      {
             g.setColor(Color.black);
             g.drawRect(40, 40, 120, 120);

             g.setColor(Color.gray);
             g.fillRect(41, 41, 119, 119); // Note 41 and 119.

             g.setColor(Color.black);
             g.draw3DRect(50, 50, 100, 100, true);

             g.setColor(Color.white);
             g.drawOval(60, 80, 80, 40);
      }
}
```

**Output Applet:**

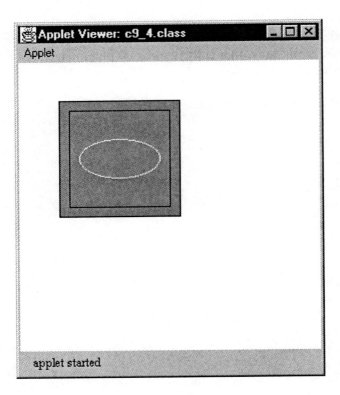

## Drawing Images

Graphic images can be inserted in an applet using the drawImage() method. For example,

```java
import java.awt.*;
import java.applet.Applet;
import java.awt.image.*;

class myPict extends Applet
{
        private Image myImage;
        // code

        public void init()
        {
                myImage = getImage(getDocumentBase(), "myfile.gif");
                prepareImage(myImage, this);
        }

        public void paint(Graphics g)
        {
                g.drawImage(myImage, x1, y1, this);
        }

        // code
}
```

Comments:

- java.awt.image.* must be imported.

- Class Image objects contain a graphics image.

- The getDocumentBase() method returns the URL object of the HTML file within which the applet is running. The filename in the getImage() method is at the URL or can be specified relative to the URL with an appropriate path.

    ```java
    public Image getImage(URL u, String filename)
    ```

- The prepareImage() method causes a thread to be created to load the image and to generate the appropriate screen representation.

    ```java
    public boolean prepareImage(Image img, ImageObserver ob)
    ```

- The drawImage() method has the format:

    ```java
    public void drawImage(Image img, int x, int y, ImageObserver ob)
    ```

- The ImageObserver object is the object whose code is responsible for drawing the pixels on screen. Usually it is the object on which the drawing will be made – such as an applet.

## Program Illustrating Image Display

**File: c9_5.html**
```
<applet code="c9_5.class" width = 300 height = 300>
</applet>
```

**File: c9_5.java**
```java
import java.awt.*;
import java.awt.image.*;
import java.applet.Applet;

public class c9_5 extends Applet
{
        private Image img;

        public void init()
        {
                setBackground(Color.white);
                img = getImage(getDocumentBase(), "myimage.gif");
                prepareImage(img, this);
        }
        public void paint(Graphics g)
        {
                g.drawImage(img, 75, 75, this);// the ImageObserver is applet - this
        }
}
```
**Output Applet:**

# INTRODUCTION TO DELEGATION EVENT HANDLING

- Java applets can respond to events such as mouse clicks, pressing keys, resizing windows, pressing buttons, and so on.

- Java uses Delegation Event Handling to handle events.

Basic idea:

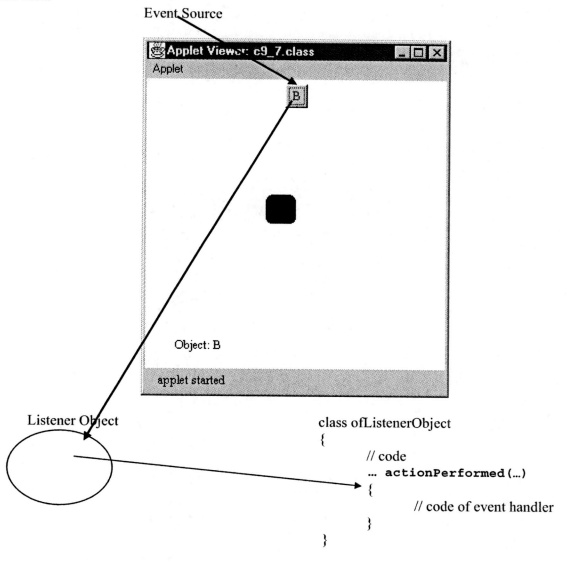

class ofListenerObject
{
    // code
    ... **actionPerformed**(...)
    {
        // code of event handler
    }
}

### Event Sources Which are Also Listeners

- Classes which contain event sources can also listen for events generated from the sources and run member functions which are event handlers. For example the below picture shows an applet containing a button. If the button is clicked an event is generated. The event is "delivered" to the applet. As a result the actionPerformed() event handler method in the applet class definition executes to handle the event.

- Many of the examples in this module will have the applet object as the listener object for the components (Buttons, etc.) on the applet. The applet class definitions will contain event handler methods to handle the events generated by components on the applet.

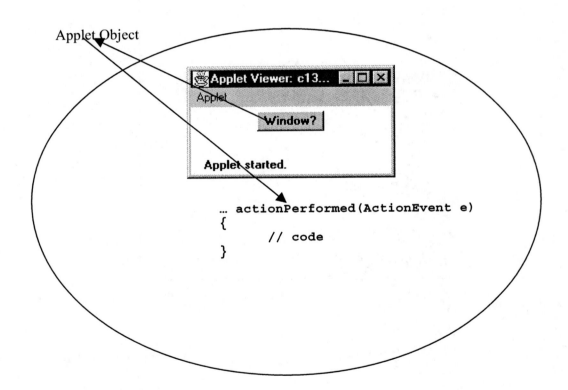

# SURVEY OF DELEGATION EVENT HANDLING FEATURES

### Types of Event Objects - Event Classes

- Event objects are created when an event is generated. There are many types of event objects.

- The classes of the various event objects form a hierarchy. The parent class of the hierarchy is class util.EventObject. The other event classes subclass from it either directly or through an intervening class.

```
java.util.EventObject

    java.awt.AWTEvent

        java.awt.event.ActionEvent ("do a command")

        java.awt.event.AdjustmentEvent ("value was adjusted")

        java.awt.event.ItemEvent ("item state has changed")

        java.awt.event.ComponentEvent (resized, moved, etc.)

        java.awt.event.FocusEvent (got focus, lost focus)

        java.awt.event.KeyEvent (key-press, key-release, etc.)

        java.awt.event.MouseEvent (mouse-down, mouse-move, etc.)

        java.awt.event.PaintEvent

        java.awt.event.TextEvent

        java.awt.event.WindowEvent

        java.awt.event.ContainerEvent
```

These event classes contain private variables which cannot be referenced directly. Some common methods for fetching event data from within an event object:

```
getSource() - returns component generating event as an Object

getID() - returns ID number of event

getX() - returns x coordinate of an event (usually mouse event)

getY() - returns y coordinate of an event

getCharKey() - returns key in key event
```

**9. Java Applets**

## Listener Interfaces

One or more listener objects must be specified to handle an event. The class of a listener object must implement the interface corresponding to the type of event for which the object is listening.   The listener interfaces are:

`ComponentListener`

`ActionListener`

`FocusListener`

`ItemListener`

`TextListener`

`AdjustmentListener`

`KeyListener`

`MouseListener`

`MouseMotionListener`

`WindowListener`

`ContainerListener`

## Adding Listener Objects

A listener object must be explicitly added with one of the following methods. Several listener objects can be defined for an event.

```
java.awt.Button
        addActionListener(ActionListener l)

 java.awt.Choice
        addItemListener(ItemListener l)

java.awt.Checkbox
        addItemListener(ItemListener l)

java.awt.CheckboxMenuItem
        addItemListener(ItemListener l)

java.awt.List (implements java.awt.ItemSelectable)
        addActionListener(ActionListener l)
                        (Single selection list)

        addItemListener(ItemListener l)
                        (Multiple selection list)

java.awt.MenuItem
        addActionListener(ActionListener l)

java.awt.Scrollbar
        addAdjustmentListener(AdjustmentListener l)

java.awt.TextField
        addActionListener(ActionListener l)

java.awt.Component
        addComponentListener(ComponentListener l)

        addFocusListener(FocusListener l)

        addKeyListener(KeyListener l)

        addMouseListener(MouseListener l)

        addMouseMotionListener(MouseMotionListener l)

java.awt.Dialog
        addWindowListener(WindowListener l)

java.awt.Frame
        addWindowListener(WindowListener l)
```

## Event Handler Methods

Each kind of event is handled by a different event handler method. (Although there are some general purpose event handlers in Delegation Event handling such as processEvent().) Some of the event handlers methods are:

```java
public void mouseClicked(MouseEvent e)
{
    // Code for mouse button click on a component.
}
public void mousePressed(MouseEvent e)
{
    // code for mouse button press on a component.
}
public void mouseReleased(MouseEvent e)
{
    // code for mouse button release on a component.
}
public void mouseEntered(MouseEvent e)
{
    // code for mouse entry to a component.
}
public void mouseExited(MouseEvent e)
{
    // code for mouse exit from a component.
}
public void actionPerformed(ActionEvent e)
{
    // Button, List (double click), MenuItem, & TextField events
}
public void itemStateChanged(ItemEvent e)
{
    // Choice, Checkbox, CheckboxMenuitem, & List (single click)
}
public void windowOpened(WindowEvent e)
{
    // code for a window open
}
public void windowClosed(WindowEvent e){}
{
    // code for a window close
}
public void windowIconified(WindowEvent e){}
{
    // code for a window iconification
}
public void windowDeiconified(WindowEvent e){}
{
    // code for a window restore
}
```

# APPLET MOUSE HANDLING

- We will now look at event handling in important specific cases starting with mouse handling. The java.awt.event subpackage contains classes, interfaces, and event handler methods for mouse handling.

- The steps to follow to implement Delegation Event mouse handling are:

    1. Import the event subpackage:

    ```
    import java.awt.event.*;
    ```

    2. Have the applet implement the MouseListener interface.

    ```
    public class xxx extends Applet implements MouseListener
    ```

    3. Specify the applet listens for mouse events with the addMouseListener(MouseListener m) method. Note this forces the applet to implement the MouseListener interface.

    ```
    addMouseListener(this); // this refers to the applet object
    ```

    4. The most direct approach then requires you to add the following mouse event handler method definitions to your applet because the MouseListener interface requires it (otherwise the browser cannot instantiate the applet).

    ```
    public void mouseClicked(MouseEvent e)
    {
            // Code for mouse button click.
    }
    public void mousePressed(MouseEvent e)
    {
            // Code for mouse button press.
    }
    public void mouseReleased(MouseEvent e)
    {
        // Code for mouse button release.
    }
    public void mouseEntered(MouseEvent e)
    {
            // code for mouse entry into a container.
    }
    public void mouseExited(MouseEvent e)
    {
            // code for mouse exit from a container.
    }
    ```

---

- Use empty blocks for types of mouse events for which the applet will not perform an action.

- Java also has a more sophisticated way of handling mouse events using inner classes with the same result.

## Mouse Example

A program which produces a black filled rectangle when the mouse is clicked down and then an adjacent rectangle when the mouse button is released. When running this program wait a bit before releasing the mouse button.

**File: c9_6.html**
```
<applet code="c9_6.class" width = 300 height = 300>
</applet>
```

**File: c9_6.java**
```java
import java.awt.*;
import java.awt.event.*;
import java.applet.Applet;

public class c9_6 extends Applet implements MouseListener
{
        private int x = 20, y = 50;

        public void init()
        {
                setBackground(Color.white);
                addMouseListener(this);
        }
        public void paint(Graphics g)
        {
                g.setColor(Color.black);
                g.fillRect(x, y, 10, 10);
        }
        public void mousePressed(MouseEvent e)
        {
                this.x = e.getX() - 10;
                this.y = e.getY() - 10;
                repaint();
        }
        public void mouseReleased(MouseEvent e)
        {
                this.x = e.getX() - 20;
                this.y = e.getY() - 20;
                repaint();
        }
        public void mouseClicked(MouseEvent e)
        { }
        public void mouseEntered(MouseEvent e)
        { }
        public void mouseExited(MouseEvent e)
        { }
}
```

Note: getX() and getY() fetch the x and y coordinates of the event.

**Output Applet:**

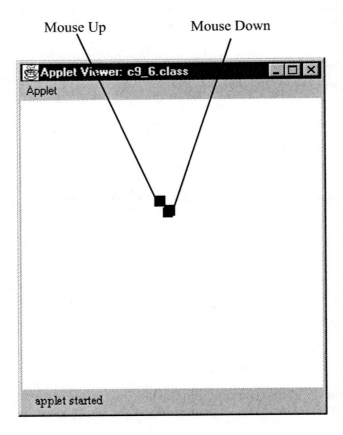

Note the lower square appears when the mouse button is pressed down. When the button is released the upper square appears. The above picture is a composite.

# WHICH MOUSE BUTTON?

If any button on the mouse is pressed or released it is a mouse event. You can detect the button that was pressed using the getModifiers() method:

**getModifiers()** (a method of the InputEvent class – the superclass of the MouseEvent class)

This method returns an integer value depending on the button pressed. The values for a standard two button mouse are:

Left button:  16
Right button:  4

Sample code:

```
if (e.getModifiers() == 16)
{
        // left button code
}
else if(e.getModifiers() == 4)
{
        // right button code
}
```

You may also want to detect the number of mouse button clicks (single-click, double-click, …). The getClickCount() method of class MouseEvent returns the click count number.

Sample code:

```
if (e.getClickCount() == 1)
{
        // single-click code
}
```

# MOUSE DRAG EXAMPLE

- When a mouse is moved over an applet mouseMove events are generated automatically every few milliseconds. When a mouse is dragged over an applet mouseDrag events are generated automatically every few milliseconds.

- These events are MouseMotion events and are handled using the MouseMotionListener interface, and the mouseMoved() and mouseDragged() handlers.

**scribe.html**
```
<applet code="scribe.class" width = 300 height = 300></applet>
```

**scribe.java**
```java
import java.awt.*;
import java.awt.event.*;
import java.applet.*;

public class scribe extends Applet implements MouseListener,
                                               MouseMotionListener
{
        private int beginX, beginY;
        private Graphics g1;

        public void init()
        {
                addMouseListener(this);
                addMouseMotionListener(this); // MouseMotion listening.
                g1 = getGraphics();
        }
        public void paint(Graphics g)
        {
                g.drawString("SCRIBE", 120, 30);
        }
        public void mousePressed(MouseEvent e)
        {
                beginX = e.getX();
                beginY = e.getY();
        }
        public void mouseDragged(MouseEvent e)
        {
                g1.drawLine(beginX, beginY, e.getX(), e.getY());
                beginX = e.getX();
                beginY = e.getY();
        }
        public void mouseReleased(MouseEvent e)
        {
                g1.drawLine(beginX, beginY, e.getX(), e.getY());
        }
```

```
        public void mouseClicked(MouseEvent e) { }
        public void mouseEntered(MouseEvent e) { }
        public void mouseExited(MouseEvent e)  { }
        public void mouseMoved(MouseEvent e)   { }
}
```

**Sample Scribe Applet Display:**

# SIMPLE BUTTONS

- Java supports many types of buttons.  This section covers simple buttons.

- A simple button is defined as an object of class Button.

- The button is normally given a label.

- The button is added to the applet using the add() method.

- A button can be added to an applet in init() or start() with only an `add(buttonObjectName);` statement.

- A button can also be added with the same statement <u>in any other applet method</u> if it is followed by a call to the validate() method which "installs" the button.  For example,

```
add(newButton1);
add(newButton2);
add(newButton3);
validate();
```

- When a button is "pushed" :

  - A button event is generated and "delivered" to the listener object.

  - The public void actionPerformed(ActionEvent e) method of the listener's class is automatically invoked.

  - Normally the method tests the nature of the event and then performs an appropriate task.

Button event handling by an applet requires:

```
public class xxx extends Applet implements ActionListener


b.addActionListener(this); // add the applet as the listener.


public void actionPerformed(ActionEvent e)// add handler to applet
```

# BUTTON EVENT EXAMPLE

- This example places one button labeled "aButton" on an applet. Each time you select this button a rounded rectangle is generated offset by 30 pixels from the previous rectangle. The descriptor of the button is also printed at the bottom of the applet window.

- The example tests which component generated the event using the equals() method.

- This example also shows how to use the *instanceof* operator to compare the event type with the Button type and thus determine if the Button generated the event. Try uncommenting the instanceof if, recompile, and test the program.

**File: c9_7.html**
```
<applet code="c9_7.class" width = 300 height = 300>
</applet>
```

**File: c9_7.java**
```
import java.awt.*;
import java.awt.event.*;
import java.applet.Applet;

public class c9_7 extends Applet implements ActionListener
{
        private Button b = new Button("aButton");  // creates Button subobject
        private int x = 30, y = 30;
        private boolean bflag = false;

        public void init()
        {
                setBackground(Color.white);
                add(b);                          // adds button to applet.
                b.addActionListener(this);// adds listening for button event.
        }
        public void paint(Graphics g)
        {
                g.setColor(Color.black);
                g.fillRoundRect(x, y, 30, 30,15, 15);
                if(bflag)  // bflag is true if button pressed.
                        g.drawString("Object: "+b.getLabel(), 30, 280);
                bflag = false;
        }
        public void actionPerformed(ActionEvent e)
        {
```

```
//                  if(e.getSource() instanceof Button)//tests for data type of
// the object generating the event. Is the object a Button object? The
// instanceof operator does data type comparisons. In English the condition is
// "is e.getSource() of data type Button".
                 if(e.getSource().equals(b))
                 {
                      x += 30;   // causes drawn figures to move down
                      y += 30;   // the display along the diagonal.
                      bflag = true;
                 }
                 repaint();
        }
}
```

Note: e.getSource() fetches the component which generated the event. It returns an Object object formally. The object is actually a Button object in memory.

**Output Applet:**

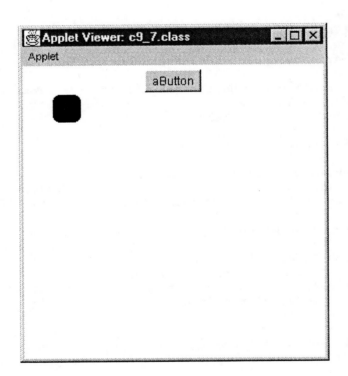

# MULTIPLE BUTTON EXAMPLE

This example places three buttons in the applet.  Each time you select a button a geometric figure  is generated offset by 30 pixels from the previous figure.

**File: c9_8.html**
```
<applet code="c9_8.class" width = 300 height = 300>
</applet>
```

**File: c9_8.java**
```java
import java.awt.*;
import java.awt.event.*;
import java.applet.Applet;

public class c9_8 extends Applet implements ActionListener
{
        private Button br = new Button("Rectangle");
        private Button bc = new Button("Circle");
        private Button bo = new Button("Oval");
        private int x = 30, y = 30;
        private int figType = 0;

        public void init()
        {
                setBackground(Color.white);
                add(br);
                add(bc);
                add(bo);
                br.addActionListener(this);
                bc.addActionListener(this);
                bo.addActionListener(this);
        }
        public void paint(Graphics g)
        {
                g.setColor(Color.black);
                switch(figType)
                {
                        case 1:
                                g.fillRoundRect(x, y, 30, 30,15, 15);
                                break;
                        case 2:
                                g.fillOval(x, y, 30, 30);
                                break;
                        case 3:
                                g.fillOval(x, y, 30, 15);
                                break;
                }
        }
```

```
public void actionPerformed(ActionEvent e)
{
        if(e.getSource() instanceof Button)// note instanceof does
        {                                  // a general test.
                if(e.getSource().equals(br))// specific button test.
                {
                        figType = 1;
                }
                else if(e.getSource().equals(bc))
                {
                        figType = 2;
                }
                else if(e.getSource().equals(bo))
                {
                        figType = 3;
                }
                x += 30;
                y += 30;
                repaint();
        }
    }
}
```

**Output Applet:** <u>**Note the buttons are "flowed" filling row after row of the applet. Then in each row they are centered on the applet. This is called a FlowLayout layout. Discussed in a few modules.**</u>

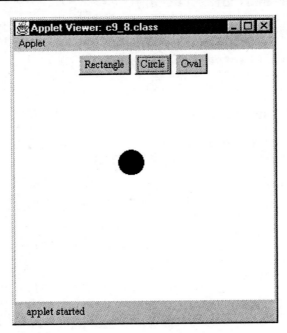

# VECTORS AND ENUMERATIONS

- Vectors are collections of objects which can be extended "indefinitely " by adding more objects.

- The objects have index numbers like array elements..

- An enumeration can be created from a vector which enables us to traverse the objects. An Enumeration is an interface which enables us to traverse a set of elements. No connection to C language enumerations.

Some Vector methods are:

**Vector(int initialCapacity, int capacityIncrement)** - constructor with parameters: initial number of elements, increments by capacityIncrement when capacity reached.

**void addElement(Object obj)** - adds element.

**Object clone()** - clones vector

**boolean removeElement(Object obj)** - removes first occurrence of element, returns true if object is an element of vector

**void removeAllElements()** - removes all elements

**Object elementAt(int index)** - returns object with specified index

**void setElementAt(Object obj, int index)** - sets element at specified index

**void removeElementAt(int index)** - removes element at specified index

**void insertElementAt(Object obj, int index)** - inserts element

**Object firstElement()** - returns first element

**Object lastElement()** - returns last element

**int size()** - number of components in vector

**boolean isEmpty()** - returns true if empty

**boolean contains(Object obj)** - returns true if vector contains obj object

**int indexOf(Object obj)** - returns index of obj object

**Enumeration elements()** - returns a VectorEnumerator of the elements in the vector with formal datatype Enumeration. The below VectorEnumerator methods can be used to traverse the vector.

*Class VectorEnumerator* **(a package class in the util package)**

**VectorEnumerator(Vector v)** - builds VectorEnumerator from Vector
**boolean hasMoreElements()** - returns true if more elements
**Object nextElement()** - returns next element

### Example:

```
// Create Vector object – empty.
Vector v = new Vector(100, 10);
MyClass m1, m2, m3;
YourClass y1, y2, y3;
...

// Add elements to the vector.
v.addElement(m1);
v.addElement(m2);
v.addElement(m3);
v.addElement(y1);
v.addElement(y2);
v.addElement(y3);

// Fetch an element of the vector.
MyClass m4 = v.elementAt(1);

// process vector like an array using its index
// number.
for(int j = 0; j < v.size(); j++)
{
    if((o = v.elementAt(j)) instanceof MyClass)
    {
        m1 = (MyClass)o;
        f(m1);  // f() and g() are methods.
        g(m1);
    }
    else if (o instanceof YourClass)
    {
        y1 = (YourClass)o;
        h(y1);  // h() and p() are methods.
        p(y1);
    }
}
```

// Using an Enumeration to iterate through (traverse) a vector of objects.

```
Enumeration e = v.elements();

while(e.hasMoreElements())
{
        Object o = e.nextElement();// automatically moves (iterates) to the next
        f(o);                      // element after fetching the current element.
        ...
}
```

Note: we cannot use the name VectorEnumerator in any of the preceding code because it is not accessible (referenceable) outside the util package. Instead we use an Enumeration interface reference to place a name on the (VectorEnumerator) object returned by v.elements().

**Program Example:**

**File: myVect.html**
```
<applet code="myVect.class" width = 400 height = 350>
</applet>
```

**File: myVect.java**
```
import java.awt.*;
import java.awt.event.*;
import java.applet.Applet;
import java.util.*;

public class myVect extends Applet implements ActionListener
{
        Vector v;
        String label;
        Enumeration e;
        String text;
        int count;

        public void init()
        {
                setBackground(Color.white);
                v = new Vector(100, 10);
                    // initial capacity, capacity increment at overflow.

                for(int j = 10; j < 100; j++)
                {
                        label = "B" + Integer.toString(j);
                        v.addElement(new Button(label));
                }
                System.out.println("Number of elements = " + v.size());
                System.out.println("Capacity = " + v.capacity());
```

```
            e = v.elements();
        while(e.hasMoreElements())
        { // The println() method calls the print() method and
          // adds a newline character. So print() is easy to use:
                System.out.print(
                    ((Button)e.nextElement()).getLabel() + " ");
        }
        System.out.println("");
        for(int j = 0; j < v.size(); j++)
        {
                add((Button)v.elementAt(j));
                ((Button)v.elementAt(j))
                        .addActionListener(this);
                count++;
        }
    }
public void actionPerformed(ActionEvent e)
{
        if(e.getSource() instanceof Button)
        {
                int index = v.indexOf(e.getSource());
                remove((Button)e.getSource());
                v.removeElementAt(index);

                if(v.size() < count - 5)
                {
                        removeAll();
                        v.removeAllElements();
                        count = 0;
                        init();
                        validate();
                }
        }
    }
}
```

## Output Applet:

Cick to make buttons disappear. Note output in Command Prompt window.

Command Window (print() and println()) Output
```
Number of elements = 90
Capacity = 100
B10 B11 B12 B13 B14 B15 B16 B17 B18 B19 B20 B21 B22 B23 B24 B25 B26 B27 B28
B29 B30 B31 B32 B33 B34 B35 B36 B37 B38 B39 B40 B41 B42 B43 B44 B45 B46 B47
B48 B49 B50 B51 B52 B53 B54 B55 B56 B57 B58 B59 B60 B61 B62 B63 B64 B65 B66
B67 B68 B69 B70 B71 B72 B73 B74 B75 B76 B77 B78 B79 B80 B81 B82 B83 B84 B85
B86 B87 B88 B89 B90 B91 B92 B93 B94 B95 B96 B97 B98 B99
```

# COMPONENT MANAGEMENT

This section describes methods which can be used to manage any Java component. Simple Button objects are the first components we have seen. We will see many more components soon. We will use Button objects in the examples.

## Adding and Removing Components

Components can be added to an applet, frame, or panel using one of the add() methods. For example,

```
add(b1);
```

If an add() is done in any method except init() or start(), then the validate() method must be executed after it to cause the component to be displayed on the applet (or other container) according to the layout of the applet (container).

```
add(b1);
// code
validate();
```

Components can be removed from an applet, frame, or panel by executing the remove() method in any method. For example,

```
remove(b1);
```

## Positioning and Sizing Components

Components such as buttons can be positioned or resized on an applet (or panel) using the setLocation() and setBounds() methods.

The setLocation() method can be used in any method:

```
obj.setLocation(x, y);
```

However, setLocation() does not work for some components in init() or start() (such as Button objects).

The setBounds() method should be used in situations where setLocation() does not work.

The setBounds() method can be used in any method.

If you use it in init() or start() then setLayout(null) must be executed first. A setLayout(null) prevents components which are not placed by setBounds() from appearing on the applet.

```
setLayout(null); // required for setBounds() in init() or start().

// code

obj.setBounds(x, y, width, height); // you choose the size
```
// OR
```
obj.setBounds(x, y, obj.getPreferredSize().width,
              obj.getPreferredSize().height); // preferred size
```

setBounds() requires you to set the size of the component. There are two ways to set the size: use the PrefferedSize (normal size), or choose a size numerically.

If you use setBounds() for one component in init() or start() then you must position all other components as well or the unpositioned components will not appear on the applet. All or nothing. In init() and start() you cannot position some components with setBounds() and have other components positioned according to some other layout (layouts are described in a few modules).

### Showing and Hiding Components

Components can be hidden (made invisible) on an applet, frame, or panel using the setVisible(false) method. For example,

```
b1.setVisible(false); // Makes a button b1 invisible
```

A hidden component is not visible and <u>loses its position</u> (the other components reflow to fill its position) if setVisible(false) is executed in init() or start().

A component keeps its position if setVisible(false) is executed from another method. However, if validate() is executed after the setVisible(false) then the hidden component loses its position.

If a component is hidden, then "clicking" on the component does not generate an event.

A hidden component can be made visible and enabled to generate events using setVisible(true). If a setVisible(true) is done in any method except init() or start(), then the validate() method must also execute after it to display the component.

```
b1.setVisible(true)

// code

validate();  // usually needed after a setVisible(true) outside of init()
                                                   // or start()
```

## Enabling and Disabling Components

Components can be disabled in an applet, frame, or panel using setEnabled(false).

A disabled component is "greyed" but visible on screen. "Clicking" on it does not generate an event. For example,

```
b1.setEnabled(false);
```

A disabled component can be reenabled with the setEnabled(boolean) method.

```
b1.setEnabled(true);
```

# APPLET AUDIO

- Java applets support audio using the AudioClip interface.

- Audio files end in a .au extension.

- An Audio file is loaded by creating an AudioClip object using a statement such as:

```
AudioClip myTape = getAudioClip(getDocumentBase(), "mySound.au");
```

- The getAudioClip() method is a method of class Applet:

```
public AudioClip getAudioClip(URL u, String filename)
```

- An AudioClip is played using the play() method:

```
myTape.play();
```

- The play() method always starts at the beginning of the playback rewinding if necessary.

- The audio is ended with the stop() method:

```
myTape.stop();
```

- An AudioClip can be played continuously with looping using the loop() method which starts the playing and then loops indefinitely:

```
myTape.loop();
```

# PROGRAM WITH AUDIO

Pressing the button starts playing a song. Pressing the button again stops playing the song. Requires a sound board in your computer to make sounds.

**File: c9_9.html**
```
<applet code="c9_9.class" width = 300 height = 300>
</applet>
```

**File: c9_9.java**
```java
import java.awt.*;
import java.awt.event.*;
import java.applet.*;

public class c9_9 extends Applet implements ActionListener
{
        private AudioClip myTape;
        private Button b = new Button("Song");
        private boolean myPlay = true;

        public void init()
        {
                myTape = getAudioClip(getDocumentBase(), "sound.au");
                add(b);
                b.addActionListener(this);
        }
        public void actionPerformed(ActionEvent e)
        {
                if(e.getSource().equals(b))
                {
                        if(myPlay)
                        {
                                myTape.play();
                                myPlay = false;
                                System.out.println("On");
                        }
                        else
                        {
                                myTape.stop();
                                myPlay = true;
                                System.out.println("Off");
                        }
                }
        }
}
```

# SECURITY ISSUES

## Three Kinds Of Applets From a Security Perspective

1. **Untrusted Applets** - applets downloaded from the Internet. Goes through byte code verification. Limited.

2. **Trusted Applets** - local applets. Does not go through byte code verification. Limited.

3. **Signed Applets** - applets signed by an "authority" which you have specified as acceptable in your browser. Can do almost anything. Origin usually irrelevant.

## Java Level Security

- The developers of Java claim to have a variety of excellent security features built-in to the Java browser environment.

- Java security has been known to been breached a number of times. Typically these security violations have resulted in new bug fix releases.

- Everybody's primary worry is downloading an applet with a virus attached. Java "solves" this problem with a variety of techniques.

## Byte Code Verification

Code checking: the Java Virtual Machine looks for code that

- is equivalent to pointer access to memory,

- violates access rights to objects,

- changes an object type or class,

- generates stack overflows or underflows,

- changes the datatypes of parameters,

- violates access rules for private, protected, etc.

## Java Class Loader

- Uses separate namespaces for local file system and network servers - no trojan horses.

- Any classes imported over the network are loaded into a private namespace tagged with their origin

- If a class from a private namespace references another class, the local filesystem class is checked first before classes in the private namespace.

- Variables and methods are accessed by name - not by address - so the variables and methods used by an applet can be easily verified. Helps prevent viruses from being introduced.

- No pointers or run-time typecasting - prevents illegal access to memory

## Digitally Signed Applets

- Java supports digitally signed applets which have significant extra capabilities.

- These applets can

    - read and write local files,

    - fetch environmental data, and

    - access other web sites in addition to the server from which the applet was downloaded.

## Browser Level Security

A security level is normally set when a browser is first used:

## Typical Applet Security Choices

**Unrestricted** - Applets can access information from anywhere.

**Firewall** - Applets from outside a firewall can access load information from outside the firewall.

**Applet Host** - Applets from a host can only load information from the host - not from your local computer or any other computer.

**No Access** - Applets cannot load information from anywhere.

# SUMMARY

This module has covered:

- Creating Java applets.

- Writing HTML scripts containing applets.

- Using applet parameters.

- Features of applet execution and applet methods.

- Applet security and environmental variables.

- Simple applet graphics.

- Applet mouse handling.

- Applet audio capabilities.

- Button implementation and handling.

# EXERCISES

1.  Add another parameter to c9_3.html called var3 and give it the value 99. Then modify the c9_3.java file to print this value in the applet display and in the MS-DOS Prompt window.

2.  Modify c9_4.java to draw a line between x = 40 and y = 40 to x = 160 and y = 160. Then draw a black arc with x = 40, y = 40, width = 160, height = 160, starting angle = 0 and ending angle = 180. Notice arc angles are measured counterclockwise. Notice that the x and y values are the x value of the left side and y value of the top side of an imaginary rectangle of the specified width and height within which the arc is drawn. The output applet should look like:

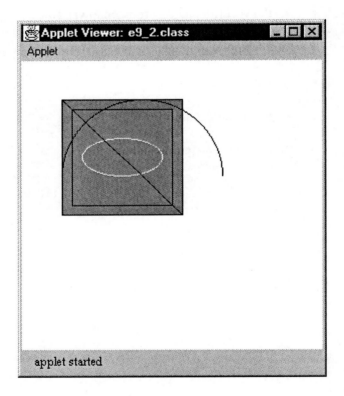

3. Modify c9_5.java to place the image at x = 150 and y = 150 in addition to the existing image drawing.

4. Modify c9_6.java to draw myimage.gif at the point where the mouse button is pressed down and then after dragging the mouse with the button down to another point in the applet to then print the same image at the new location when the button is released.

5. Revamp c9_8.java so that a button with the label "Figures" appears on screen. If this button is clicked then it is removed from the applet and the three button display of c9_8.java is activated. Then clicking these buttons will draw figures on the screen. If the "Figures" button is not clicked, then clicking the other buttons does not generate drawings. Hint: remove(buttonName) removes a button. The remove() method is in class awt.Container.java.

# 10.  More Java Classes

## OBJECTIVES

At the end of this module you should be able to:

- Describe and use features of the Applet, Graphics, and URL classes.

- Switch between Web pages from an applet in supporting browsers.

# APPLET CLASS

- The Applet class has numerous features. We have seen some its features such as audio playback and image display. In this section we will survey some of the features of the Applet class.

- The Applet class is subclassed from the Panel class as the following hierarchy shows.

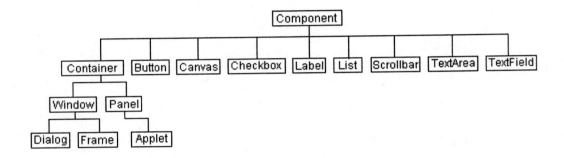

- We will see details of many of these classes in the next few modules.

## Useful Applet Methods

- Applet *Control Methods* such as:

  init(), start(), stop(), etc. methods which manage the executing applet.

  **setSize(int width, int height)** - resize the applet.


- Applet *Imaging Methods* such as:

  **getImage(URL u)** - Access an image. Image loaded when needed.

  **getImage(URL u, String filename)** - Access image file. Load image when needed.


- Applet *Audio Methods* such as:

  **getAudioClip(URL u)** - Access an audio file.

  **getAudioClip(URL u, String s)** - Access an audio file.

  **play(URL u, String filename)** - plays audio file specified by URL u and String filename.

  **play(URL u)** - plays audio file specified by URL u.


- *General Applet methods* such as:

  **getDocumentBase()** - returns the URL object of .html document file within which the applet resides.

  **getCodeBase()** - returns the URL object of the applet .class file itself.

# GRAPHICS CLASS METHODS

The Graphics class contains many methods which are useful such as:

The drawing methods for rectangles, ovals, lines, etc. discussed in module 9.

**void clipRect(int x, int y, int width, int height)** - clips (like scissors on a a photograph) a Graphics object to the width and height specified starting from x and y. The graphic object cannot draw outside the clip area.

**Color getColor()** - returns the current color.

**void setColor(Color c)** - sets the current color.

**Font getFont()** - returns the current font.

**void setFont(Font f)** - sets the current font.

**void copyArea(int x, int y, int width, int height, int destx, int desty)** - copies the area specified by x, y, width and height to the specified destination coordinates which are measured from the specified x and y values (not the applet coordinates origin).

**boolean drawImage(Image I, int x, int y, ImageObserver o)** - draws the image starting from x and y (upper left corner) for the ImageObserver o.

**boolean drawImage(Image I, int x, int y, int width, int height, ImageObserver o)** - draws image starting at specified x and y position (the upper left corner). Scales image to width and height if needed.

# PROGRAMS WITH GRAPHICS

## Example 1

This example shows how to create a Graphics object for applet drawing using getGraphics(). The new Graphics object is clipped to draw in a restricted area using clipRect(). Press button to see clipped drawing.

**File: c10_1.html**
```
<applet code="c10_1.class" width = 350 height = 300></applet>
```

**File: c10_1.java**
```java
import java.awt.*;
import java.awt.event.*;
import java.applet.Applet;

public class c10_1 extends Applet implements MouseListener
{
        private Graphics g1;
        private Image i1;

        public void init()
        {
                setBackground(Color.white);
                addMouseListener(this);

                i1 = getImage(getDocumentBase(), "myimage.gif");
                prepareImage(i1, this);

                g1 = getGraphics();
                g1.clipRect(150, 150, 50, 50);// clip drawing area
        }
        public void paint(Graphics g)
        {
                g.drawImage(i1, 20, 20, this);

                g.drawRect(19, 19, 152, 152); // box around image
                g.drawRect(59, 39, 52, 52); // box around area matching
                                            // clipped drawing
                g.drawRect(109, 129, 152, 152);// box around image
                g.drawRect(149, 149, 51, 51); // box around clip area
        }
        public void mousePressed(MouseEvent e)
        {
                g1.drawImage(i1, 110, 130, this); // draw image in
                                                  // clip area
        }
        public void mouseReleased(MouseEvent e) { }
        public void mouseClicked(MouseEvent e)  { }
        public void mouseEntered(MouseEvent e)  { }
        public void mouseExited(MouseEvent e)   { }
}
```

**Output Applet:**

Clipped drawable region

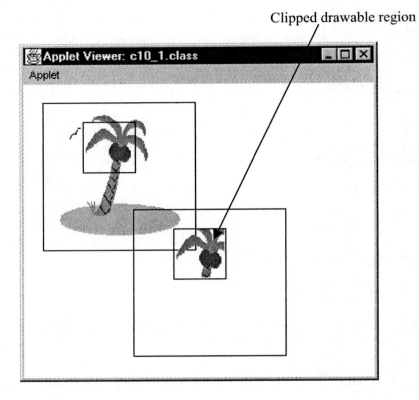

**10. More Java Classes**

## Example 2

Paints the screen with a graphic display. When the button is pushed, part of the graphic is copied to another part of the applet window.

**File: c10_2.html**

```
<applet code="c10_2.class" width = 300 height = 300>
</applet>
```

**File: c10_2.java**

```java
import java.awt.*;
import java.awt.event.*;
import java.applet.Applet;

public class c10_2 extends Applet implements ActionListener
{
        private Graphics g1;
        private Button b = new Button("Duplicate");

        public void init()
        {
                setBackground(Color.white);
                add(b);
                g1 = getGraphics();
                b.addActionListener(this);
        }
        public void paint(Graphics g)
        {
                g.setColor(Color.gray);
                g.fillRect(40, 40, 120, 120);

                g.setColor(Color.black);
                g.drawRect(40, 40, 120, 120);

                g.setColor(Color.black);
                g.draw3DRect(50, 50, 100, 100, false);

                g.setColor(Color.white);
                g.drawOval(60, 80, 80, 40);
        }
        public void actionPerformed(ActionEvent e)
        {
                if(e.getSource().equals(b))
                {
                        g1.copyArea(50, 50, 101, 101, 100,100);
                }            // Copy inner box only. Note 101.
        }
}
```

**10. More Java Classes**

**Output applet display after pushing button.**

The duplicate

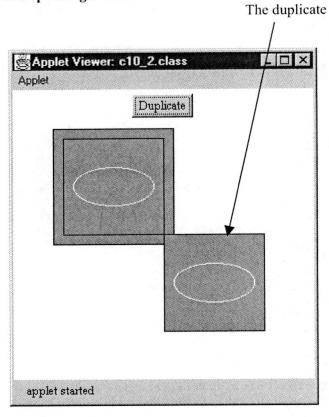

**10. More Java Classes**

# URL CLASS

- The URL class of the java.net package is used to specify a URL and then to fetch the contents of the URL.

## URL Constructors

URL objects can be defined with statements such as:

```
URL myURL = new URL("http://mystuff.company.com");
URL myImage = new URL(myURL, "myimages/mypicture.gif");
```

- The URL constructor can throw the MalformedURLException and therefore often appears in a try expression with a catch for the exception.

## URL Images

Once a URL containing an *image* is obtained its contents can be fetched with statements such as:

```
Image i1 = getImage(myImage);
```

## URL Audio

An *audio* URL is accessed with code such as:

```
URL myURL = new URL("http://mystuff.company.com");
URL myAudio = new URL(myURL, "mySounds/sound1.au");

AudioClip a1 = getAudioClip(myAudio);
```

or

```
URL myURL = new URL("http://mystuff.company.com");
AudioClip a1 = getAudioClip(myURL, "mySounds/sound1.au");
```

- An audio file can be played directly with code such as:

```
URL myURL = new URL("http://mystuff.company.com");
play(myURL, "mySounds/sound1.au");
```

or

```
URL myURL = new URL("http://mystuff.company.com/mySounds/sound1.au");
play(myURL);
```

# SWITCHING WEB PAGES IN AN APPLET

- Inside an applet on a web page you can cause the web page to be replaced with another URL using the showDocument() method.

- This method is in java.applet.AppletContext. The java.applet package must be imported to use showDocument().

  ```
  void showDocument(URL u)
  ```

- The showDocument() method requires an AppletContext object to execute.

- The getAppletContext() method of java.applet.getAppletContext returns the current AppletContext. An example of the type of statement which runs showDocument() is:

  ```
  getAppletContext().showDocument(u);
  ```

- The *showDocument() method does not work in appletviewer*. It works in popular Web browsers like Netscape and Internet Explorer.

# EXAMPLE OF A WEB PAGE SWITCH

Note: For those using the early Java version Java 1.02, c10_3a.java is a Java 1.02 version of the below program. It is used with c10_3a.html.

File: c10_3.html
```
<applet code="c10_3.class" width = 300 height = 300>
</applet>
```

File: c10_3.java
```
import java.awt.*;
import java.awt.event.*;
import java.net.*;
import java.applet.*;

public class c10_3 extends Applet implements ActionListener
{
        private Button b = new Button("Next Document");
        private URL u;

        public void init()
        {
                add(b);
                b.addActionListener(this);
                try
                {
                        u = new URL("file:///C|work/class/c9_4.html");
                }
                catch(Exception e)
                {  }
        }
        public void actionPerformed(ActionEvent e)
        {
                if(e.getSource().equals(b))
                {
                        System.out.println(
                            "Tried to display another html.");
                        getAppletContext().showDocument(u);
                }
        }
}
```

# SUMMARY

This module has examined the features of the

- Applet class,

- Graphics class,

- URL class.

In addition we examined switching between Web pages in an applet.

# 11. *Buttons, Lists, Fonts and Color*

## OBJECTIVES

At the end of this module you should be able to:

- Select fonts for applet displays.

- Specify colors for applet displays.

- Describe and create the various kinds of Java buttons: push buttons, checkbox buttons, choice buttons, and "radio" buttons.

- Describe and create single and multiple choice lists.

- Set and change button features such as color and labeling.

# FONTS

- All Java versions have a number of "so-called built-in" fonts available for printing text: Monospaced, SansSerif, Serif, Dialog, DialogInput, and ZapfDingbats (UNICODE \u2700 and following). Actually font names are mapped onto fonts available on specific platforms. The fonts are therefore platform specific.

- To use a font follow these steps:

    1. Declare a Font variable.

    2. Allocate storage for a font object specifying font characteristics.

    3. Select the font with the setFont() method.

    4. Draw a string with the drawstring() method or some other method.

## Font Variables

Font variables are declared with statements such as:

```
Font f1;
```

## Allocating storage for a Font object

- Storage is allocated for a Font object using a statement specifying the font name, font style and the point size. For example,

```
f1 = new Font("SansSerif", Font.BOLD, 12);
```

- The format of the Font constructor is:

```
public Font(String fontname, int style, int pointSize)
```

## Specifying a Font

- The allowed values for the style argument are the static Font variables:

    Font.PLAIN

    Font.BOLD

    Font.ITALIC

## Font Handling Methods

- The current font can be fetched with the getFont() member.

```
Font f = g.getFont();
```

- The name of the current font can be obtained with the getName() method of class java.awt.Font. For example you can print the name of the current font with the statement:

```
System.out.println(g.getFont().getName());
```

where g is the current Graphics object.

An example of a program using a variety of fonts is:

**File: c11_1.html**
```
<applet code="c11_1.class" width = 300 height = 200></applet>
```

**File: c11_1.java**
```java
import java.awt.*;
import java.applet.*;

public class c11_1 extends Applet
{
        private Font f1, f2, f3, f4, f5, f6, f7, f8;

        public void init()
        {
                setBackground(Color.white);
                f1 = new Font("Monospaced", Font.BOLD, 16);
                f2 = new Font("SansSerif", Font.BOLD, 16);
                f3 = new Font("SansSerif", Font.BOLD|Font.ITALIC, 16);
                f4 = new Font("Serif", Font.BOLD, 16);
                f5= new Font("Monospaced", Font.BOLD, 12);
                f6= new Font("Serif", Font.BOLD, 12);
                f7 = new Font("Monospaced", Font.PLAIN, 12);
                f8 = new Font("SansSerif", Font.PLAIN, 10);
        }

        public void paint(Graphics g)
        {
                g.drawString("Normal Print", 80, 40);

                g.setFont(f1);
                g.drawString("Monospaced Bold 16", 80, 55);

                g.setFont(f2);
                g.drawString("SansSerif Bold 16", 80, 70);

                g.setFont(f3);
                g.drawString("SansSerif Bold Italic 16", 80, 85);

                g.setFont(f4);
                g.drawString("Serif Bold 16", 80, 100);

                g.setFont(f5);
                g.drawString("Monospaced Bold 12", 80, 115);

                g.setFont(f6);
                g.drawString("Serif Bold 12", 80, 130);

                g.setFont(f7);
                g.drawString("Monospaced Plain 12", 80, 145);

                g.setFont(f8);
                g.drawString("SansSerif Plain 10", 80, 160);
        }
```

The output applet window is:

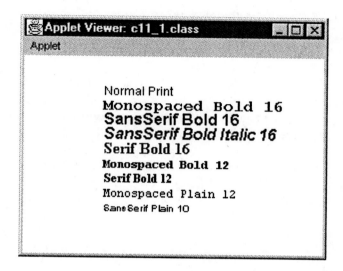

**11. Buttons, Lists, Fonts and Color**

## Positioning Text

- Java uses the FontMetrics class to position text on an applet.

- FontMetrics class objects contain the character widths and heights of a font.

- FontMetrics objects are created using the getFontMetrics() method of the Graphics class.

- The getAscent(), getDescent(), and getHeight() methods of FontMetrics return a font's height information in pixels (as pictured below).

- The stringWidth(String s) method of FontMetrics returns the width of the String argument in pixels for the font specified by the FontMetrics object.

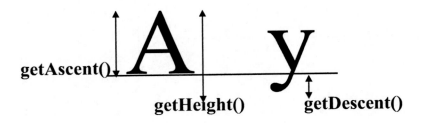

*Example:*

**File: c11_2.html**
```
<applet code="c11_2.class" width = 300 height = 200>
</applet>
```

**File: c11_2.java**
```
import java.awt.*;
import java.applet.*;

public class c11_2 extends Applet
{
        private Font f1;
        private String s = "My SansSerif Font";

        public void init()
        {
                setBackground(Color.white);
                f1 = new Font("SansSerif", Font.BOLD, 16);
        }
```

```
public void paint(Graphics g)
{
        g.setFont(f1);

        FontMetrics fm1 = g.getFontMetrics();// Fetch font data.

        int mystringWidth = fm1.stringWidth(s);
                                        // Width of String s

        int mystringHeight = fm1.getAscent();
                                        // Font Ascent in pixels

        Dimension d = getSize();          // Size of applet area.

        g.drawString(s, (d.width - mystringWidth)/2,
                        (d.height - mystringHeight)/2);
    }
}
```

**Output Applet**

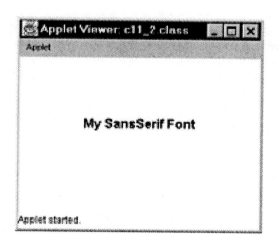

# COLOR

- Colors can be set in Java methods using the setColor() method as discussed in module 9.

- Some of the standard colors are red, white, blue, black, yellow, green, gray, lightGray, darkGray, pink, magenta, orange and cyan.

- The awt.Color.java file contains a list of available colors.

- Color objects can also be defined specifying RGB colors or more general colors with a specified transparency.  An RGB color object can be defined with code such as:

```
Color myColor1 = new Color(0xrrggbb);

Color myColor2 = new Color(R, G, B);

g.setColor(myColor1);
```

where R, G and B are int values specifying the RGB color (all range from 0 through 255). The hexadecimal form is 0xrrggbb where the hexadecimal digit pairs rr, gg and bb specify the amount of red, green and blue in the color. The values of the hex digit pairs range from 0 to 255.

- Colors can also be set with the setForeground() and setBackground() methods.  For example, the next program sets a black background color and a white foreground color:

**File: c11_3.html**
```
<applet code="c11_3.class" width = 300 height = 200>
</applet>
```

**File: c11_3.java**
```
import java.awt.*;
import java.applet.*;

public class c11_3 extends Applet
{
        private Font f1;
        private String s = "My SansSerif Font";

        public void init()
        {
                setBackground(new Color(0x880099));
                setForeground(Color.white);
                f1 = new Font("SansSerif", Font.BOLD, 16);
        }
```

```
public void paint(Graphics g)
    {
            g.setFont(f1);
            FontMetrics fm1 = g.getFontMetrics();
            int mystringWidth = fm1.stringWidth(s);
            int mystringHeight = fm1.getAscent();
            Dimension d = getSize();
            g.drawString(s, (d.width - mystringWidth)/2,
                            (d.height - mystringHeight)/2);
    }
}
```

**Output of c11_3.java**

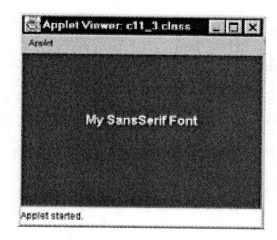

# CHOICE BUTTONS

- Choice buttons are buttons which display a list of selections. After clicking on a selection an event is generated containing the selection information.

- An itemStateChanged() method normally executes code based on the selection made.

- Two methods in class awt.Choice which are useful in retrieving the selection information are:

```
String getSelectedItem()     // returns label of selected choice

int getSelectedIndex()       // returns index number of selected choice.
                             // The first selection has index number zero.
```

## Implementing Choice Buttons

- A procedure for implementing choice buttons is:

    1.  Define a Choice variable and allocate an object for it.

    ```
    Choice myChoice = new Choice();
    ```

    2.  Add the items to the Choice object.

    ```
    myChoice.add("choice 1");
    ```

## Choice Button Event Handling

- Specify the applet implements ItemListener

- Add the applet as the listener object with a statement such as:

```
myChoice.addItemListener(this);
```

Define an itemStateChanged(ItemEvent e) event handler method which executes when the selection is made using getSelectedItem() or get SelectedIndex() to determine the choice.

## Choice Button Example

**File: c11_4.html**
```
<applet code="c11_4.class" width = 300 height = 300></applet>
```

**File: c11_4.java**
```java
import java.awt.*;
import java.awt.event.*;
import java.applet.Applet;

public class c11_4 extends Applet implements ItemListener
{
        private Choice myChoice = new Choice(); // define Choice button
        private int x = 60, y = 60;
        private int figType = 0;

        public void init()
        {
                setBackground(Color.white);
                myChoice.add("Rectangle"); // add selections to the button
                myChoice.add("Circle");
                myChoice.add("Oval");
                add(myChoice);          // add button to the applet
                myChoice.addItemListener(this); // add event listening for
                                                // button
        }
        public void paint(Graphics g)
        {
                g.setColor(Color.black);
                g.drawString("Painting: figType = " + figType, 10,295);
                switch(figType)
                {
                        case 1:
                                g.fillRoundRect(x, y, 30, 30,15, 15);
                                break;
                        case 2:
                                g.fillOval(x, y, 30, 30);
                                break;
                        case 3:
                                g.fillOval(x, y, 30, 15);
                                break;
                }
        }
```

```
public void itemStateChanged(ItemEvent e)// handles Choice event
{
        if(e.getSource() instanceof Choice)
        {
                figType =
                ((Choice)e.getSource()).getSelectedIndex() + 1;
                x += 30;
                y += 30;

                repaint();
                if( x >= 215 || y >= 215)
                {
                        x = 60;
                        y = 60;
                }
        }
}
}
```

**Output Applet:**

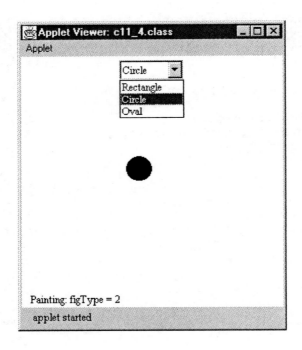

# CHECKBOX BUTTONS

- Checkbox buttons are buttons which are either checked (state = true) or unchecked (state = false).

- The state of a Checkbox can always be obtained using the getState() method. The state can be set with setState(boolean state).

- A Checkbox object begins by default in the unchecked or false state. It then can toggle between checked and unchecked with mouse clicks.

## Procedure for Implementing Checkboxes

- A procedure for using checkbox buttons is:

    1. Define a Checkbox object with statements such as:

    ```
    Checkbox clockIt;

    clockIt = new Checkbox("Clock It?");
    ```

    2. Define an itemStateChanged() method if you want to respond to a Checkbox event.

- A programmer may choose not to listen for Checkbox events. It may only be necessary to fetch the current state of the Checkbox (using getState()) at appropriate points in the program.

## Checkbox Example

**File: c11_5.html**
```
<applet code="c11_5.class" width = 300 height = 300>
</applet>
```

**File: c11_5.java**
```
import java.awt.*;
import java.awt.event.*;
import java.applet.Applet;

public class c11_5 extends Applet implements ItemListener
{
        private Checkbox clockIt;
        private String label;
        private boolean state;
```

```
public void init()
{
        setBackground(Color.white);
        clockIt = new Checkbox("Clock it?");// create Checkbox object
        add(clockIt); // add Checkbox to applet
        clockIt.addItemListener(this);   // add Item event listening
                                         // for Checkbox. The applet
                                         // is the listener object.
}
public void paint(Graphics g)
{
        g.drawString("Label = " + label, 40,80);
        g.drawString("State = " + state, 40,120);
}
public void itemStateChanged(ItemEvent e)
{
        if(e.getSource() instanceof Checkbox)
        {
                label = ((Checkbox)e.getSource()).getLabel();
                state = ((Checkbox)e.getSource()).getState();
                repaint();
        }
}
}
```

**Output Applet:**

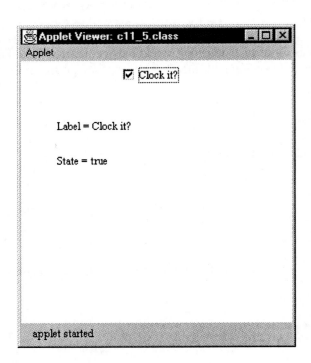

**11. Buttons, Lists, Fonts and Color**

# "RADIO" BUTTONS

- "Radio" buttons are similar in concept to the buttons on old-fashioned radios. Push one button down and the currently pushed button pops up.

- A group of "radio" buttons can have no buttons pushed or one button pushed.

- "Radio" buttons are implemented by grouping a set of Checkbox buttons into a CheckboxGroup object. A CheckboxGroup object is not a component although it is composed of components. It maps to the CheckboxGroup equivalent on the platform.

## Procedure for Implementing "Radio" Buttons

- A procedure for using "radio" buttons is:

    1. Define a CheckboxGroup object and allocate storage for it in init().

    2. Add Checkbox buttons. <u>Add an addItemListener() call for each button.</u>

    3. An itemStateChanged() method then executes if a Checkbox button is selected. The code in method can determine the pressed button and respond appropriately.

Note: the add() method cannot be used to add a CheckboxGroup to an applet.

## "Radio" Button Example

**File: c11_6.html**
```
<applet code="c11_6.class" width = 300 height = 300></applet>
```

**File: c11_6.java**
```java
import java.awt.*;
import java.awt.event.*;
import java.applet.Applet;

public class c11_6 extends Applet implements ItemListener
{
        private CheckboxGroup stations;
        private Checkbox c1, c2, c3;
        private String label = "Love101FM";
        private boolean state = true;
        public void init()
        {
                setBackground(Color.white);
                setLayout(null);
                stations = new CheckboxGroup();// allocate CheckboxGroup
                        // add buttons to CheckboxGroup object
                add(c1 = new Checkbox("Love101FM", stations, true));
                add(c2 = new Checkbox("News77FM", stations, false));
                add(c3 = new Checkbox("Music88FM", stations, false));
                        // position buttons on applet
                c1.setBounds(30, 50, 90, 20);
                c2.setBounds(30, 80, 90, 20);
                c3.setBounds(30, 110, 90, 20);
                        // add Item event listening for each button
                c1.addItemListener(this);
                c2.addItemListener(this);
                c3.addItemListener(this);
        }
        public void paint(Graphics g)
        {
                g.drawString("Label = " + label, 110,150);
                g.drawString("State = " + state, 110,170);
        }
        public void itemStateChanged(ItemEvent e)// Item event handler
        {
                if(e.getSource() instanceof Checkbox)
                {
                        label = ((Checkbox)e.getSource()).getLabel();
                        state = ((Checkbox)e.getSource()).getState();
                        if(e.getSource().equals(c3))
                                System.out.println("Great music.");
                        repaint();
                }
        }
}
```

**Output Applet:**

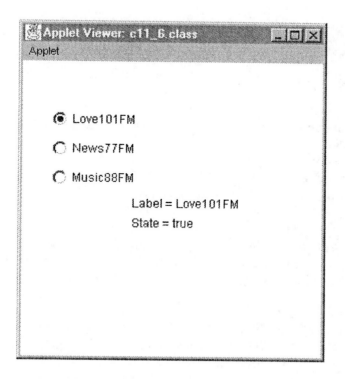

# LISTS

- A List object generates a display area that contains a vertical list of items.

- When you define a list you specify the number of visible items. If the list actually contains more than the specified number of items, then a scrollbar is automatically added to enable you to traverse the entire list.

- List objects can be defined which allow you to select only one item OR allow you to select several items.

- To select an item in a one-selection-only list you *double-click* on the item. This generates a List action event which runs the actionPerformed() method.

- There are two strategies for handling multiple selection lists. The preferred strategy from a human factors point of view is to add a "Done" or "OK" button next to the List object. The end user selects items with single clicks and then clicks on the button to trigger an event. The button event causes the actionPerformed() method to execute.

- An alternate multiple selection List strategy is to tell the end user to single click selections for all items up to the last item. Double-click the last item to generate an event which causes the actionPerformed() method to execute. This is usually not a good idea.

- Each selection made in a multiple selection List generates an ItemEvent which is handled by the itemStateChanged(ItemEvent e) handler method. The class of the listener object must implement ItemListener. The List object must specify a listener with addItemListener().

- The getSelectedItem() and getSelectedItems() methods fetch the item or items selected from a list as String objects.

- The getSelectedIndex() and getSelectedIndexes() methods fetch the item or items selected from a list as int index numbers. List index numbers start with zero.

## List Constructor

- The most convenient List constructor has the format:

```
List(int NumVisibleItemsPlusOne, boolean MultipleSelections)
```

where setting the second argument to false results in a single selection list and setting it to true gives a multiple selection list.

---

## Methods for List Selection(s)

**int getSelectedIndex()** - returns index number of selection. Returns -1 on failure.

**int [] getSelectedIndexes()** - returns an array of selected item index values.

**String getSelectedItem()** - returns String containing selected item name.

**String [] getSelectedItems()** - returns String array containing selected names.

**void deselect(int index)** - deselects a selected item.

**Object getItem()** - returns index number of a selected item as an Integer object with the formal data type Object. Used in itemStateChanged() event handler for a multiple selection list.

## Single Selection List Example

**File: c11_8.html**
```
<applet code="c11_8.class" width = 300 height = 300>
</applet>
```

**File: c11_8.java**
```java
import java.awt.*;
import java.awt.event.*;
import java.applet.Applet;

public class c11_8 extends Applet implements ActionListener
{
        private List myList = new List(4, false);// single selection list
        private int x = 60, y = 60;
        private int figType = 0;

        public void init()
        {
                setBackground(Color.white);
                        // add selections to the list
                myList.add("Rectangle");
                myList.add("Rounded Rectangle");
                myList.add("Circle");
                myList.add("Vertical Oval");
                myList.add("Horizontal Oval");
                        // add list to applet
                add(myList);
                        // add action listening for the list
                myList.addActionListener(this);
        }
```

```java
public void paint(Graphics g)
{
        g.setColor(Color.black);
        g.drawString("Painting: figType = " + figType, 10,295);
        switch(figType)
        {
                case 1:
                        g.fillRect(x, y, 30, 30);
                        break;
                case 2:
                        g.fillRoundRect(x, y, 30, 30,15, 15);
                        break;
                case 3:
                        g.fillOval(x, y, 30, 30);
                        break;
                case 4:
                        g.fillOval(x, y, 15, 30);
                        break;
                case 5:
                        g.fillOval(x, y, 30, 15);
                        break;
        }
}
public void actionPerformed(ActionEvent e)
{
        if(e.getSource() instanceof List)// handles list action event
        {
                figType = ((List)e.getSource())
                        .getSelectedIndex() + 1;
                x += 30;
                y += 30;
                repaint();
                if( x >= 215 || y >= 215)
                {
                        x = 60;
                        y = 60;
                }
        }
}
}
```

**11. Buttons, Lists, Fonts and Color**

**Output Applet:**

<u>Double</u> click on the scrollbar to view hidden selections.

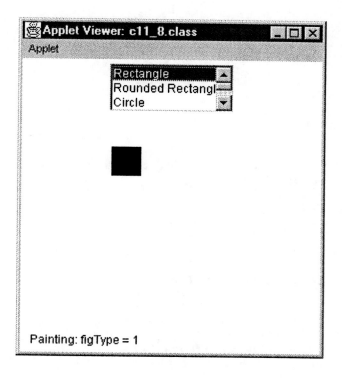

**11. Buttons, Lists, Fonts and Color**

# JAVA PROGRAMMING

## Multiple Selection List Example

**File: c11_9.html**

```
<applet code="c11_9.class" width = 300 height = 300>
</applet>
```

**File: c11_9.java**

```java
import java.awt.*;
import java.awt.event.*;
import java.applet.Applet;

public class c11_9 extends Applet implements ActionListener,
                                            ItemListener
{
        private List myList = new List(4, true); // multiple selection list
        private Button b;
        private int x = 60, y = 60;
        private int figType = 0;
        private Graphics g;

        public void init()
        {
                setBackground(Color.white);
                        // add selections to the list
                myList.add("Rectangle");
                myList.add("Rounded Rectangle");
                myList.add("Circle");
                myList.add("Vertical Oval");
                myList.add("Horizontal Oval");
                add(myList);
                b = new Button("Done");
                add(b);
                g = getGraphics();
                        // add action listening for "Done" button
                b.addActionListener(this);
                        // add Item listening for Item events from list.
                        // listen for each selection made.
                myList.addItemListener(this);
        }
        public void myPaint(Graphics g)
        {
                g.setColor(Color.black);
                g.drawString("Painting: figType = " + figType,
                                                10,100+y);
                switch(figType)
                {
                        case 1:
                                g.fillRect(x, y, 30, 30);
                                break;
```

```
                    case 2:
                            g.fillRoundRect(x, y, 30, 30,15, 15);
                            break;
                    case 3:
                            g.fillOval(x, y, 30, 30);
                            break;
                    case 4:
                            g.fillOval(x, y, 15, 30);
                            break;
                    case 5:
                            g.fillOval(x, y, 30, 15);
                            break;
                }
            }
            public void actionPerformed(ActionEvent e)
            {
                    if(e.getSource() instanceof Button)
                    {
                            x = 60;
                            y = 60;
                                    // fetch the selections as Strings
                            String [] sArray = myList.getSelectedItems();
                            for(int index = 0;index < sArray.length;
                                                        index++)
                                {
// This is an inefficient way to process the selections that are made.
// See the next example for a better approach.
                                    if(sArray[index].equals("Rectangle"))
                                    {
                                            figType = 1;
                                    }
                                    else if(sArray[index].equals(
                                                    "Rounded Rectangle"))
                                    {
                                            figType = 2;
                                    }
                                    else if(sArray[index].equals("Circle"))
                                    {
                                            figType = 3;
                                    }
                                    else if(sArray[index].equals(
                                                        "Vertical Oval"))
                                    {
                                            figType = 4;
                                    }
                                    else if(sArray[index].equals(
                                                        "Horizontal Oval"))
                                    {
                                            figType = 5;
                                    }
```

**11.  Buttons, Lists, Fonts and Color**

```
                            x += 30;
                            y += 30;
                            myPaint(g);
                            if( x >= 215 || y >= 215)
                            {
                                    x = 60;
                                    y = 60;
                            }
                            myList.deselect(figType - 1);
                    }
            }
      }
      public void itemStateChanged(ItemEvent e) // Item event handler.
            // This method executes when a list selection is made.
      {
            int choice = ((Integer)e.getItem()).intValue();
            System.out.println("Item Selected: " + choice);
      }
}
```

**Output Applet:**
Click once on each of your selections. When finished then click on the Done button.

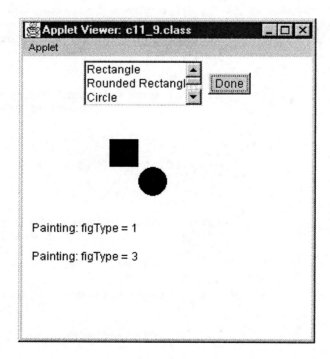

## A Better Multiple Selection List Example Using getSelectedIndexes()

**File: c11_10.html**

```
<applet code="c11_10.class" width = 300 height = 300>
</applet>
```

**File: c11_10.java**

```java
import java.awt.*;
import java.awt.event.*;
import java.applet.Applet;

public class c11_10 extends Applet implements ActionListener,
                                              ItemListener
{
        private List myList = new List(4, true);
        private Button b;
        private int x = 60, y = 60;
        private int figType = 0;
        private Graphics g;

        public void init()
        {
                setBackground(Color.white);
                myList.add("Rectangle");
                myList.add("Rounded Rectangle");
                myList.add("Circle");
                myList.add("Vertical Oval");
                myList.add("Horizontal Oval");
                add(myList);
                b = new Button("Done");
                add(b);
                g = getGraphics();
                b.addActionListener(this);
                myList.addItemListener(this);
                                // listen for each selection
        }
        public void myPaint(Graphics g)
        {
                g.setColor(Color.black);
                g.drawString("Painting: figType = " + figType,
                                                10,100+y);
                switch(figType)
                {
                        case 1:
                                g.fillRect(x, y, 30, 30);
                                break;
```

**11. Buttons, Lists, Fonts and Color**

```java
                        case 2:
                                g.fillRoundRect(x, y, 30, 30,15, 15);
                                break;
                        case 3:
                                g.fillOval(x, y, 30, 30);
                                break;
                        case 4:
                                g.fillOval(x, y, 15, 30);
                                break;
                        case 5:
                                g.fillOval(x, y, 30, 15);
                                break;
                }
        }
        public void actionPerformed(ActionEvent e)
        {
                if(e.getSource() instanceof Button)
                {
                        x = 60;
                        y = 60;
// Use index numbers for more efficient processing of selections made.
                        int [] iArray = myList.getSelectedIndexes();
                        for(int index = 0;index < iArray.length;
                                                        index++)
                        {
                                x += 30;
                                y += 30;
                                figType = iArray[index] + 1;
                                myPaint(g);
                                if( x >= 215 || y >= 215)
                                {
                                        x = 60;
                                        y = 60;
                                }
                                myList.deselect(iArray[index]);
                        }
                }
        }
        public void itemStateChanged(ItemEvent e)
        {
                int choice = ((Integer)e.getItem()).intValue();
                System.out.println("Item Selected: " + choice);
        }
}
```

**11. Buttons, Lists, Fonts and Color**

# SUMMARY

This module has introduced the various kinds of buttons: Choice buttons, Checkbox buttons, and "radio" buttons.

Single and multiple choice lists were described. The specification of fonts and colors was also described.

**11. Buttons, Lists, Fonts and Color**
325

# EXERCISES

1. Rewrite c11_2.java to place the character string in the vertical center of the applet and flush right against the right edge of the applet area.

2. Enhance c11_4.java so that it has a checkbox which enables or disables the selection of choices to draw a figure. The checkbox label should read "Enable Drawing?".

3. Enhance the radio button program c11_6.java to display "Listening to station ____" when the corresponding station button is selected. The applet display should show the complete list of stations selected which should grow each time a station selection is made.

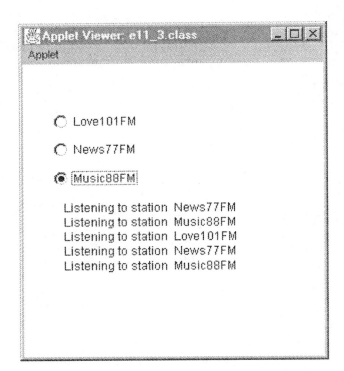

# 12.  Fill-in Text and Scrollbars

## OBJECTIVES

At the end of this module you should be able to describe and use:

- Labels,

- TextFields,

- Text Areas,

- and Scrollbars.

# LABELS

- Until now we have used the drawString() method of the Graphics class to place text in an applet.

- Text can also be placed with primitive formatting on an applet display using class Label objects.

## Sample Program with Labels

**File: c12_1.html**
```
<applet code="c12_1.class" width = 300 height = 200>
</applet>
```

**File: c12_1.java**
```java
import java.awt.*;
import java.applet.*;

public class c12_1 extends Applet
{
        public void init()
        {
                setBackground(Color.white);
                Label lab1 = new Label("This is a passage of normal text.");
                add(lab1);
                lab1.setBackground(Color.black);
                lab1.setForeground(Color.white);

                Label lab2 = new Label("There is more to come.");
                add(lab2);
        }
}
```

Output Applet:

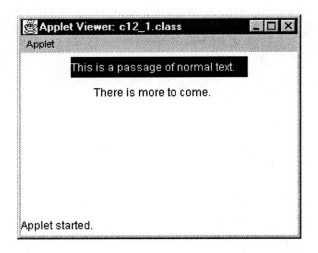

**12. Fill-in Text and Scrollbars**

# TEXTFIELDS

- Java enables you to create fill-in text boxes called text fields. Each fill-in box is an object of class TextField.

## The Four Kinds of TextField Initializations

- There are four kinds of TextField initializations. Each one has a different constructor.

  1. Blank text field.

     ```
     TextField()
     ```

  2. Blank text field with a specified length (not necessarily the number of visible characters).

     ```
     TextField(int length)
     ```

  3. Text field containing a specified string of characters

     ```
     TextField(String s)
     ```

  4. Text field containing a specified string in a specified length.

     ```
     TextField(String s, int length)
     ```

- End users click on a text field to enter or change data unless its not editable.

- They can use the standard editing keys. Automatic tabbing between fields is supported.

- The text can overflow the display width. The arrow keys can be used to access hidden characters.

- When the end user presses ENTER or RETURN in a text field, an event is generated which causes an actionEvent object to be created. The event can be handled with an actionPerformed() method in the class of the listener object.

- A text field can be declared unchangeble with a statement such as:

  ```
  t.setEditable(false);
  ```

- TextFields are described in more detail in Appendix B. Appendix D describes limiting the number of characters in a text field.

## Example of TextFields

The following example shows how to test for a TextField event and how to test for a specific TextField object. The text of the object generating the event can be fetched with the getText() method in the actionPerformed() event handler.

**File: c12_2.html**
```
<applet code="c12_2.class" width = 300 height = 300></applet>
```

**File: c12_2.java**
```java
import java.awt.*;
import java.awt.event.*;
import java.applet.Applet;

public class c12_2 extends Applet implements ActionListener
{
        private TextField t1, t2, t3 , t4;
        private String text = "";
        private Graphics g1;
        private int j = 0;

        public void init()
        {
                t1 = new TextField();
                add(t1);
                t2 = new TextField(25);
                add(t2);
                t3 = new TextField("Text");
                t3.setEditable(false);
                add(t3);
                t4 = new TextField("More Text", 20);
                add(t4);
                g1 = getGraphics();
// Set up action listening for text fields.
                t1.addActionListener(this);
                t2.addActionListener(this);
                t4.addActionListener(this);
        }
        public void actionPerformed(ActionEvent e)
        {    // handler for text field action events.
                if(e.getSource() instanceof TextField)
                {
                        if(e.getSource().equals(t1))
                                text = "Field 1: " + t1.getText();
                        else if(e.getSource().equals(t2))
                                text = "Field 2: " + t2.getText();
                        else if(e.getSource().equals(t4))
                                text = "Field 4: " + t4.getText();
                        g1.drawString(text, 40, 160 + 15 * j++);
                }
        }
}
```

**Output Applet:**

Note the text inserted in the text fields.

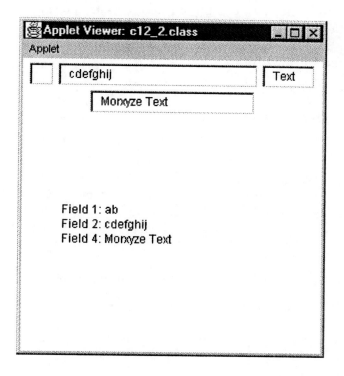

# TEXT AREAS

- Java also enables you to create multi-line fill-in text boxes called text areas. Each fill-in text area is an object of class TextArea.. Text areas are also used to display data.

## Four Kinds of TextArea Initialization

- There are four kinds of TextArea initializations. Each one has a different constructor.

    1. Blank text area (large blank area).

       ```
       TextArea()
       ```

    2. Blank text area with a specified number of rows and columns. In some Java versions you get the rows number minus one actual rows and the columns number minus one actual columns.

       ```
       TextArea(int rows, int columns)
       ```

    3. Text area containing a specified string of characters (large area)

       ```
       TextArea(String s)
       ```

    4. Text area containing a specified string in a specified area of rows and columns.

       ```
       TextArea(String s, int rows, int columns)
       ```

- End users click on a text area to enter or change data.

- End users can use the standard editing keys.

- The text can overflow the display area. End users can use the arrow keys or scrollbars to access hidden characters.

- When the end user presses ENTER or RETURN in a text area, the cursor moves to the next line. No event is created. To signal the end of text input, click on a button as the following example shows. The data entry events supported by text areas are keyEvents and TextEvents (Appendix D).

- A text area can be declared unchangeble with a statement such as:

    ```
    t.setEditable(false);
    ```

## A Program Illustrating TextAreas

The following example shows how to set up a button as an event to indicate a text area edit is finished. The text of the TextArea can be fetched with the getText() method. The commented add() statements can be uncommented to produce additional text areas. These areas can be best viewed with the applet display maximized.

**File: c12_3.html**
```
<applet code="c12_3.class" width = 400 height = 300>
</applet>
```

**File: c12_3.java**
```
import java.awt.*;
import java.awt.event.*;
import java.applet.Applet;

public class c12_3 extends Applet implements ActionListener
{
        private TextArea t1, t2, t3 , t4;
        private Button b1, b2;
        private String text = "";
        private Graphics g1;
        private int j = 0;

        public void init()
        {
                setBackground(Color.white);
                b1 = new Button("Finished 1");
                add(b1);
                t1 = new TextArea();
// Can be seen by enlarging to full screen:
//              add(t1);
                t2 = new TextArea(4, 8);
                add(t2);
                t3 = new TextArea("Can't Edit Text");
                t3.setEditable(false);
// Can be seen by enlarging to full screen:
//               add(t3);
                t4 = new TextArea("More Text",5, 9);
                add(t4);
                b2 = new Button("Finished 2");
                add(b2);
                g1 = getGraphics();
                b1.addActionListener(this);
                b2.addActionListener(this);
        }
```

```
// End users normally click a button to indicate end of text entry to a
// text area. Button events are handled as action events.
        public void actionPerformed(ActionEvent e)
        {
                if(e.getSource() instanceof Button)
                {

                        if(e.getSource().equals(b1))
                                text = "Field 2: " + t2.getText();
                        else if(e.getSource().equals(b2))
                                text = "Field 4: " + t4.getText();

                        g1.drawString(text, 40, 160 + 15 * j++);
                }
        }
}
```

**Output Applet:**

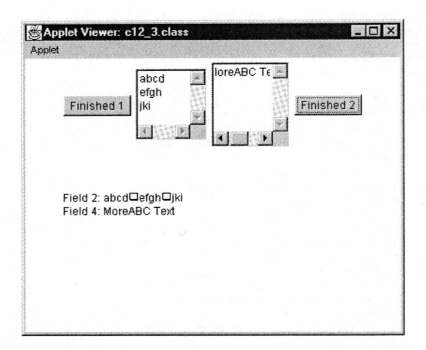

Note: the "boxes" in the Field2 output above are graphic representations of '\n'.

**12. Fill-in Text and Scrollbars**

# SCROLLBARS

- Scrollbars are a bit less interesting now then they were in earlier Java versions. In recent versions of Java most components that need scrollbars actually have scrollbars built into them. Nevertheless these scrollbars can be useful.

- Scrollbars are often used to select values or features such as color choices. A scrollbar has one int value which is reset by clicking on the scrollbar arrows or by moving the slide bar. Basically scrollbars can generate a number within a range visually by making mouse clicks and drags. The generated number can be used for a variety of purposes such as setting coordinates for graphic displays or numbers for computations.

- Scrollbars look best when used with a BorderLayout layout (module 13) with the scrollbar placed in the East, West, or South borders. They expand to fill the border.

- Scrollbars placed on applets without reshaping are of small size and not appealing.


**Scrollbar Initialization**

- Scrollbar objects can be created in three different ways using the constructors:

```
Scrollbar()   // creates vertical scrollbar by default.

Scrollbar(int orientation)   // orientation = Scrollbar.VERTICAL or
                             //               Scrollbar.HORIZONTAL
                             // Otherwise it throws an exception:
                             //               IllegalArgumentException

Scrollbar(int orientation, int startValue, int visibleSize,
          int minimum, int maximum)
```

- The first two constructors require the scrollbar's values to be set with the setValues() method:

```
void setValues(int startValue, int visibleSize, int minimum, int maximum)
```

- The third constructor sets the values directly.

- The four values set in the third constructor and the setValues() method are:

  startValue - the initial value of the scrollbar.

  visibleSize - the difference in value of the bottom (right) edge of the bar minus the value of the top (left) edge of the bar. The visibleSize value is mapped in a non-linear way into a proportionate pixel size of the slidebar.

  minimum - the minimum value which a scrollbar can have.

  maximum - the largest value a scrollbar can have is the maximum value.

## Scrollbar Methods

- The current value of a scrollbar is returned by the getValue() method:

  ```
  int getValue()
  ```

- Scrollbar values are set by:

  - A click on the arrow gadgets changes the scrollbar value and generates an event: the default change in value is 1. The setUnitIncrement() method can specify a different value.

  - Clicking on the space around the slide bar causes the scrollbar to "page". The default change in value is 10. The setBlockIncrement() method can implement a different "page" change value.

  - Dragging the slide bar with the mouse generates a Scrollbar event to take place setting a value.

  - Scrollbar events can be handled with the adjustmentValueChanged(AdjustmentEvent e) event handler. The listener object's class must implement the AdjustmentListener interface.

## An Example Containing Scrollbars

**File: c12_4.html**

```
<applet code="c12_4.class" width = 500 height = 300></applet>
```

**File: c12_4.java**

```java
import java.awt.*;
import java.awt.event.*;
import java.applet.Applet;

public class c12_4 extends Applet implements ActionListener,
                                              AdjustmentListener
{
        private Button b;
        private Scrollbar scrollAmt, scrollType;
        private TextField T1, T2, T3;
        private String value = "", type = "";
        private Graphics g1;
        private int j = 0;

        public void init()
        {
                setBackground(Color.white);
                b = new Button("Button Event");
                T1 = new TextField("Percentage: (1-100) ",15);
                T1.setEditable(false);
                scrollAmt = new Scrollbar(Scrollbar.HORIZONTAL, 1, 1, 1,
                                                               100);
                scrollType = new Scrollbar(Scrollbar.VERTICAL);
                T2 = new TextField("1", 10);
                T2.setEditable(false);
                T3 = new TextField("215", 10);
                T3.setEditable(false);
                add(b);
                add(T1);
                add(scrollAmt);
                add(T2);
                add(scrollType);
                add(T3);
                scrollType.setValues(215, 20, 200, 500);

                scrollAmt.setUnitIncrement(5);
                scrollType.setUnitIncrement(3);
                scrollAmt.setBlockIncrement(15);
                scrollType.setBlockIncrement(20);

                g1 = getGraphics();
                b.addActionListener(this);
                scrollAmt.addAdjustmentListener(this);
                scrollType.addAdjustmentListener(this);
```

```
        }
public void actionPerformed(ActionEvent e)
{
        g1.drawString("Other Event: " + ((Button)e.getSource())
                            .getLabel(), 40, 100 + 15 * j++);
}
public void adjustmentValueChanged(AdjustmentEvent e)
{
        if(e.getSource().equals(scrollAmt))
        {
                value = Integer.toString(
                        ((Scrollbar)e.getSource()).getValue());
                T2.setText(value);
                g1.drawString("Value: " + value,40, 100+15*j++);
        }
        else if(e.getSource().equals(scrollType))
        {
                type = Integer.toString(
                        ((Scrollbar)e.getSource()).getValue());
                T3.setText(type);
                g1.drawString("Type: " + type,100,100 + 15*j++);
        }
    }
}
}
```

**Output Applet:**

The "Value:" amounts are selected on the horizontal scrollbar. The "Type:" amounts are sgenerated by the vertical scrollbar. The other events are generated by button clicks.

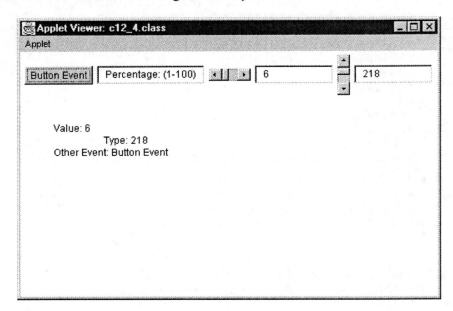

---

**12. Fill-in Text and Scrollbars**

## SUMMARY

This module has examined the features and coding of:

- Labels

- TextFields

- TextAreas

- Scrollbars

**12. Fill-in Text and Scrollbars**

# EXERCISES

1. Create an applet with a label stating: "Last Name:" followed by a 20 column text field. When the user presses ENTER the typed name should be displayed in the lower half of the applet. Use the editing keys to edit the last name entry: the arrow keys, backspace, the delete key, and the Insert key. Then make the text field unchangeable and try to enter a name. Remember to click on text field before data entry.

2. Transform exercise 1 into a two row text area with the prompt label "Full name". The text area should have 20 columns. Display the entries in the lower part of the applet in "firstname lastname" format. Note the newline character appears as a box character if displayed with drawString().

3. Make the following changes in c12_4.java to implement a dynamic scrollbar. The scrollAmt scrollbar will reset the maximum and starting value of the other scrollbar scrollType each time a value is selected with the scrollAmt scrollbar. Here are the changes:

   i.   Set the startValue of scrollAmt to 100 and also the corresponding text field.

   ii.  Set the startValue of scrollType to 50 and also the corresponding text field. Set its minimum to 0 and maximum to 100.

   iii. Add code to the event handler block setting the new scrollType startValue and maximum to the value selected on the scrollAmt scrollbar. Set the T3 text to the new startValue also.

# 13. Layouts, Panels, Frames, Canvases, and Menus

## OBJECTIVES

At the end of this module you should be able to:

- Describe and create Layouts, Panels, Frames, Canvases, and Menus.

- Embed the GUI parts discussed in earlier modules within Panels and Frames such as buttons, scrollbars, lists, text fields, and text areas.

- Create subpanels.

- Create complex GUI screens.

# OVERVIEW OF GUI CONSTRUCTS

The hierarchy of basic components in Java is:

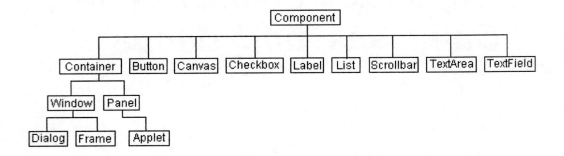

The role and purpose of some of these classes can be summarized as:

## Frame Class

This class enables you to create a window with a border, a layout, a title, and a MenuBar with associated menus.

## Panel Class

This class allows you to specify "building blocks" for applets. Panels can contain <u>components</u>.

## Canvas Class

This class enables you to create a graphical display area which handles events generated by user input. Think artist's canvas. Canvases cannot contain components (except for pop-up menus). Canvases are for drawing.

Two important classes which are superclasses of Window, Panel, and Frame are the

Component class

Container class

These classes are described next.

# SOME COMPONENT CLASS METHODS

**Dimension getSize()** - This method returns a Dimension object containing the width and height of a component. Dimension objects have a public width variable and a public height variable.

**Rectangle getBounds()** - returns a Rectangle object containing the variables x and y (coordinates of the upper left corner), and the variables width and height (specifying the width and height of a component).

**boolean contains(int x, int y)** - returns true if (x,y) coordinates inside component.

```
if(b1.contains(150, 150))
```

**void paint(Graphics g)** - paints the screen display.

**void repaint()** - repaints a display; calls paint() by default.

**void repaint(int x, int y, int width, int height )** - repaints specified rectangle of component.

**13. Layouts, Panels, Frames, Canvasses, and Menus**

# SOME CONTAINER CLASS METHODS

**void add(Component co)** - adds a component to the current container.

**void add(String name, Component comp)** - adds a component to the current container. The name can be the location of the component (BorderLayout), or the name assigned to the component within a layout (CardLayout).

**void setLayout(LayoutManager Lm)** - sets the layout manager for the current component. The layout manager is responsible for positioning the components inside the container.

**void validate()** - places all the components on the current container's display according to the specified layout. validate() is normally executed in methods other than init() and start(). It should be executed after one or more new components are added in an event handler or in any method other than init() or start().

# LAYOUTS

- An applet can be divided into parts using a layout class. A layout class is often called a layout manager. The five original built-in Java layout managers are

  - FlowLayout - like text flow.

  - BorderLayout - four border regions around a center.

  - GridLayout - rectangular fixed-size, equally-sized grid with one cell per component.

  - CardLayout - like a stack of playing cards - each card can hold a component. Only one card visible at a time.

  - GridBagLayout - a flexibly-sized grid (size of largest component determines vertical size of each row). A component can occupy several cells. Very flexible.

We will examine the three most popular layouts FlowLayout, BorderLayout, and GridLayout next. The other layouts are described in Appendix B.

## FlowLayout Manager

- Flows components in rows onto a container like words are flowed in a word processor.

- The FlowLayout manager provides the default layout for an applet or for a component of an applet such as a panel. The components placed in an applet or panel are placed in sequential order in the order that they are added.

- The vertical and horizontal spacing between components can be specified using the FlowLayout constructor:

  ```
  FlowLayout(int align, int horizontalGap, int verticalGap)
  ```

- The values of the align parameter can be any of the static variable values FlowLayout.LEFT, FlowLayout.CENTER and FlowLayout.RIGHT.

- Other FlowLayout constructors are:

  ```
  FlowLayout()   // default align = CENTER, gaps = 5

  FlowLayout(int align)   // default gaps = 5
  ```

## Example with a FlowLayout

**File: c13_1.html**
```
<applet code="c13_1.class" width = 300 height = 300></applet>
```

**File: c13_1.java**
```java
import java.awt.*;
import java.awt.event.*;
import java.applet.Applet;

public class c13_1 extends Applet implements ActionListener
{
        private TextArea t1, t2, t3 , t4;
        private Button b1, b2;
        private String text = "";
        private Graphics g1;
        private int j = 0;

        public void init()
        {
                setBackground(Color.white);
                setLayout(new FlowLayout(FlowLayout.RIGHT, 15, 35));
                b1 = new Button("Finished 1");
                add(b1);
                t1 = new TextArea();
//                add(t1);
                t2 = new TextArea(4, 8);
                add(t2);
                t3 = new TextArea("Can't Edit Text");
                t3.setEditable(false);
//                add(t3);
                t4 = new TextArea("More Text",5, 9);
                add(t4);
                b2 = new Button("Finished 2");
                add(b2);
                g1 = getGraphics();
                b1.addActionListener(this);
                b2.addActionListener(this);
        }
        public void actionPerformed(ActionEvent e)
        {
                if(e.getSource() instanceof Button)
                {
                        if(e.getSource().equals(b1))
                                text = "Field 2: " + t2.getText();
                        else if(e.getSource().equals(b2))
                                text = "Field 4: " + t4.getText();
                        g1.drawString(text, 40, 160 + 15 * j++);
                }
        }
}
```

**Output Applet:**

Note:

- The program is the same as c12_3.java except for the setLayout() statement.

- The components are right justified because of the FlowLayout.RIGHT align value.

- The horizontal spacing between components is 15 and the vertical spacing is 35.

- The height of each row is set by the tallest component in the row. The other components in the row are vertically centered on the tallest component.

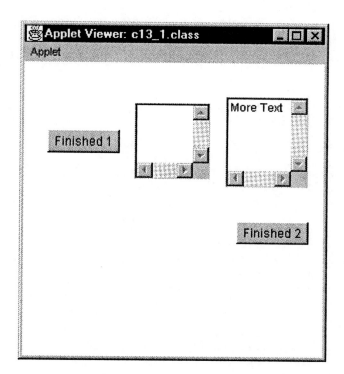

**13.  Layouts, Panels, Frames, Canvasses, and Menus**

## BorderLayout Manager

- The BorderLayout manager defines five areas on an applet or panel: North, South, East, West, and Center.

- The areas are visible in the applet generated from the following program:

## Simple Panels

The next example has a Panel in it. A Panel is a rectangular display area. It is very much lke an applet. It is often used as a building block for an applet. We add() components to a Panel object. The components are flowed on the pnel just like an applet. After adding components to a panel we usually add the panel to an applet. In the following example we add the panel to the North section of the BorderLayout on the applet.

## Example with a BorderLayout

**File: c13_2.html**
```
<applet code="c13_2.class" width = 300 height = 300></applet>
```

**File: c13_2.java**
```java
import java.awt.*;
import java.applet.Applet;

public class c13_2 extends Applet
{
        private Button b1, b2, b3, b4;
        private Scrollbar scr1, scr2;
        private Panel p = new Panel();
        public void init()
        {
                setBackground(Color.white);
                setLayout(new BorderLayout());
                b1 = new Button("Yankees");
                b2 = new Button("Red Sox");
                p.add(b1);      // add button to panel
                p.add(b2);      // add button to panel
                add("North", p); // add panel to North
                scr1 = new Scrollbar(Scrollbar.VERTICAL, 1, 1, 1, 100);
                add("East", scr1);
                b3 = new Button("Dodgers");
                add("West", b3);
                scr2 = new Scrollbar(Scrollbar.HORIZONTAL, 1, 1, 1,100);
                add("South", scr2);
                b4 = new Button("Giants");
                add("Center", b4);
        }
}
```

**Output Applet Showing BorderLayout:**

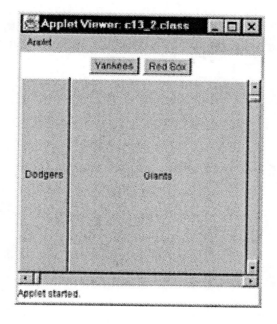

Note:

• The height of the North section is set by the height of the buttons plus 10 pixels (five above and five below the buttons). The width of North is the width of the applet.

• The height of the South section is set by the height of the scrollbar. The width of South is the width of the applet.

• The height of the East section is set by the distance between the North and South edges. The width of East is the width of the scrollbar.

• The height of the West section is set by the distance between the North and South edges. The width of West is the width of the Dodgers button plus 10 pixels (five pixels of space on either side of the button).

• The components and panel expand to fill the BorderLayout regions. The panel expanded horizontally to fill the North. The scrollbar in the South expanded horizontally to fill the South. The scrollbar in the East expanded vertically to fill the East. The Dodgers button in the West expanded vertically to completely fill the West.

## GridLayout Manager

The GridLayout manager divides the output display area into a specified number of rows and columns of regions with equally sized grid cells.

The format of the constructor is:

```
GridLayout(int rows, int columns)
```

## Example with a GridLayout

**File: c13_3.html**
```
<applet code="c13_3.class" width = 400 height = 300></applet>
```

**File: c13_3.java**
```java
import java.awt.*;
import java.applet.Applet;

public class c13_3 extends Applet
{
        private Button b1, b2, b3, b4, b5, b6, b7;
        private Panel p = new Panel();

        public void init()
        {
                setBackground(Color.white);
                setLayout(new GridLayout(2,3));
                b1 = new Button("Button 1");
                add(b1);
                b2 = new Button("Button 2");
                add(b2);
                b3 = new Button("Button 3");
                add(b3);
                b4 = new Button("Button 4");
                add(b4);
                b5 = new Button("Button 5");
                add(b5);
                b6 = new Button("Button 6"); // adding buttons to panel
                p.add(b6);
                b7 = new Button("Button 7");
                p.add(b7);
                add(p);         // add panel to last grid cell
        }
}
```

**Output applet with GridLayout visible**

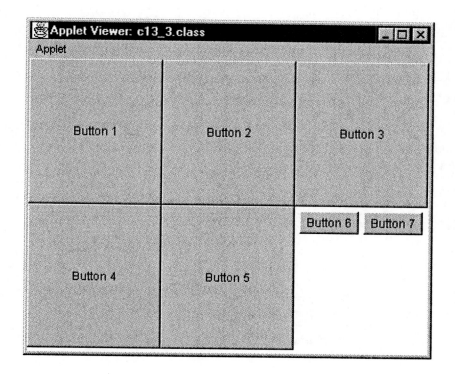

Note:

- The Button (and other) components expand to completely fill their cells.

- The order of the add() statements determines the filling of the cells. The cells are filled from left to right row by row.

- The Panel expanded to fill its cell. The components on the panel retain their size since the panel has a FlowLayout on it by default.

# CANVASES

- Canvases are rectangular areas within a display which can hold drawn graphical figures and handle events connected with it such as a mouseUp() in its display area. It is like a painter's canvas. "Draw" on it.

- Canvases are normally created by defining a class which subclasses from class Canvas and then creating an object instantiating the class.

- Canvases are rectangular and have a coordinate system whose origin is the upper left hand corner (the x = 0 and y = 0 point). Drawings are placed on a canvas with coordinates measured relative to the upper left hand corner.

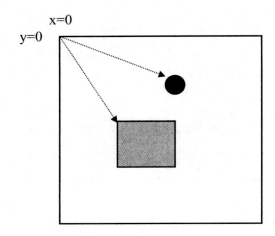

## Procedure for Creating a Canvas Subclass

- The following steps are often used to create a canvas:

    1. Define a class which extends class Canvas.

    2. The class contains one or more constructors which often use setSize() to size the canvas area. Constructors also may set background and foreground colors as well as performing other chores.

       `void setSize(int width, int height)` - resizes the width and height of a canvas.

    3. The class also can contain the following:

       - A paint() method which sets colors and draws figures and images. *Figures are drawn with pixel coordinates relative to the upper left hand corner of the canvas.* A Graphics object for drawing in other methods of the canvas class can be obtained by using getGraphics(). For example, g1 = getGraphics();

       - Mouse event handlers to act on events taking place within the canvas.

Note: A canvas subclass cannot add components except for a popup menu.

## Canvas Management

- To add a canvas to an applet use an add() method.

- To position a canvas on an applet use the methods:

    `void setLocation(int x, int y)` - places upper left corner of canvas at x and y coordinates.

    `void setBounds(int x, int y, int width, int height)` - places upper left corner of canvas at x and y coordinates, and sets width and height of canvas.

## Example Program Using a Canvas Subclass

File: c13_4.html
```
<applet code="c13_4.class" width = 400 height = 300></applet>
```

File: c13_4.java
```java
import java.awt.*;
import java.awt.event.*;
import java.applet.Applet;

public class c13_4 extends Applet implements MouseListener
{
        private newCanvas nc;
        private Graphics g1;
        public void init()
        {
                setBackground(Color.white);
                setLayout(null);
                nc = new newCanvas(100, 100);
                add(nc);
                nc.setLocation(200, 200);
                g1 = getGraphics();
                addMouseListener(this);
        }
        public void paint(Graphics g)
        {
                g.setColor(Color.black);
                g.fillOval(100, 100,  50, 100);
        }
        public void mouseReleased(MouseEvent e)
        {
                g1.drawString("Not Canvas: Mouse", 10, 10);
        }

        public void mouseClicked(MouseEvent e)
        {
                // Code for mouse button click on a component.
        }
        public void mousePressed(MouseEvent e)
        {
                // code for mouse button press on a component.
        }
        public void mouseEntered(MouseEvent e)
        {
                // code for mouse entry to a component.
        }
        public void mouseExited(MouseEvent e)
        {
                // code for mouse exit from a component.
        }
}
```

```
class newCanvas extends Canvas implements MouseListener
{
        private int width;
        private int height;
        private Graphics g1;
        public newCanvas(int width, int height)
        {
                this.width = width;
                this.height = height;
                setBackground(Color.black);
                setForeground(Color.white);
                setSize(width,height);
                addMouseListener(this);
        }
        public void paint(Graphics g)
        {
                g1 = getGraphics();
                g.setColor(Color.white);
                g.fillOval(20, 20, 40, 40);
        }
        public void mouseReleased(MouseEvent e)
        {
                g1.drawString("Canvas: Mouse", 10, 10);
        }
        public void mouseClicked(MouseEvent e)  { }
        public void mousePressed(MouseEvent e)  { }
        public void mouseEntered(MouseEvent e)  { }
        public void mouseExited(MouseEvent e)   { }
}
```

**Output Applet:**

Click on the black square canvas and click outside the canvas to see the messages.

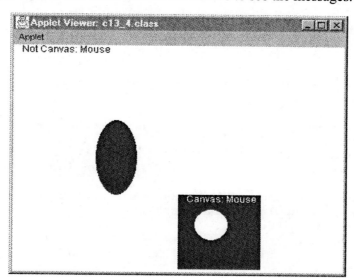

# GRAPHIC BUTTONS

- A canvas class can be used to create a graphic button. Graphical buttons can also be created using the JButton class of the Swing package. See Appendix on Swing package.

- The graphical button is created by drawing a graphic design on a canvas.

- When the mouse is positioned on the canvas and a mouse button is pressed a mouse event is created which simulates a Button click. The example below shows an applet listening for such a "button" click.

- The graphic can be enhanced to show a "pressed"and ünpressed" button look as the following example demonstrates.

**File: gButtonApp.html**
```
<applet code="gButtonApp.class" width=470 height=300></applet>
```

**File: gButtonApp.java**
```java
import java.awt.*;
import java.awt.image.*;
import java.awt.event.*;
import java.applet.Applet;

public class gButtonApp extends Applet implements MouseListener
{
        private gButton gb;
        private Graphics g1;
        private Image img;
        private boolean pushed = false;

        public void init()
        {
                setBackground(Color.white);
                setLayout(null);
                img = getImage(getDocumentBase(), "myimage.gif");
                prepareImage(img, this);
                g1 = getGraphics();
                gb = new gButton(img,50,50);// create graphical canvas button
                add(gb);
                gb.setLocation(200, 30);
                gb.addMouseListener(this);// listen for canvas mouse events
        }
        public void mouseReleased(MouseEvent e)// react to canvas event
        {    // draws on applet if canvas button pushed
                pushed = !pushed;
                if(!pushed)
                        g1.clearRect(50, 150, 240, 140);
```

```
                else
                {
                        g1.setColor(Color.lightGray);
                        g1.fillRect(50, 150, 240, 140);

                        g1.drawImage(img, 50, 150, 100,100, this);
                        g1.drawImage(img, 120, 190, 100,100, this);
                        g1.drawImage(img, 190, 150, 100,100, this);
                }
        }
        public void mouseClicked(MouseEvent e) { }
        public void mousePressed(MouseEvent e) { }
        public void mouseEntered(MouseEvent e) { }
        public void mouseExited(MouseEvent e)   { }
}

class gButton extends Canvas implements MouseListener
{
        private int width;
        private int height;
        private Graphics g;
        private Image i;
        private boolean pushed = false;

        public gButton(Image i, int width, int height)
        {
                this.width = width;
                this.height = height;
                this.i = i;
                setBackground(Color.gray);
                setForeground(Color.white);
                setSize(width,height);
                addMouseListener(this);
        }
        public void bPushed()// creates pushed look on canvas
        {
                g.clearRect(0, 0, width, height);
                g.drawImage(i, 4, 4, width-8, height-8, Color.white,
                                                                this);
                g.setColor(Color.gray);
                g.draw3DRect( 0, 0, width-2, height-2, false);
                g.draw3DRect( 1, 1, width-4, height-4, false);
                g.draw3DRect( 2, 2, width-6, height-6, false);
                g.setColor(Color.black);
                g.drawString("Palms", width/2 -18, height - 5);
        }
        public void bNotPushed() // creates not pushed look on canvas
        {
                g.clearRect(0, 0, width, height);
                g.drawImage(i, 1, 1, width-4, height-4, Color.white,
                                                                this);
```

**13. Layouts, Panels, Frames, Canvasses, and Menus**

```
            g.setColor(Color.gray);
            g.draw3DRect( 0, 0, width-2, height-2, true);
            g.setColor(Color.black);
            g.drawString("Palms", width/2 -18, height - 5);
    }
    public void paint(Graphics g)
    {
            this.g = getGraphics();
            bNotPushed();
            pushed = false;
    }
    public void mouseReleased(MouseEvent e)// reacts to canvas mouse event
    {
            pushed = !pushed;
            if(!pushed)
                    bNotPushed();
            else
                    bPushed();
    }
    public void mouseClicked(MouseEvent e){ }
    public void mousePressed(MouseEvent e){ }
    public void mouseEntered(MouseEvent e){ }
    public void mouseExited(MouseEvent e) { }
}
```

**Graphic Button Applet**

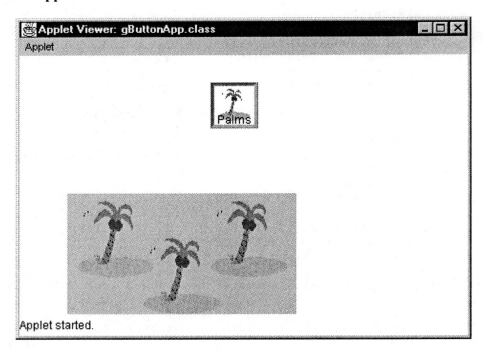

# CREATING TOOLBARS

- Another application of canvases. A canvas subclass can be used to create a toolbar. The Swing package has a simple way of creating toolbars. See the Appendix on the Swing package.

- The MouseMoved() event handler can be used to put toolbar help strings on screen.

- The MousePressed() event handler can be used to launch a toolbar application.

- The below example is "primitive"on purpose – A real application would use one image, properly sized as the toolbar image. The use of 4 large images which must be resized is done to show you how costly it is in terms of time to resize images on the fly.

**File: toolApp.html**
```
<applet code="toolApp.class" width=320 height=300></applet>
```

**File: toolApp.java**
```java
import java.awt.*;
import java.awt.image.*;
import java.awt.event.*;
import java.applet.Applet;

public class toolApp extends Applet
{
        private myTBar tb;
        private Graphics g1;
        Label lab = new Label("");
        private Image picts[] = new Image[4];

        public void init()
        {
                setBackground(Color.white);
                setLayout(null);
                picts[0] = getImage(getDocumentBase(), "palms.jpg");
                picts[1] = getImage(getDocumentBase(), "mars.jpg");
                picts[2] = getImage(getDocumentBase(), "moon.jpg");
                picts[3] = getImage(getDocumentBase(), "mercury.jpg");
                for(int j = 0; j < 4;j++)
                        prepareImage(picts[j], this);

                g1 = getGraphics();
                tb = new myTBar(picts, g1, 120, 30, this);// create toolbar
                add(tb);
                tb.setLocation(100, 30);
        }
}
```

```
class myTBar extends Canvas implements MouseListener,
                                        MouseMotionListener
{
        private int width;
        private int height;
        private Graphics g1;
        private Image picts[];
        private Font f;
        private toolApp a;
        public myTBar(Image picts[], Graphics g, int width, int height,
                                                        toolApp a)
        {
                this.width = width;
                this.height = height;
                g1 = g;
                this.picts = picts;
                this.a = a;
                setBackground(Color.lightGray);
                setForeground(Color.white);
                setSize(width,height);
                f = new Font("SanSerif", Font.BOLD,10);
                addMouseListener(this);// listening for application lanch
                addMouseMotionListener(this);//listening for help tip display
        }
        public void paint(Graphics g)
        {
                g.setColor(Color.gray);
                g.draw3DRect( 1, 1, 27, 28, true);
                g.draw3DRect( 30, 1, 28, 28, true);
                g.draw3DRect( 60, 1, 28, 28, true);
                g.draw3DRect( 90, 1, 28, 28, true);

                g.drawImage(picts[0], 3, 3, 24, 24, Color.lightGray,
                                                            this);
                g.drawImage(picts[1], 32, 3, 24, 24, this);
                g.drawImage(picts[2], 62, 3, 24, 24, this);
                g.drawImage(picts[3], 92, 3, 24, 24, this);
        }
        public void mousePressed(MouseEvent e)
        {
                int x = e.getX();

                g1.clearRect(50, 150, 151, 101);
                g1.setColor(Color.black);
                if(x <= 30)    // figures out which application to launch.
                {              // toolbar images are 30 pixels wide.
                      g1.drawImage(picts[0], 50, 150, 100, 100, this);
                }
                else if ( x <= 60)
                {
```

**13. Layouts, Panels, Frames, Canvasses, and Menus**

```
                g1.drawImage(picts[1], 50, 150, 100, 100, this);
        }
        else if ( x <= 90)
        {
                g1.drawImage(picts[2], 50, 150, 125, 100, this);
        }
        else
                g1.drawImage(picts[3], 50, 150, 150, 100, this);
}
public void mouseMoved(MouseEvent e)
{
        int x = e.getX();

        g1.setFont(f);
        g1.setColor(Color.black);
        if(x <= 30)       // Sets toolbar help string label a mouse
        {                 // moves over toolbar.
                a.remove(a.lab);
                a.lab = new Label("Palms");
                a.add(a.lab);
                a.validate();
                a.lab.setBounds(103, 80, 100, 20);
        }
        else if ( x <= 60)
        {
                a.remove(a.lab);
                a.lab = new Label("Mars");
                a.add(a.lab);
                a.validate();
                a.lab.setBounds(133, 80, 100, 20);
        }
        else if ( x <= 90)
        {
                a.remove(a.lab);
                a.lab = new Label("Moon");
                a.add(a.lab);
                a.validate();
                a.lab.setBounds(163, 80, 100, 20);
        }
        else
        {
                a.remove(a.lab);
                a.lab = new Label("Mercury");
                a.add(a.lab);
                a.validate();
                a.lab.setBounds(193, 80, 100, 20);
        }
}
```

## 13. Layouts, Panels, Frames, Canvasses, and Menus

```
public void mouseEntered(MouseEvent e)// adds label to applet on entry
{                                      // onto toolbar.
        a.add(a.lab);
}


public void mouseExited(MouseEvent e)// refreshes label after moving
{                                     // off toolbar.
        a.remove(a.lab);
        a.lab = new Label("");
}

public void mouseDragged(MouseEvent e)
{ }
public void mouseClicked(MouseEvent e)
{ }
public void mouseReleased(MouseEvent e)
{ }
}
```

**Applet Showing Canvas Toolbar Example:**

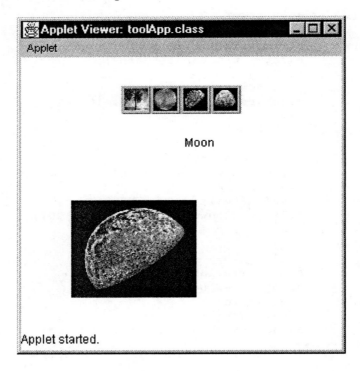

# PANELS

- Canvases are for drawings. Panels are for components (and drawings).

- A panel is an entity which can hold components. When a component is added to a panel the component retains its normal size unless it is resized or unless a layout placed on the panel requires it.

- Panels have a default FlowLayout. Components placed on them are flowed from row to row with the components in each row centered with 5 pixels between them.

- A layout such as a BorderLayout or a GridLayout can be specified for a panel. Then components and subpanels can be placed within the specified layout.

- Panels are rectangular and have a coordinate system whose origin is the upper left hand corner (the x = 0 and y = 0 point). Components can be placed on a panel with coordinates measured relative to the upper left hand corner.

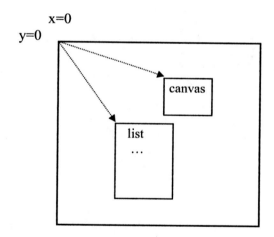

- An applet has a default panel implicitly defined for it.

- A panel can be placed within a layout on an applet using the add() method.

**13. Layouts, Panels, Frames, Canvasses, and Menus**

## Procedures for Building Panels

There are two ways to create a panel:

1. Define a Panel object. Then add components and specify its features with method calls.

2. Define a class which subclasses from Panel. The class definition normally includes:

   - One or more constructors which set a layout, place components on the panel, and set other features of the panel such as adding listener objects.

   - A paint() method specifying drawings on the panel.

   - Event handlers for events for which the the panel object listens.

## 1. Building a Panel object

Define a Panel object

```
Panel pobj = new Panel();
```

Specify a layout or use the default flowlayout:

```
pobj.setLayout(...);
```

Add components:

```
pobj.add(...);
```

If setLayout(null) is specified, position components with setLocation() or setBounds().

Add appropriate listener objects for events (such as MouseEvents) originating in the panel:

```
pobj.add<Event Type>Listener(listenerObject);
```

## 2. Building a Panel Subclass

1. Subclass from Panel and implement any needed interfaces such as possibly ActionListener and ItemListener.

2. Define one or more constructors which:

- Specify a layout or use the default flowlayout:

```
setLayout(…);
```

- Add components:

```
add(…);
```

- If setLayout(null) is specified, position components with setLocation() or setBounds().

- Add appropriate listener objects for events originating in the panel:

```
add<Event Type>Listener(listenerObject);
```

3. Add a paint() method to specify drawings on the panel.

4. Add any needed event handlers if it "listens to itself" for some events originating in its components.

5. Add any other relevant methods and member variables.

## Placing Panels on Applets (or Other Containers)

- A common procedure for building an applet with one or more subpanels is:

    1. Specify a layout for the applet.

    2. Define Panel objects and/or objects of a subclass of Panel placing the objects on the container as needed.

    3. Define and add other components, variables and methods.

## A Sample Program with Panels

**File: c13_5.html**
```
<applet code="c13_5.class" width = 450 height = 300></applet>
```

**File: c13_5.java**
```java
import java.awt.*;
import java.awt.event.*;
import java.applet.Applet;

public class c13_5 extends Applet implements MouseListener,
                            ActionListener, ItemListener
{
        private Panel p1, p2, p3, p5, p6;
        private myPanel p4 = new myPanel();
        private Graphics g6;
        private newCanvas nc;
        private Button b1, b2, b3, b4, b5;
        private TextField tf1;
        private List L1;
        private Choice c1;

        public void init()
        {
                setBackground(Color.white);
                setLayout(new GridLayout(2,3));
                p1 = new Panel();
                p2 = new Panel();
                p3 = new Panel();
                p5 = new Panel();
                p6 = new Panel();
                p1.setLayout(new BorderLayout());
                b1 = new Button("North"); p1.add("North", b1);
                b2 = new Button("South"); p1.add("South", b2);
                b3 = new Button("East"); p1.add("East", b3);
                b4 = new Button("West"); p1.add("West", b4);
                b5 = new Button("Center"); p1.add("Center", b5);

                nc = new newCanvas(150, 150);
                p2.setLayout(null);
                p2.add(nc);
                nc.setLocation(0,0);

                tf1 = new TextField("Grid 3", 20);
                p3.setLayout(null);
                p3.add(tf1);
                tf1.setBounds(25, 20, 100, 20);
```

```java
        L1 = new List(4, false);
        L1.add("Rectangle");
        L1.add("Square");
        L1.add("Circle");
        L1.add("Oval");
        p5.add(L1);

        c1 = new Choice();
        c1.add("Rose");
        c1.add("Daisy");
        c1.add("Lilac");
        p6.add(c1);
        add(p1); add(p2); add(p3); add(p4); add(p5); add(p6);

        g6 = p6.getGraphics(); // make object to draw on p6

        p6.addMouseListener(this); // set mouse listening for p6 only

        b1.addActionListener(this);
        b2.addActionListener(this);
        b3.addActionListener(this);
        b4.addActionListener(this);
        b5.addActionListener(this);
        c1.addItemListener(this);
        L1.addActionListener(this);
        tf1.addActionListener(this);
}
public void paint(Graphics g)
{
        // paint methods
}
public void mousePressed(MouseEvent e)
{    // draws on canvas object nc
        nc.gc.drawString("p6: Mouse Pressed", 5,110);
}
public void actionPerformed(ActionEvent e)
{
        // draws on panel object p6
        g6.drawString("p1 button pressed.", 20, 90);

        // code for Button, List (double click), MenuItem,
        // and TextField events.
}
public void mouseClicked(MouseEvent e)
{
        // Code for mouse button click on a component.
}
public void mouseReleased(MouseEvent e)
{
        // code for mouse button release on a component.
}
```

### 13.  Layouts, Panels, Frames, Canvasses, and Menus

```
        public void mouseEntered(MouseEvent e)
        {
                // code for mouse entry to a component.
        }
        public void mouseExited(MouseEvent e)
        {
                // code for mouse exit from a component.
        }
        public void itemStateChanged(ItemEvent e)
        {
                // code for Choice, Checkbox, CheckboxMenuitem,
                // and List (single click) events.
        }
}

class myPanel extends Panel implements ActionListener
{
        Button b;
        Graphics gp;

        myPanel()
        {
                setLayout(null);
                add(b = new Button("myPanelButton"));
                b.setBounds(10, 30, 100, 20);
                b.addActionListener(this);
        }
        public void actionPerformed(ActionEvent e)
        {
                gp = getGraphics();
                gp.drawString("p4 button pressed.", 20, 90);
        }
}

class newCanvas extends Canvas implements MouseListener
{
        private int width;
        private int height;
        Graphics gc;
        private Font f;

        public newCanvas(int width, int height)
        {
                this.width = width;
                this.height = height;
                setSize(width, height);
                setBackground(Color.black);
                setForeground(Color.white);
                f = new Font("Serif", Font.BOLD, 12);
                addMouseListener(this);
        }
```

**13. Layouts, Panels, Frames, Canvasses, and Menus**

```java
public void paint(Graphics g)
{
        gc = getGraphics();
        g.setColor(Color.white);
        g.fillOval(48, 30, 40, 40);
        g.setFont(f);
        g.drawString("Click Mouse Here",25, 15);
}
public void mouseClicked(MouseEvent e)
{
        // Code for mouse button click on a component.
}
public void mousePressed(MouseEvent e)
{
        gc.drawString("Canvas: Mouse Pressed",5, 90);
}
public void mouseReleased(MouseEvent e)
{
        // code for mouse button release on a component.
}
public void mouseEntered(MouseEvent e)
{
        // code for mouse entry to a component.
}
public void mouseExited(MouseEvent e)
{
        // code for mouse exit from a component.
}
}
```

**Output applet:**

Note gridLayout with 6 panels.  Please follow these steps:

1. Click on p6 to see mousePressed() event handler output.
2. Click on a BorderLayout button.
3. Click on canvas.
4. Click on myPanelButton.

You should see:

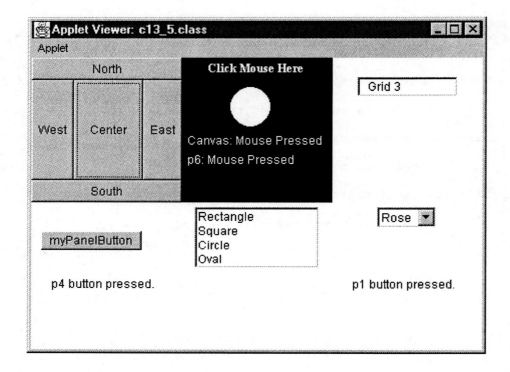

# EXERCISES

Now please do exercises 1, 2 and 3 at the end of the module.

**13. Layouts, Panels, Frames, Canvasses, and Menus**

# FRAMES

- A frame is a window with a border, a layout, a title, and possibly a menubar.

- A frame can be generated from an applet class as shown in this section or it can be generated from a standalone Java program using a main() method. Creating frames in standalone Java programs will be described in the last section of this module.

- A frame can have any of the components which we have placed in applets. In addition it has some extra features:

  MenuBars and menus

  A pack() method to pack the components in the frame as tightly as possible using the preferred size of the components.

  A setVisible(true) method to make a frame visible.

  A setVisible(false) method to make a frame invisible.

  A dispose() method to deallocate the frame and its associated system resources.

- An applet has some features which frames do not have:

  Fetching graphic files with getImage().

  Fetching audio files with getAudioClip().

  Fetching the language environment with getLocale() for the purpose of internationalization with UNICODE.

- We will see how to run applets from Java standalone programs later in this module so we can take advantage of these applet features. Basically the approach is to put an applet in a frame generated from main() in a standalone Java program.

## Procedure for Creating a Frame

- To create a frame subclass:

    Subclass from class Frame. Usually, implement WindowListener.

    Place one or more constructors in the new class. The constructor (s) normally setSize() the frame to the desired size. If the size of the frame is not set then the generated frame may be "amputated" or full screen. The constructors play a role analogous to the applet init() method. A constructor will normally specify a layout, add components, …

    A frame class will often add a start() method which calls the setVisible(true) method to display the frame. Alternately, the setVisible(true) can be executed on the frame object directly.

    Add a paint() method to paint the frame.

    Add any of the components and methods you would put in an applet class definition. They play the same role in the frame class that you are defining.

    Use the unique frame features listed previously.

    Add any needed event handlers for window events:

```
public void windowClosing(WindowEvent e)
{
        dispose(); // support the "Close" menu
               //
               // selection and the [X] box
}
public void windowOpened(WindowEvent e) { … }
public void windowClosed(WindowEvent e){ … }
public void windowIconified(WindowEvent e){ … }
public void windowDeiconified(WindowEvent e) { … }
public void windowActivated(WindowEvent e) { … }
public void windowDeactivated(WindowEvent e){ … }
```

- After defining the new frame class, define an applet class creating an object of the frame type.

- You can specify the frame is to be packed as tightly as possible with a statement such as

```
frameobj.pack();
```

- Then the frame can be displayed with the start() or the setVisible(true) methods.

- The following program creates a frame by clicking on a button (and makes it disappear by clicking again on the button.)

## Program with a Frame

**File: c13_6.html**
```
<applet code="c13_6.class" width = 200 height = 50>
</applet>
```

**File: c13_6.java**
```java
import java.awt.*;
import java.awt.event.*;
import java.applet.Applet;

public class c13_6 extends Applet implements ActionListener,
                                              WindowListener
{
        private myFrame f;
        private Button b;
        private boolean win = true;

        public void init()
        {
                setBackground(Color.white);
                b = new Button("Window?");
                add(b);
                b.addActionListener(this);
        }
        public void actionPerformed(ActionEvent e)
        {   // displays the frame.
            if(e.getSource() instanceof Button)
            {
                    if(win)
                    {
                            f = new myFrame("MYFRAME");
                            f.addWindowListener(this);
//                          f.pack();
                            f.start();
                            win = false;
                    }
                    else
                    {
                            f.dispose();
                            win = true;
                    }
            }
        }
}
```

```java
        public void windowClosing(WindowEvent e)
        {   // Keeps button in sync with showing frame.
                win = true;
        }
        public void windowOpened(WindowEvent e) {}
        public void windowClosed(WindowEvent e){}
        public void windowIconified(WindowEvent e){}
        public void windowDeiconified(WindowEvent e){}
        public void windowActivated(WindowEvent e){}
        public void windowDeactivated(WindowEvent e){}
}

class myFrame extends Frame implements WindowListener, MouseListener,
                                        ActionListener, ItemListener
{
        private Panel p1, p2, p3, p4, p5, p6;
        private Graphics g6;
        private newCanvas nc;
        private Button b1, b2, b3, b4, b5;
        private TextField tf1;
        private TextArea ta1;
        private List L1;
        private Choice c1;

        public myFrame(String s)
        {
                super(s); // Puts name on title bar of frame.
                setSize(450,300); // Sets the size of the frame.
                setBackground(Color.white);
                setLayout(new GridLayout(2,3));
                p1 = new Panel();
                p2 = new Panel();
                p3 = new Panel();
                p4 = new Panel();
                p5 = new Panel();
                p6 = new Panel();
                p1.setLayout(new BorderLayout());
                p1.setBounds(1,1, 200, 150);
                b1 = new Button("North"); p1.add("North", b1);
                b2 = new Button("South"); p1.add("South", b2);
                b3 = new Button("East"); p1.add("East", b3);
                b4 = new Button("West"); p1.add("West", b4);
                b5 = new Button("Center"); p1.add("Center", b5);
                nc = new newCanvas(150, 150);
                p2.setLayout(null);
                p2.add(nc);
                nc.setLocation(0,0);
                tf1 = new TextField("Grid 3", 20);
```

**13. Layouts, Panels, Frames, Canvasses, and Menus**

```
                p3.setLayout(null);
                p3.add(tf1);
                tf1.setBounds(25, 20, 100, 20);
                ta1 = new TextArea("Grid 4", 4, 8);
                p4.add(ta1);
                L1 = new List(4, false);
                L1.add("Rectangle");
                L1.add("Square");
                L1.add("Circle");
                L1.add("Oval");
                p5.add(L1);
                c1 = new Choice();
                c1.add("Rose");
                c1.add("Daisy");
                c1.add("Lilac");
                p6.add(c1);
                        // Adds panels to the frame.
                add(p1); add(p2); add(p3); add(p4); add(p5); add(p6);

                p6.addMouseListener(this); // set mouse listening for p6

                addWindowListener(this);
                b1.addActionListener(this);
                b2.addActionListener(this);
                b3.addActionListener(this);
                b4.addActionListener(this);
                b5.addActionListener(this);
                c1.addItemListener(this);
                L1.addActionListener(this);
                tf1.addActionListener(this);
        }
public void start()
{
                setVisible(true);
}
public void paint(Graphics g)
{
                g6 = p6.getGraphics(); // make object to draw on p6

                // drawing methods
}
public void mousePressed(MouseEvent e)
{   // draws on canvas nc.
        nc.gc.drawString("p6: Mouse Pressed", 5,110);
}
public void actionPerformed(ActionEvent e)
{   // draws on panel p6.
        g6.drawString("p1 Button pressed", 20, 90);
}
```

```java
        public void windowClosing(WindowEvent e)
        {
                dispose();
        }
        public void windowOpened(WindowEvent e) {}
        public void windowClosed(WindowEvent e){}
        public void windowIconified(WindowEvent e){}
        public void windowDeiconified(WindowEvent e){}
        public void windowActivated(WindowEvent e){}
        public void windowDeactivated(WindowEvent e){}
        public void mouseClicked(MouseEvent e)
        {
          // Code for mouse button click on a component.
        }
        public void mouseReleased(MouseEvent e)
        {
          // code for mouse button release on a component.
        }
        public void mouseEntered(MouseEvent e)
        {
          // code for mouse entry to a component.
        }
        public void mouseExited(MouseEvent e)
        {
          // code for mouse exit from a component.
        }
        public void itemStateChanged(ItemEvent e)
        {
          // code for Choice, Checkbox, CheckboxMenuitem,
          // and List (single click) events.
        }
}


class newCanvas extends Canvas implements MouseListener
{
        private int width;
        private int height;
        Graphics gc;
        private Font f;

        public newCanvas(int width, int height)
        {
                this.width = width;
                this.height = height;
                setSize( width, height);
                setBackground(Color.black);
                setForeground(Color.white);
                f = new Font("Serif", Font.BOLD, 12);
                addMouseListener(this);
        }
        public void paint(Graphics g)
        {
```

**13. Layouts, Panels, Frames, Canvasses, and Menus**

```
            gc = getGraphics();
            g.setColor(Color.white);
            g.fillOval(48, 30, 40, 40);
            g.setFont(f);
            g.drawString("Click Mouse Here",25,15);
    }
    public void mouseClicked(MouseEvent e)
    { }
    public void mousePressed(MouseEvent e)
    {
            gc.drawString("Canvas: Mouse Pressed",5, 90);
    }
    public void mouseReleased(MouseEvent e)
    { }
    public void mouseEntered(MouseEvent e)
    { }
    public void mouseExited(MouseEvent e)
    { }
}
```

**Output applet and generated frame:**

Note: Select with mouse to open frame. Then click mouse on white circle. Then click mouse outside canvas (lower right corner?). Then try clicking on components (no actions defined for the other components. Add actions if you wish.) .

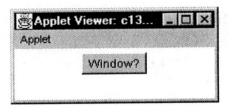

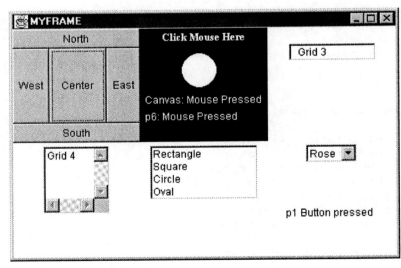

---

**13. Layouts, Panels, Frames, Canvasses, and Menus**

# MENUS AND SHORTCUTS

Java enables you to create menus and a menubar on a frame. Menus can have submenus and subsubmenus, and so.

## Procedure to Install a Menu in a Frame

1.  Define a menuBar object within the frame class.

    Example:

    ```
    Menubar mbar;
    mbar = new Menubar();
    ```

2.  Define Menu objects for each submenu.

    Example:

    ```
    Menu msela, mselb;
    msela = new Menu("MyItem1");
    mselb = new Menu("MyItem2");
    msela.setEnabled(false);// grays and disables menu
                            // selection.
    ```

3.  Add MenuItem objects to Menu objects install menu items at the "lowest" levels of the menu. Keyboard shortcuts are supported.

    Example:
    ```
    msela.add(m1 = new MenuItem("Item1"));
    msela.add(m2 = new MenuItem("Item2"));

    msela.add(m3 = new MenuItem("Item3",
                   new MenuShortcut('a')));   // ctrl-a executes

    msela.add(m4 = new MenuItem("Item4",
                   new MenuShortcut('b', true)));
                            // ctrl-shift-b executes this item.
    ```

4.  Add CheckboxMenuItems at the "lowest" level of the menu. If clicked a CheckboxMenuItem displays a ⌐ . The state of a CheckboxMenuItem can be fetched with the getState() method.

    Example:
    ```
    msela.add(m3 = new CheckboxMenuItem("Go for it?"));
    boolean m3State = m3.getState();
    ```

**13. Layouts, Panels, Frames, Canvasses, and Menus**

5. Add horizontal line separators as needed.

      Example:

```
msela.add("-");
```

OR

```
msela.addSeparator();
```

6. Add the submenu objects to the main menu items.

      Example:

```
msela.add(subMenuSelb);
```

7. Add the main menu items to the menu bar.

      Example:

```
mbar.add(msel);
```

8. Add the menubar to the frame.

      Example:

```
setMenuBar(mbar);
```

9. Event handling for frames:

- The frame class must implement ActionListener to listen to its MenuItem events and must implement ItemListener to listen to its CheckboxMenuItem events.

- MenuItem listener objects are specified with addActionListener() and CheckboxMenuItem listener objects are added with addItemListener().

- MenuItem events are handled with the ActionPerformed() method. CheckboxMenuItems are handled with the ItemStateChanged() event handler.

**13. Layouts, Panels, Frames, Canvasses, and Menus**

**Output applet showing menus for the following c13_7.java on next page.**

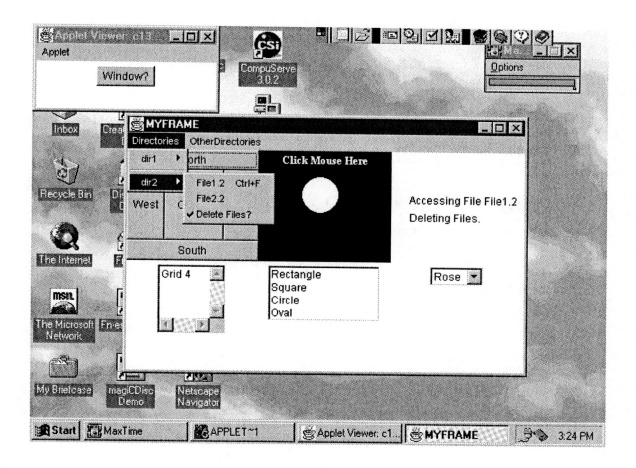

## Program with a Frame and Menubar

**File: c13_7.html**
```
<applet code="c13_7.class" width = 200 height =50>
</applet>
```

**File: c13_7.java**
```java
import java.awt.*;
import java.awt.event.*;
import java.applet.Applet;

public class c13_7 extends Applet implements ActionListener,
                                             WindowListener
{
        private myFrame f;
        private Button b;
        private boolean win = true;

        public void init()
        {
                setBackground(Color.white);
                b = new Button("Window?");
                add(b);
                b.addActionListener(this);
        }
        public void actionPerformed(ActionEvent e)
        {
                if(e.getSource() instanceof Button)
                {
                        if(win)
                        {
                                f = new myFrame("MYFRAME");
                                f.addWindowListener(this);
//                              f.pack();
                                f.start();
                                win = false;
                        }
                        else
                        {
                                f.dispose();
                                win = true;
                        }
                }
        }
        public void windowClosing(WindowEvent e)
        {
                win = true;
        }
```

```java
        public void windowOpened(WindowEvent e) {}
        public void windowClosed(WindowEvent e){}
        public void windowIconified(WindowEvent e){}
        public void windowDeiconified(WindowEvent e){}
        public void windowActivated(WindowEvent e){}
        public void windowDeactivated(WindowEvent e){}
}

class myFrame extends Frame implements WindowListener, MouseListener,
                                       ActionListener, ItemListener
{
        private Panel p1, p2, p3, p4, p5, p6;
        private Graphics g6;
        private MenuBar mb1;
        private Menu myDirs, OtherDirs, myFiles1, myFiles2, myFiles3;
        private MenuItem m1, m2, m3, m4, m5, m6, m7, m8;
        private CheckboxMenuItem cm1;
        private newCanvas nc;
        private Button b1, b2, b3, b4, b5;
        private otherCanvas oc;
        private TextArea ta1;
        private List L1;
        private Choice c1;
        private int j;
        private String text;

        public myFrame(String s)
        {
                super(s);
                setSize(450,300);
                setBackground(Color.white);
                mb1 = new MenuBar();
                myDirs = new Menu("Directories");
                OtherDirs = new Menu("OtherDirectories");
                myFiles1 = new Menu("dir1");
                myFiles2 = new Menu("dir2");
                myFiles1.add(m1 = new MenuItem("File1.1"));
                myFiles1.add(m2 = new MenuItem("File2.1"));
                myFiles1.add(m3 = new MenuItem("File3.1"));
//                 myFiles1.enable(false);
                myFiles2.add(m4 = new MenuItem("File1.2",
                                        new MenuShortcut('f')));
                myFiles2.add(m5 = new MenuItem("File2.2"));
                myFiles2.add(cm1 = new CheckboxMenuItem(
                                        "Delete Files?"));
                myDirs.add(myFiles1);
                myDirs.add("-");  // Horizontal line separator.
                myDirs.add(myFiles2);
                mb1.add(myDirs);
                myFiles3 = new Menu("dir3");
```

**13. Layouts, Panels, Frames, Canvasses, and Menus**

```
myFiles3.add(m6 = new MenuItem("File1.3"));
myFiles3.add(m7 = new MenuItem("File2.3"));
myFiles3.add(m8 = new MenuItem("File3.3"));
OtherDirs.add(myFiles3);
mb1.add(OtherDirs);
setMenuBar(mb1);

setLayout(new GridLayout(2,3));
p1 = new Panel();
p2 = new Panel();
p3 = new Panel();
p4 = new Panel();
p5 = new Panel();
p6 = new Panel();
p1.setLayout(new BorderLayout());
p1.setBounds(1,1, 200, 150);
b1 = new Button("North"); p1.add("North", b1);
b2 = new Button("South"); p1.add("South", b2);
b3 = new Button("East"); p1.add("East", b3);
b4 = new Button("West"); p1.add("West", b4);
b5 = new Button("Center"); p1.add("Center", b5);
nc = new newCanvas(150, 150);
p2.setLayout(null);
p2.add(nc);
nc.setLocation(0,0);
p3.setLayout(null);
oc = new otherCanvas(150, 150);
p3.add(oc);
oc.setLocation(0,0);
ta1 = new TextArea("Grid 4", 4, 8);
p4.add(ta1);
L1 = new List(4, false);
L1.add("Rectangle");
L1.add("Square");
L1.add("Circle");
L1.add("Oval");
p5.add(L1);
c1 = new Choice();
c1.add("Rose");
c1.add("Daisy");
c1.add("Lilac");
p6.add(c1);
add(p1); add(p2); add(p3); add(p4); add(p5); add(p6);

m1.addActionListener(this);
m2.addActionListener(this);
m3.addActionListener(this);
m4.addActionListener(this);
m5.addActionListener(this);
m6.addActionListener(this);
m7.addActionListener(this);
```

**13.  Layouts, Panels, Frames, Canvasses, and Menus**

```java
                m8.addActionListener(this);
                cm1.addItemListener(this);

                addWindowListener(this);
//                b1.addActionListener(this);
//                b2.addActionListener(this);
//                b3.addActionListener(this);
//                b4.addActionListener(this);
//                b5.addActionListener(this);
//                c1.addItemListener(this);
//                L1.addActionListener(this);
        }
        public void start()
        {
                setVisible(true);
        }
        public void paint(Graphics g)
        {
                g6 = getGraphics();
                // drawing methods
        }
        public void windowClosing(WindowEvent e)
        {
                dispose();
        }
        public void actionPerformed(ActionEvent e) // handles menuitem events
        {
                if(e.getSource().equals(m1))
                {
                        text = "Hot File ";
                        j = 20;
                }
                else if(e.getSource().equals(m2))
                {
                        text = "Cool File ";
                        j = 40;
                }
                else
                {
                        text = "Accessing File ";
                        j = 60;
                }
                text +=  ((MenuItem)e.getSource()).getLabel();
                oc.goc.drawString(text, 20, j);
        }
        public void itemStateChanged(ItemEvent e)
        {
                if(e.getSource().equals(cm1))
                {
                        oc.goc.drawString("Deleting Files.", 20, 80);
                }
        }
}
```

**13. Layouts, Panels, Frames, Canvasses, and Menus**

```
public void windowOpened(WindowEvent e) {}
public void windowClosed(WindowEvent e){}
public void windowIconified(WindowEvent e){}
public void windowDeiconified(WindowEvent e){}
public void windowActivated(WindowEvent e){}
public void windowDeactivated(WindowEvent e){}
public void mouseClicked(MouseEvent e)
{
  // Code for mouse button click on a component.
}
public void mousePressed(MouseEvent e)
{
  // code for mouse button press on a component.
}
public void mouseReleased(MouseEvent e)
{
  // code for mouse button release on a component.
}
public void mouseEntered(MouseEvent e)
{
  // code for mouse entry to a component.
}
public void mouseExited(MouseEvent e)
{
  // code for mouse exit from a component.
}
}

class newCanvas extends Canvas implements MouseListener
{
        private int width;
        private int height;
        Graphics gc;
        private Font f;

        public newCanvas(int width, int height)
        {
                this.width = width;
                this.height = height;
                setSize( width, height);
                setBackground(Color.black);
                setForeground(Color.white);
                f = new Font("Serif", Font.BOLD, 12);
                addMouseListener(this);
        }
        public void paint(Graphics g)
        {
                gc = getGraphics();
                g.setColor(Color.white);
                g.fillOval(48, 30, 40, 40);
```

**13. Layouts, Panels, Frames, Canvasses, and Menus**

```java
                g.setFont(f);
                g.drawString("Click Mouse Here",25,15);
        }
        public void mouseClicked(MouseEvent e) { }
        public void mousePressed(MouseEvent e)
        { }
        public void mouseReleased(MouseEvent e)
        { }
        public void mouseEntered(MouseEvent e)
        { }
        public void mouseExited(MouseEvent e)
        { }
}

class otherCanvas extends Canvas implements MouseListener
{
        private int width;
        private int height;
        Graphics goc;
        private Font f;

        public otherCanvas(int width, int height)
        {
                this.width = width;
                this.height = height;
                setSize( width, height);
                setBackground(Color.white);
                f = new Font("Serif", Font.BOLD, 10);
                addMouseListener(this);
        }
        public void paint(Graphics g)
        {
                goc = getGraphics();
        }
        public void mouseClicked(MouseEvent e)
        { }
        public void mousePressed(MouseEvent e)
        { }
        public void mouseReleased(MouseEvent e)
        { }
        public void mouseEntered(MouseEvent e)
        { }
        public void mouseExited(MouseEvent e)
        { }
}
```

# STANDALONE GUI FRAME-BASED PROGRAMS

- The Java programs which we have considered up to now in this module have been run in appletviewer and start execution from an applet class.

- We will now consider standalone programs with a main() method which creates a frame and which can be run by the Java interpreter, java.

**Procedure to Create a Stand-alone Frame-based GUI Program**

- One strategy is to define a class to hold a main() method, and create and show your frame from there.

- A key requirement is to setSize() the frame. Otherwise, the frame may have different sizes on different platforms.

- The following program will create a frame in a window when it executes. It contains the myFrame class and the canvas classes from c13_7.java with one significant change: the addition of a setSize() method to the constructor method of myFrame. The output frame is identical to the frame of c13_7.java.

---

## Example of a Stand-alone GUI Program

**File: c13_8.java**

```java
import java.awt.*;
import java.awt.event.*;

public class c13_8
{
        public static void main(String args[])
        {
                myFrame1 mf = new myFrame1("My Standalone Frame");
                mf.start();
        }
}

class myFrame1 extends Frame implements WindowListener, MouseListener,
                                        ActionListener, ItemListener
{
        private Panel p1, p2, p3, p4, p5, p6;
        private Graphics g6;
        private MenuBar mb1;
        private Menu myDirs, OtherDirs, myFiles1, myFiles2, myFiles3;
        private MenuItem m1, m2, m3, m4, m5, m6, m7, m8;
        private CheckboxMenuItem cm1;
        private newCanvas nc;
        private Button b1, b2, b3, b4, b5;
        private otherCanvas oc;
        private TextArea ta1;
        private List L1;
        private Choice c1;
        private int j;
        private String text;

        public myFrame1(String s)
        {
                super(s);
                setSize(450,300);
                setBackground(Color.white);
                mb1 = new MenuBar();
                myDirs = new Menu("Directories");
                OtherDirs = new Menu("OtherDirectories");
                myFiles1 = new Menu("dir1");
                myFiles2 = new Menu("dir2");
                myFiles1.add(m1 = new MenuItem("File1.1"));
                myFiles1.add(m2 = new MenuItem("File2.1"));
                myFiles1.add(m3 = new MenuItem("File3.1"));
//                  myFiles1.enable(false);
                myFiles2.add(m4 = new MenuItem("File1.2"));
                myFiles2.add(m5 = new MenuItem("File2.2"));
```

```
myFiles2.add(cm1 = new CheckboxMenuItem(
                    "Delete Files?"));
myDirs.add(myFiles1);
myDirs.add("-");   // Horizontal line separator.
myDirs.add(myFiles2);
mb1.add(myDirs);
myFiles3 = new Menu("dir3");
myFiles3.add(m6 = new MenuItem("File1.3"));
myFiles3.add(m7 = new MenuItem("File2.3"));
myFiles3.add(m8 = new MenuItem("File3.3"));
OtherDirs.add(myFiles3);
mb1.add(OtherDirs);
setMenuBar(mb1);

setLayout(new GridLayout(2,3));
p1 = new Panel();
p2 = new Panel();
p3 = new Panel();
p4 = new Panel();
p5 = new Panel();
p6 = new Panel();
p1.setLayout(new BorderLayout());
p1.setBounds(1,1, 200, 150);
b1 = new Button("North"); p1.add("North", b1);
b2 = new Button("South"); p1.add("South", b2);
b3 = new Button("East"); p1.add("East", b3);
b4 = new Button("West"); p1.add("West", b4);
b5 = new Button("Center"); p1.add("Center", b5);
nc = new newCanvas(150, 150);
p2.setLayout(null);
p2.add(nc);
nc.setLocation(0,0);
p3.setLayout(null);
oc = new otherCanvas(150, 150);
p3.add(oc);
oc.setLocation(0,0);
ta1 = new TextArea("Grid 4", 4, 8);
p4.add(ta1);
L1 = new List(4, false);
L1.add("Rectangle");
L1.add("Square");
L1.add("Circle");
L1.add("Oval");
p5.add(L1);
c1 = new Choice();
c1.add("Rose");
c1.add("Daisy");
c1.add("Lilac");
p6.add(c1);
add(p1); add(p2); add(p3); add(p4); add(p5); add(p6);
```

**13. Layouts, Panels, Frames, Canvasses, and Menus**

```java
                m1.addActionListener(this);
                m2.addActionListener(this);
                m3.addActionListener(this);
                m4.addActionListener(this);
                m5.addActionListener(this);
                m6.addActionListener(this);
                m7.addActionListener(this);
                m8.addActionListener(this);
                cm1.addItemListener(this);

                addWindowListener(this);
//                b1.addActionListener(this);
//                b2.addActionListener(this);
//                b3.addActionListener(this);
//                b4.addActionListener(this);
//                b5.addActionListener(this);
//                c1.addItemListener(this);
//                L1.addActionListener(this);
        }
        public void start()
        {
                setVisible(true);
        }
        public void paint(Graphics g)
        {
                g6 = getGraphics();
                // drawing methods
        }
        public void windowClosing(WindowEvent e)
        {
                System.exit(0); // ends program.
        }
        public void actionPerformed(ActionEvent e)
        {
                if(e.getSource().equals(m1))
                {
                        text = "Hot File ";
                        j = 20;
                }
                else if(e.getSource().equals(m2))
                {
                        text = "Cool File ";
                        j = 40;
                }
                else
                {
                        text = "Accessing File ";
                        j = 60;
                }
                text +=  ((MenuItem)e.getSource()).getLabel();
                oc.goc.drawString(text, 20, j);
        }
}
```

**13. Layouts, Panels, Frames, Canvasses, and Menus**

```java
public void itemStateChanged(ItemEvent e)
{
        if(e.getSource().equals(cm1))
        { // draws on the oc canvas.
                oc.goc.drawString("Deleting Files.", 20, 80);
        }
}
public void windowOpened(WindowEvent e) {}
public void windowClosed(WindowEvent e){}
public void windowIconified(WindowEvent e){}
public void windowDeiconified(WindowEvent e){}
public void windowActivated(WindowEvent e){}
public void windowDeactivated(WindowEvent e){}

public void mouseClicked(MouseEvent e)
{
  // Code for mouse button click on a component.
}
public void mousePressed(MouseEvent e)
{
  // code for mouse button press on a component.
}
public void mouseReleased(MouseEvent e)
{
  // code for mouse button release on a component.
}
public void mouseEntered(MouseEvent e)
{
  // code for mouse entry to a component.
}
public void mouseExited(MouseEvent e)
{
  // code for mouse exit from a component.
}
}

class newCanvas extends Canvas implements MouseListener
{
        private int width;
        private int height;
        Graphics gc;
        private Font f;

        public newCanvas(int width, int height)
        {
                this.width = width;
                this.height = height;
                setSize( width, height);
                setBackground(Color.black);
                setForeground(Color.white);
```

```java
                    f = new Font("Serif", Font.BOLD, 12);
                    addMouseListener(this);
          }
          public void paint(Graphics g)
          {
                    gc = getGraphics();
                    g.setColor(Color.white);
                    g.fillOval(48, 30, 40, 40);
                    g.setFont(f);
                    g.drawString("Click Mouse Here",25,15);
          }
          public void mouseClicked(MouseEvent e)
          { }
          public void mousePressed(MouseEvent e)
          { }
          public void mouseReleased(MouseEvent e)
          { }
          public void mouseEntered(MouseEvent e)
          { }
          public void mouseExited(MouseEvent e)
          { }
}

class otherCanvas extends Canvas implements MouseListener
{
          private int width;
          private int height;
          Graphics goc;
          private Font f;
          public otherCanvas(int width, int height)
          {
                    this.width = width;
                    this.height = height;
                    setSize( width, height);
                    setBackground(Color.white);
                    f = new Font("Serif", Font.BOLD, 10);
                    addMouseListener(this);
          }
          public void paint(Graphics g)
          {
                    goc = getGraphics();
          }
          public void mouseClicked(MouseEvent e)
          { }
          public void mousePressed(MouseEvent e)
          { }
          public void mouseReleased(MouseEvent e)
          { }
          public void mouseEntered(MouseEvent e)
          { }
          public void mouseExited(MouseEvent e)
          { }
}
```

**13. Layouts, Panels, Frames, Canvasses, and Menus**

# RUNNING APPLETS FROM STANDALONE JAVA

- The Java interpreter can run Java applets - with little or no change sometimes - if we embed the Java applet in a frame. One problem is access to graphic and audio files. The Java interpreter does not support easy access to these resources with methods like getImage() or getAudioClip().

- The following example runs the c13_6 applet:

**File: AppletHolder.java**
```java
import java.awt.*;
import java.awt.event.*;
import java.applet.Applet;

class AppletHolder
{
        public static void main(String args[])
        {
                myFrameA f = new myFrameA("My Applet", 300, 300);
                c13_6 a = new c13_6();
                f.add(a);
                a.init();
                a.start();
                f.show();
        }
}

class myFrameA extends Frame implements WindowListener
{

        public myFrameA(String s, int width, int height)
        {
                super(s);
                setSize(width, height);
                addWindowListener(this);
        }
        public void windowClosing(WindowEvent e)
        {
                System.exit(0); // Ends standalone program.
        }
        public void windowOpened(WindowEvent e) {}
        public void windowClosed(WindowEvent e){}
        public void windowIconified(WindowEvent e){}
        public void windowDeiconified(WindowEvent e){}
        public void windowActivated(WindowEvent e){}
        public void windowDeactivated(WindowEvent e){}
}
```

**Frame containing applet**

**A generated window:**

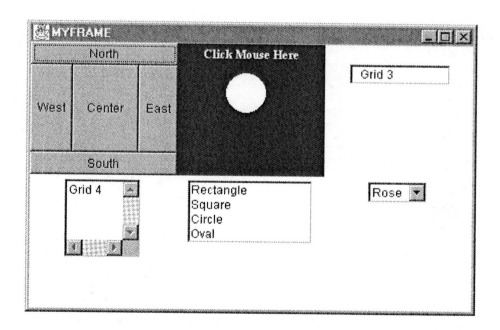

**13. Layouts, Panels, Frames, Canvasses, and Menus**

# SUMMARY

This module has introduced the ideas of GUI Java programming.  It shows how to specify

Layouts

Panels

Canvases

Frames

Menus

Standalone GUI Programs

We also saw how to embed components such as button, text areas, text fields, and other components in panels and frames.

# EXERCISES

1. Modify c13_1.java to center the components on the applet with a horizontal gap of 40 and vertical gap of 45.

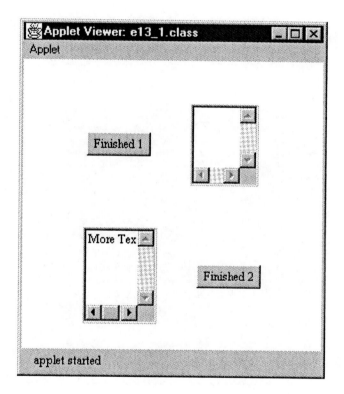

2. Add a BorderLayout to c13_4.java placing the canvas in c13_4.java in the center of the layout. Then add north, south, east and west buttons as in c13_2.java to the program. Place an actionPerformed() in the program which will remove any button which is clicked using the remove() method of java.awt.container. When running the applet follow these steps: (1) click in canvas area to generate "Canvas: mouse" message, (2) remove north button, (3) click in empty north area and observe message.

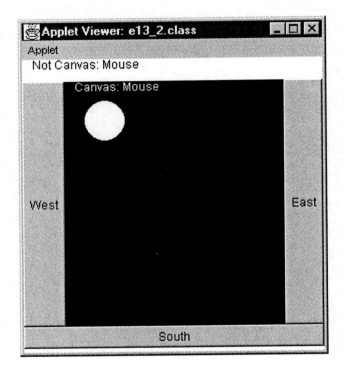

3. Revamp c13_5.java changing the overall layout to BorderLayout. Eliminate the Choice panel (p6). Place the canvas in the center. Place the five button panel in the east. Place the List in the west. Place the text field in the north. Place the myPanel panel in the south. Eliminate the "p1 button pressed" drawString. When you run the applet, click on the canvas and click outside the canvas to display the messages. Hints: p3.setLayout(null) must be deleted to see the north region. The setLayout(null) must also be deleted in MyPanel to see the button in the south region.

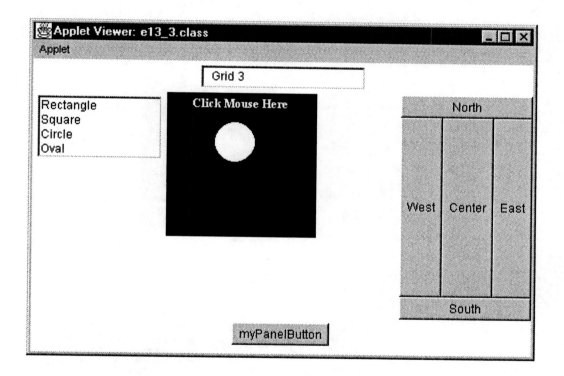

4. Modify c13_6.java so that a new frame is generated each time you click on the "Window?" button. As you create new frames click on the title bar of each frame and drag it to some corner of the screen. A window closing event should cause dispose() to execute.

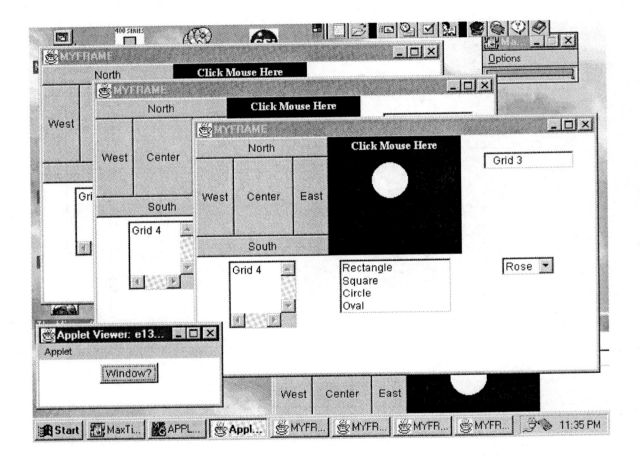

5. Modify the mouseReleased() method in class newCanvas of c13_5.java to generate a pop-up frame when the mouse is pressed on the canvas area. The pop-up frame will display the message, "You clicked on the canvas" in centered 14 point bold SansSerif type. The pop-up frame should disappear if you click anywhere on it with the mouse. When you run the program keep clicking on the canvas to generate pop-up's and click on the pop-up's to dispose of them.

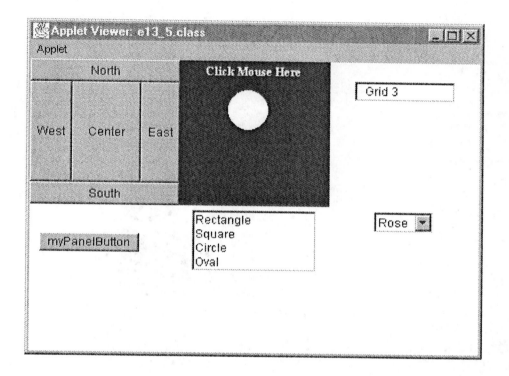

**13. Layouts, Panels, Frames, Canvasses, and Menus**

6. Add a menubar to the pop-up in exercise 5 with two top selections: "Main Choice 1" and "Main Choice 2". Then for each selection add two menu items: "Submenu Choice 1" and "Submenu Choice 2". If a menu item is selected, then print the message "Menu Choice: " followed by the label of the selected menu item at x = 25 and y = 125.

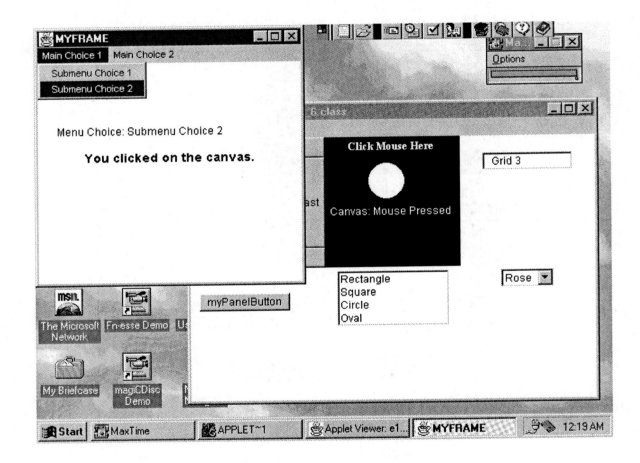

# 14. *Animation & Double Buffering*

## OBJECTIVES

At the end of this module you should be able to:

- Describe and create graphic displays using double buffering to improve graphics displays.

- Create animations.

# GRAPHICS IMAGES AND GRAPHICS CONTEXTS

- Java applets have a graphics display area upon which we have painted lines, graphic figures and images from .gif files.

- Graphics areas are called *graphics contexts* in Java. They are complex data structures hose internal details are hidden from us - the Java programmers. They are also subject to change since they are not defined in the Java language standard. Therefore, we should not code based on the hidden detailed graphics context representation which is inaccessible anyway.

- The contents of the graphics image of a Java applet are often specified in the paint() method of the applet's class.

- It is useful to define other graphics contexts within a Java program. These can be used for double buffering.

- Double buffering in Java is the creation of an Image object to store graphical data. It is similar to creating a buffer array to store numeric data. After building the double buffer image it is displayed on screen at some appropriate point in the evolution of an applet.

- The purposes of double buffering are:

    - To quickly display an image on screen in one burst rather than painting it slowly on screen.

    - To enable a variety of methods to contribute to the creation of an image.

## Creating New Graphics Contexts

Several methods are important in creating new graphics contexts:

**Graphics getGraphics()** - This awt.Component method returns a graphics context for *this* component.

**Image createImage(int width, int height)** - This awt.Component method creates a drawable image for the purposes of double buffering.

**boolean prepareImage(Image img, ImageObserver o)** - This awt.Component method creates a thread and loads the image from the file. An appropriate screen display is prepared. Returns true if the image is already fully prepared.

**boolean drawImage(Image i, int x, int y, int width, int height, ImageObserver o)** - This awt.Graphics method draws the specified image placing the upper left corner at x and y. The image is *scaled* to the specified width and height. The ImageObserver object specifies the entity for whom the image is drawn.

**boolean drawImage(Image i, int x, int y, int width, int height, Color c, ImageObserver o)** - This awt.Graphics method draws the specified image placing the upper left corner at x and y. The image is *scaled* to the specified width and height. The ImageObserver object specifies the entity for whom the image is drawn. The specified color c is the background color for the displayed image.

## Procedure for Implementing Double Buffering

1.  Define an object of class Image using the createImage() method. This method creates a drawable image. The getImage() method (module 9) produces an image from a graphics file. However the image it creates is not drawable.

    Example:
    ```
    Image myImage;
    ...
    myImage = createImage(200, 400);
    ```

2.  Define an object of class Graphics which will be the "channel" for drawing on the Image object. This object is the graphics context of the Image object.

    Example:
    ```
    Graphics myGraph;
    ...
    myGraph = myImage.getGraphics();
    ```

3.  Use myGraph to draw on the graphics context.

    Example:
    ```
    myGraph.drawRect(50, 50, 100, 100);
    ```

4.  After placing all the desired graphics on the image, it can be displayed on an applet, panel, canvas or frame with the drawImage() method. Note: we use the Graphics object of the container (applet, frame, …) to draw on the container.

    Example:
    ```
    g.drawImage(myImage, 50, 50, this);
    ```

## Program Illustrating Graphics Contexts
**File: c14_1.html**
```
<applet code="c14_1.class" width = 300 height = 300></applet>
```

**File: c14_1.java**
```java
import java.awt.*;
import java.awt.event.*;
import java.applet.Applet;

public class c14_1 extends Applet implements ActionListener
{
        private Image i1, i2, i3;
        private Graphics g1, g2, g3;
        private List myList = new List(3, false);
        private int x = 60, y = 60;
        private int figType = 0;

        public void init()
        {
                setBackground(Color.white);
                        // create 3 double buffers.
                i1 = createImage(100, 100);
                i2 = createImage(100, 100);
                i3 = createImage(100, 100);
                g1 = i1.getGraphics();
                g2 = i2.getGraphics();
                g3 = i3.getGraphics();
                build1(g1);
                build2(g2);
                build3(g3);
                myList.add("Rectangle");
                myList.add("Circle");
                myList.add("Oval");
                add(myList);
                myList.addActionListener(this);
        }
        void build1(Graphics g)
        {
                g.fillRect(x, y, 30, 30);
        }
        void build2(Graphics g)
        {
                g.fillOval(x, y, 30, 30);
        }
        void build3(Graphics g)
        {
                g.fillOval(x, y, 30, 15);
        }
```

**14. Animation & Double Buffering**

```
public void paint(Graphics g)
{
        g.setColor(Color.black);
        g.drawString("Painting: figType = " + figType, 10,295);
        switch(figType)
        {
                case 1:
                        g.drawImage(i1, 0, 0, this);
                        break;
                case 2:
                        g.drawImage(i2, 100, 100, this);
                        break;
                case 3:
                        g.drawImage(i3, 175, 175, this);
                        break;
        }
}
public void actionPerformed(ActionEvent e)
{
        if(e.getSource() instanceof List)
        {
                figType = ((List)e.getSource())
                                .getSelectedIndex() + 1;
        }
        repaint();
}
}
```

**Output Applet**
Click <u>twice</u> on your selection.

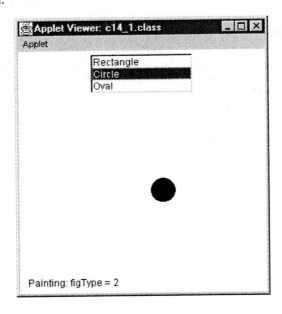

**14. Animation & Double Buffering**

# GRAPHICS DOUBLE BUFFERING

- Graphics double buffering consists of creating one or more graphics contexts and then drawing on them.

- The next program implements double buffering for three graphics contexts with more complex graphics and paints them on the applet display in a checkerboard pattern when the button is selected.

**File: c14_2.html**
```
<applet code="c14_2.class" width = 300 height = 400>
</applet>
```

**File: c14_2.java**
```java
import java.awt.*;
import java.awt.event.*;
import java.applet.Applet;

public class c14_2 extends Applet implements ActionListener
{
        private Image i1, i2, i3;
        private Graphics g1, g2, g3;
        private Button b = new Button("Show Image");
        private int x = 60, y = 60;
        private int figType = 0;

        public void init()
        {
                setBackground(Color.white);
                add(b);
                i1 = createImage(100, 100);
                i2 = createImage(100, 100);
                i3 = createImage(100, 100);
                g1 = i1.getGraphics();
                g2 = i2.getGraphics();
                g3 = i3.getGraphics();
                build1(g1);
                build2(g2);
                build3(g3);
                b.addActionListener(this);
        }
```

```java
void build1(Graphics g)
{
        g.setColor(Color.black);
        g.fillRect(0, 0, 100, 100);
        g.setColor(Color.white);
        g.drawOval(1, 1, 97, 97);
        g.drawRect(20, 20, 60, 60);
        g.drawOval(40, 40, 20, 20);
}
void build2(Graphics g)
{
        g.setColor(Color.black);
        g.fillRect(0, 0, 100, 100);
        g.setColor(Color.white);
        g.drawRect(15, 15, 70, 70);
        g.drawOval(30, 30, 40, 40);
        g.drawRect(45, 45, 10, 10);
}
void build3(Graphics g)
{
        g.setColor(Color.black);
        g.fillRect(0, 0, 100, 100);
        g.setColor(Color.white);
        g.drawOval(1, 1, 97, 97);
        g.drawOval(15, 15, 70, 70);
        g.drawOval(30, 30, 40, 40);
        g.drawOval(45, 45, 10, 10);
}
public void paint(Graphics g)
{
        if(figType > 0)
        {
                g.drawImage(i1, 0, 0, 100, 100, this);
                g.drawImage(i1, 200, 0, 100, 100, this);

                g.drawImage(i2, 100, 100, 100, 100, this);

                g.drawImage(i3, 200, 200, 100, 100, this);
                g.drawImage(i3, 0, 200, 100, 100, this);
        }
}
public void actionPerformed(ActionEvent e)
{
        if(e.getSource() instanceof Button)
        {
                figType = 1;
                repaint();
        }
}
}
```

**14. Animation & Double Buffering**

**Output Applet:**

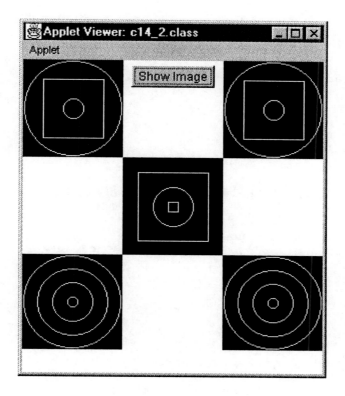

# USING DOUBLE BUFFERS TO LOG DRAWINGS

A double buffer can be used to log drawings made in methods other than the paint() method so that they may be automatically refreshed when a window is placed in front of the applet and removed, etc.

**Example**

**File: logger.html**
```
<applet code="logger.class" width = 300 height = 400>
</applet>
```

**File: logger.java**
```java
import java.awt.*;
import java.awt.event.*;
import java.applet.Applet;

public class logger extends Applet implements ActionListener,
                                              ItemListener
{
        private List myList = new List(4, true);
        private Button b;
        private int x = 60, y = 60;
        private int figType = 0;
        private Graphics g;
        Image img;  // double buffer used for logging graphics.

        public void init()
        {
                setBackground(Color.white);
                myList.add("Rectangle");
                myList.add("Rounded Rectangle");
                myList.add("Circle");
                myList.add("Vertical Oval");
                myList.add("Horizontal Oval");
                add(myList);
                b = new Button("Done");
                add(b);
                b.addActionListener(this);
                myList.addItemListener(this);//listen for each selection
                img = createImage(300, 300);
        }
        public void paint(Graphics g)
        {
                g.drawImage(img, 0, 100, 300, 300, this);
        }
        public void myPaint(Graphics g)
        {
                g.drawString("Painting: figType = " + figType,
                                                10,100+y);
```

```
                switch(figType)
                {
                        case 1:
                                g.fillRect(x, y, 30, 30);
                                break;
                        case 2:
                                g.fillRoundRect(x, y, 30, 30,15, 15);
                                break;
                        case 3:
                                g.fillOval(x, y, 30, 30);
                                break;
                        case 4:
                                g.fillOval(x, y, 15, 30);
                                break;
                        case 5:
                                g.fillOval(x, y, 30, 15);
                                break;
                }
        }
        public void actionPerformed(ActionEvent e)
        {
                if(e.getSource() instanceof Button)
                {
                        g = img.getGraphics();
                        int [] iArray = myList.getSelectedIndexes();
                        g.clearRect(0, 0, 300, 300);
                        g.setColor(Color.lightGray);
                        g.fillRect(0, 0, 300, 300);
                        x = y = 0;
                        g.setColor(Color.black);
                        for(int index = 0;index < iArray.length;
                                                        index++)
                        {
                                x += 30;
                                y += 30;
                                figType = iArray[index] + 1;
                                myPaint(g);
                                myList.deselect(iArray[index]);
                        }
                        repaint();
                }
        }
        public void itemStateChanged(ItemEvent e)
        {
                int choice = ((Integer) e.getItem()).intValue();
                System.out.println("Item Selected: " + choice);
        }
}
```

**14.  Animation & Double Buffering**

**Ouput applet (total automatic refresh by paint()) :**

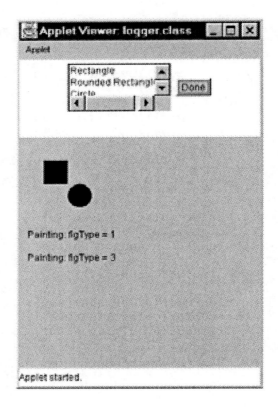

**14. Animation & Double Buffering**

# ANIMATIONS

- Animations can be created in Java either through

    - Creating a series of images which are rapidly drawn on screen to create the illusion of motion.

    - Or, by drawing a series of images on screen with timed incremental moves to create the illusion of motion.

- Complex animations can be created using multithreaded drawing programs which simultaneously draw various parts of the displayed image.

- An important part of the Java support for animation is the MediaTracker class and its methods which enable you to assemble and manage a sequence of images which produce smooth animations when combined with double-buffering and multithreading techniques.

- We shall now look at a series of animation examples:

    1. A simple animation with no multithreading or use of MediaTracker.

    2. A multi-threaded animation.

    3. A multithreaded animation with a set of images managed by MediaTracker methods.

## Simple Single Thread Animation

**File: c14_3.html**

```
<applet code="c14_3.class" width = 350 height = 350>
</applet>
```

**File: c14_3.java**

```java
import java.awt.*;
import java.awt.event.*;
import java.applet.Applet;

public class c14_3 extends Applet implements ActionListener
{
        private Image i1;
        private Graphics g1;
        private Button b = new Button("Show Animation");
        private int x = 60, y = 60;
        private int figType = 0;

        public void init()
        {
                setBackground(Color.white);
                i1 = createImage(100, 100); // double buffer
                g1 = i1.getGraphics();
                build1(g1);
                add(b);
                b.addActionListener(this);
        }
        void build1(Graphics g)
        {
                g.setColor(Color.black);
                g.fillOval(0, 0, 100, 100);
                g.setColor(Color.white);
                g.drawOval(1, 1, 97, 97);
                g.drawOval(15, 15, 70, 70);
                g.drawOval(30, 30, 40, 40);
                g.drawOval(45, 45, 10, 10);
        }
        public void paint(Graphics g)
        {
                if(figType > 0)
                {
                    for(;;)
                        for(int k = 0; k < 250; k++) // animation.
                                g.drawImage(i1, k, k, 100, 100, this);
                }
        }
}
```

```
public void actionPerformed(ActionEvent e)
{
        if(e.getSource() instanceof Button)
        {
                figType = 1;
                repaint();
        }
}
}
```

**Output Applet Displaying Motion**

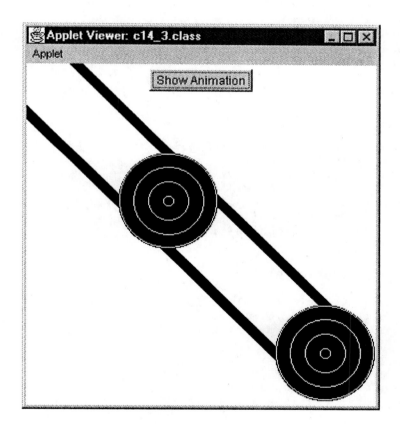

### Animation Using Two Threads to Display Moving Graphics

**File c14_4.html**
```
<applet code="c14_4.class" width = 350 height = 350></applet>
```

**File: c14_4.java**
```java
import java.awt.*;
import java.awt.event.*;
import java.applet.Applet;

public class c14_4 extends Applet implements ActionListener
{
        private Button b = new Button("Clash of the Titans");
        private ImThread it1, it2;
        private Graphics gg, g1, g2;
        private Image i1, i2;
        static boolean run = true;

        public void init()
        {
                setBackground(Color.white);
                add(b);
                b.addActionListener(this);
                gg = getGraphics();
                i1 = createImage(100, 100);
                g1 = i1.getGraphics();
                build1(g1);
                i2 = createImage(100, 100);
                g2 = i2.getGraphics();
                build1(g2);
        }
        void build1(Graphics g)
        {
                g.setColor(Color.black);
                g.fillOval(0, 0, 100, 100);
                g.setColor(Color.white);
                g.drawRect(0, 0, 99, 99);
                g.drawOval(1, 1, 97, 97);
                g.drawOval(15, 15, 70, 70);
                g.drawOval(30, 30, 40, 40);
                g.drawOval(45, 45, 10, 10);
        }
        public void actionPerformed(ActionEvent e)
        {
                if(e.getSource() instanceof Button)
                        if(run)
                        {
                                it1 = new ImThread(1, i1, gg);
                                it2 = new ImThread(2, i2, gg);
                                run = false;
```

```
                        }
                        else
                        {
                                it1.stop();
                                it2.stop();
                                run = true;
                        }
                }
        }

class ImThread extends Applet implements Runnable
{
        private Thread t;
        private Image i;
        private Graphics gg;
        private int figType = 0;

        public ImThread(int type, Image i, Graphics gg)
        {
                figType = type;
                this.gg = gg;
                this.i = i;
                t = new Thread(this);
                t.start();
        }
        public void run()
        {
            for(;;)
            {
            if(figType == 1)
            {
                    for(int k = 0; k < 300; k++)
                    {
                            gg.drawImage(i, k, k, 100, 100, this);
                    }
            }
            else if(figType == 2)
            {
                    for(int k = 0; k < 300; k++)
                    {
                            gg.drawImage(i, k, 250-k, 100, 100,
                                                            this);
                    }
            }
            if(c14_4.run) break;
            }
        }
}
```

**14. Animation & Double Buffering**

**Output Applets**

Click button to start animation.

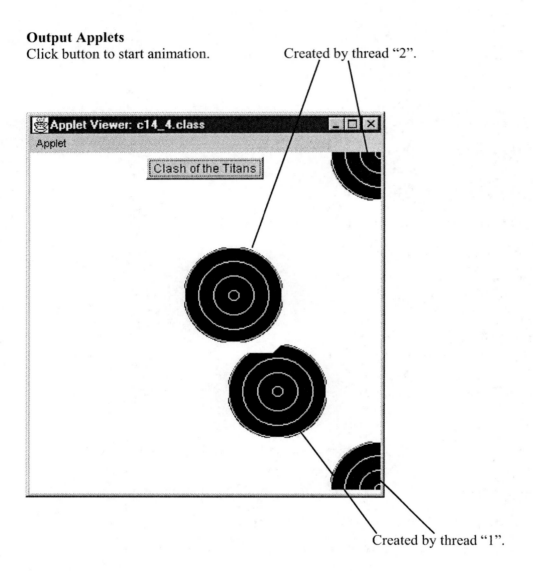

Created by thread "2".

Created by thread "1".

## Animation Using Four Threads

*This is a teaching example for threading.  This animation would be smoother on one thread.*

**File c14_5.html**
```
<applet code="c14_5.class" width = 350 height = 350></applet>
```

**File: c14_5.java**
```java
import java.awt.*;
import java.awt.event.*;
import java.applet.Applet;

public class c14_5 extends Applet implements ActionListener
{
        private Button b = new Button("Show Pinwheel");
        private ImThread it1, it2, it3, it4;
        private Graphics gg, g1, g2, g3, g4, g5, g6;
        private Image i1, i2, i3, i4;

        public void init()
        {
                setBackground(Color.white);
                add(b);
                b.addActionListener(this);

                i1 = createImage(50, 50);
                g1 = i1.getGraphics();
                build1(g1);
                i2 = createImage(50, 50);
                g2 = i2.getGraphics();
                build2(g2);
                i3 = createImage(50, 50);
                g3 = i3.getGraphics();
                build3(g3);
                i4 = createImage(50, 50);
                g4 = i4.getGraphics();
                build4(g4);
                gg = getGraphics();
        }
        void build1(Graphics g)
        {
                g.setColor(Color.black);
                g.fillRect(0, 0, 50, 50);
                g.setColor(Color.white);
                g.drawRect(0, 0, 50, 50);
                g.drawLine(0, 0, 49, 49);
                g.drawLine(0, 49, 49, 0);
        }
}
```

```java
        void build2(Graphics g)
        {
                g.setColor(Color.black);
                g.fillRect(0, 0, 50, 50);

                g.setColor(Color.white);
                g.drawRect(0, 0, 50, 50);
                g.drawLine(12, 0, 38, 50);
                g.drawLine(50, 12, 0, 38);
        }
        void build3(Graphics g)
        {
                g.setColor(Color.black);
                g.fillRect(0, 0, 50, 50);

                g.setColor(Color.white);
                g.drawRect(0, 0, 50, 50);
                g.drawLine(25, 0, 25, 50);
                g.drawLine(0, 25, 50, 25);
        }
        void build4(Graphics g)
        {
                g.setColor(Color.black);
                g.fillRect(0, 0, 50, 50);

                g.setColor(Color.white);
                g.drawRect(0, 0, 50, 50);
                g.drawLine(38, 0, 12, 50);
                g.drawLine(0, 12, 50, 38);
        }
        public void actionPerformed(ActionEvent e)
        {
                if(e.getSource() instanceof Button)
                {
                        it1 = new ImThread(i1, gg);
                        it2 = new ImThread(i2, gg);
                        it3 = new ImThread(i3, gg);
                        it4 = new ImThread(i4, gg);
                }
        }
}

class ImThread extends Applet implements Runnable
{
        private Thread t;
        private Image i;
        private Graphics gg;
```

```
public ImThread(Image i, Graphics gg)
{
        this.gg = gg;
        this.i = i;
        t = new Thread(this);
        t.start();
}
public void run()
{
        for(;;)
        {
                gg.drawImage(i, 150, 150, 50, 50, this);
        }
}
}
```

**Output Applet:**
Rotating pinwheel.

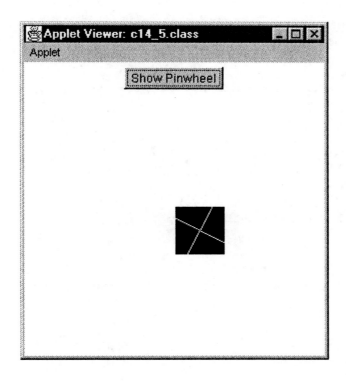

## Class MediaTracker

The MediaTracker class is defined to manage a set of images such as a set of .gif files. Images are registered as part of a set and then managed by the following methods. Often the images are variations on each other which combine to produce an animation.

MediaTracker methods can be used to cause the program to pause until all images in an animation are loaded, or to force the loading of images.

Images are loaded asynchronously. A Java program does not wait for an image to loaded before proceeding to the next statement unless MediaTracker methods are used.

Some of the important methods in this class are:

**MediaTracker(Component c)** - constructor creating MediaTracker object. The Component c is the component upon which the images will be drawn.

>     Example:
>                     MediaTracker m = new MediaTracker(this);

**void addImage(Image i, int id_num)** - adds an image to a group of images. The added image is given id number id_num. Id numbers can be unique or a set of images can be given the same id.

>     Example:
>                     m.addImage(myImage, my_id);

**void waitForAll()** - forces loading of all images and blocks (pauses) program execution until all images are loaded. Will throw an InterruptedException if its thread receives an interrupt().

>     Example:
>                     m.waitForAll();

**void waitForID(int id_num)** - Forces loading of all images with specified id and blocks (pauses) program execution until the image with id = id_num is loaded. Throws InterruptedException if another thread interrupts current thread.

      Example:
```
m.waitForID(my_id);
```

**boolean checkAll(boolean do_load)** - checks for all images. If do_load == true, then it loads missing images. If do_load == false, then it does not load missing images.

      Example:
```
if(m.checkAll(true))
```

**boolean checkID(int  id_num)** - checks to see if image with specified id is loaded. Returns true if loaded.

      Example:
```
if(m.checkID(mu_id))
```

**boolean checkID(int id_num, boolean do_load)** - checks to see if image with id id_num is loaded. If do_load == true, then it loads the image if it isn't loaded. Method returns true if loaded.

      Example:
```
if(m.checkID(my_id, true))
```

## Program Illustrating the use MediaTracker

**File: c14_6.html**
```html
<applet code="c14_6.class" width = 300 height = 300>
</applet>
```

**File: c14_6.java**
```java
import java.awt.*;
import java.awt.event.*;
import java.net.*;
import java.applet.Applet;

public class c14_6 extends Applet implements ActionListener
{
        private Button b = new Button("CocoNuts");
        private ImThread it1, it2;
        private Graphics gg, g1, g2;
        private Image i1, i2;

        private Image myImages[] = new Image[10];
                // create MediaTracker object.
        private MediaTracker m = new MediaTracker(this);

        public void init()
        {
                setBackground(Color.white);
                add(b);
                b.addActionListener(this);

                i1 = createImage(100, 100); // black background
                g1 = i1.getGraphics();
                build1(g1);

                i2 = createImage(100, 100); // white background
                g2 = i2.getGraphics();
                build2(g2);

                for(int j = 0; j < 10;j++)
                {
                        String iFile = new String("T" +
                                        String.valueOf(j+1) + ".gif");
                        try
                        {
                                myImages[j] = getImage(
                                        getDocumentBase(), iFile);
                        }
                        catch(Exception e) { }
                                // register image with MediaTracker object.
                        m.addImage(myImages[j], j);
                }
```

**14. Animation & Double Buffering**

```
                try
                {
                        m.waitForAll();// pause until all images are loaded.
                }
                catch(Exception e) { }
                gg = getGraphics();
        }
        void build1(Graphics g)
        {
                g.setColor(Color.black);
                g.fillRect(0, 0, 100, 100);
        }
        void build2(Graphics g)
        {
                g.setColor(Color.white);
                g.fillRect(0, 0, 100, 100);

                g.setColor(Color.black);
                g.drawRect(0, 0, 99, 99);
        }
        public void actionPerformed(ActionEvent e)
        {
                if(e.getSource() instanceof Button)
                {
                        it1 = new ImThread(1, i1, gg, m, myImages,
                                                        0, 150);
                        it2 = new ImThread(2, i2, gg, m, myImages,
                                                        200, 150);
                }
        }
}

class ImThread extends Applet implements Runnable
{
        private Thread t;
        private Image i, myImages[];
        private Graphics gg;
        private int x, y, type;
        private MediaTracker m;
        public ImThread(int type, Image i, Graphics gg, MediaTracker m,
                                        Image myImages[], int x, int y)
        {
                this.gg = gg;
                this.i = i;
                this.x = x;
                this.y = y;
                this.myImages = myImages;
                this.type = type;
                this.m = m;
                t = new Thread(this);
                t.start();
```

**14. Animation & Double Buffering**

```
        }
        public void run()
        {
                for(int k = 0;; k++)
                {
                        if(m.checkID(k%10))
                        {
                                gg.drawImage(i, x, y, 100, 100, this);
                                gg.drawImage(myImages[k%10], x, y, 100,
                                                           100, this);
//                                  if(type == 1)
//                                          gg.drawImage(myImages[k%10],x,y,
// Smoother image: draws background also.    100,100,Color.black,this);
//                                  else
//                                          gg.drawImage(myImages[k%10],x,y,
//                                             100,100,Color.white,this);
                        }
//                  try
//                  {
// Adds smoothness:               t.sleep(50);
//                  }
//                  catch(Exception e) {  }
                }
        }
}
```

**Output Applet**
**it1 thread**

**it2 thread**

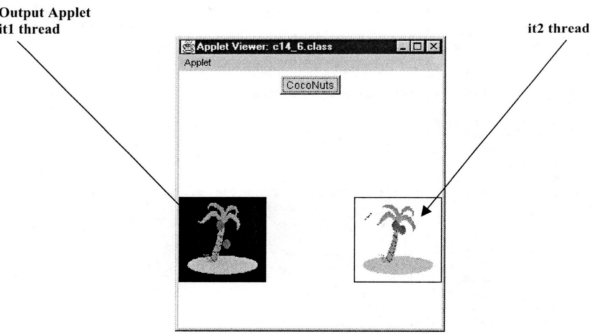

**14.  Animation & Double Buffering**

# SUMMARY

This module has described double buffering and animation. The topics which were covered include:

- Using double buffering to create smoother image displays.

- Managing images with the MediaTracker class methods.

- Simple animation techniques.

- Using multithreading to produce complex animations.

# EXERCISES

1. Modify c14_2.java so that the i2 graphics image has the graphics file myimage.gif.

2. Enhance c14_4.java by adding a third thread with a double buffered image of myimage.gif moving horizontally across the screen at midscreen. Then replace everything in both other double buffers with myimage.gif. The result should be three copies of myimage.gif moving across the screen.

3.  Starting from c14_6.java install the graphics animation files T1.gif through T10.gif in the program using MediaTracker to manage them. Then add another thread which runs this animation at x = 100 and y = 150. The background for this animation should be gray with a black box around it. The animation will look like:

# 15.  *Java Terminal and File I/O*

## OBJECTIVES

At the end of this module you should be able to:

- Describe and perform terminal input and output in Java programs.

- Describe and perform file input and output.

- Perform random access in files.

# FILE I/O IN APPLETS AND STANDALONE JAVA PROGRAMS

- File reading and writing are privileges. A person or program with these privileges could damage your files.

- So Java prevents ordinary applets from reading or writing files.

- Digitally signed applets can read and write your files (assuming they were signed by an entity that your browser is set up to accept).

- Standalone Java programs can read and write your files since they are programs on your computer.

- In this module we will primarily use standalone Java programs to explore file I/O. The methods and techniques seen in this module will work equally well in digitally signed applets.

# TERMINAL INPUT AND OUTPUT

Java enables you to read keyboard input into a Java program and to send output to the terminal screen.

**Frankly, it is far preferable to use the applet approaches shown in earlier modules using TextFields and TextAreas to read input from an applet page, and the drawString() method to print character strings on an applet display.**

The Standard I/O input and output "channels" are:

| Standard Input | System.in | - a static variable of type InputStream in class System. |
|---|---|---|
| Standard Output | System.out | - a static variable of type PrintStream in class System. |
| Standard Error Output | System.err | - a static variable of type PrintStream in class System. |

## Sending Output to the Terminal Screen

**void println( ... )** - A method of class PrintStream which displays its argument on the terminal screen. Arguments include the primitive data types, String objects, char arrays, and objects (which are printed as `String.valueOf(object)`). A newline is always printed at the end of the output. `System.out.println()` prints a newline only.

Example:
```
System.out.println("my string");
```

**void print( ... )** - A method of class PrintStream which displays its argument on the terminal screen. Arguments include the primitive data types, String objects, char arrays, and objects (which are printed as `String.valueOf(object)`). A newline is not printed at the end of the output. The println() method calls the print() method.

Example:
```
System.out.print("my string");
```

**void flush()** - A method of class PrintStream which causes characters in the output buffer to be delivered to their destination. Often used after a print() call if the character string being printed does not contain a newline. A newline also causes the buffer contents to be delivered to the destination.

Example:
```
System.out.flush();
```

## Reading Input from the Keyboard

**int read()** - A method of class InputStream which reads one character from the keyboard. This method returns -1 when it reads the end of file character which is ctrl-D in UNIX and ctrl-Z in PC operating system environments. This method throws an IOException if an I/O error occurred.

Example:

```
while((c = System.in.read()) != -1)     // reads characters
                                  // until it reads end of input.
```

**long skip(long num)** - A method of class InputStream which skips over num characters of keyboard input. It returns the number of characters actually skipped over. Some keyboard inputs may not contain num characters and so it may not skip over the specified number. This method throws an IOException if an I/O error occurred.

Example:

```
System.in.skip(5L);   // skip over 5 bytes.
```

## Standalone Program with Terminal I/O

**Procedure:**

        edit c15_1.java
        javac c15_1.java
        java c15_1

Type a sequence of characters, press the ENTER key, and then type ctrl-Z (on PCs) or ctrl-D (in UNIX or LINUX environments).

**File: c15_1.java**

```
class c15_1                                // File: c15_1.java
{
        public static void main(String args[])
        {
                char carr[] = new char[20];
                int c;

                System.out.print("Type some input: "); // no newline output.
                System.out.flush();        // flushes buffer to terminal.
                try
                {
                        if((c = System.in.read()) == -1)
                                return;
                        else
                                carr[0] = (char) c;
                        System.in.skip(3L);        // skips 3 characters.
                } catch(Exception e) { }

                for(int j = 1; j < 19; j++)
                {
                        try
                        {                // read one character from keyboard
                                if((c = System.in.read()) == -1)
                                        break;
                                else
                                        carr[j] = (char) c;
                        } catch(Exception e) { break; }
                }
                System.out.println("\nOutput: " + carr);

        }
}
```

Output:

```
Type some input: abcdefghijk
^Z
Output: aefghijk
```

---

**Program Notes:**

- We use a char array to allow us to perform simple output using println().

- Since the read() method returns int, and we wish to test for end of input which is -1, we use an int variable c to store the input keyboard character.

- The print() method was used since we did not wish to add a newline to the prompt string. We must use the flush() method to force delivery of the prompt to the screen from the output buffer.

# FILE INFORMATION METHODS

Java uses class File methods to retrieve information about files and directories. Some File methods perform file and directory manipulation. This class does not support file I/O.

Some important methods of class File are:

## Constructors

**File(String fileName)** - creates a File object for a specified disk file.

**File(String directory, String fileName)** - creates a File object for a specified disk file in a specified directory.

## File Information

**String getName()** - returns a String object containing the filename.

**String getPath()** - returns a String object containing the path of the file object.

**String getAbsolutePath()** - returns a String containing the absolute path of the file.

**String getParent()** - returns the name of the parent directory.

**String toString()** - returns a String object containing the object's pathname.

**long length()** - returns the size of the file in bytes.

**long lastModified()** - returns the time since the last modification of the file. Should only be used for comparisons of modification times. Its absolute value is not meaningful.

## File Tests

**boolean exists()** - returns true if the file exists.

**boolean canWrite()** - returns true if the file is writeable.

**boolean canRead()** - returns true if the file is readable.

**boolean isFile()** - returns true if the file is a file and not a directory.

**boolean isDirectory()** - returns true if the file is actually a directory.

**boolean isAbsolute()** - returns true if the file is specified with an absolute pathname.

## Directory Manipulation

**boolean mkdir()** - creates a directory with the name specified by the current File object and returns true if successful.

**String [] list()** - returns a list of the files in the directory specified by the current object.

**boolean delete()** - deletes the file associated with the current object and returns true on success.

**boolean renameTo(File newFileName)** - renames the file associated with the object.

## Program Illustrating the use of File Methods

**Commands:**
```
javac c15_2.java
java c15_2
```

**File: c15_2.java**
```java
import java.io.*;

public class c15_2
{
        public static void main(String args[])
        {
                File f = new File("c15_2.java");

                System.out.println("File: "      + f.getName());

                System.out.println("Path: "      + f.getPath());

                System.out.println("Parent: "    + f.getParent());

                System.out.println("Is a File? "+ (f.isFile()?"true":"false"));

                System.out.println("Readable: " + (f.canRead()?"true":"false"));

                System.out.println("Size: "      + f.length());
        }
}
```

**Output:**
```
File: c15_2.java
Path: \work\c15_2.java
Parent: \work
Is a File? true
Readable: true
Size: 610
```

# TYPES OF FILE I/O

- Java supports several types of file reading and writing.

- This section compares the various types and points out when each type should be used.

- Some browsers, such as NetScape, do not support file access for security reasons for normal applets. Digitally signed applets can read and write local files.

- Some browsers such as Hot Java let you specify allowed file access.

- The classes supporting file I/O are located in java.io and java.io classes must be imported in programs performing file I/O.

- Some important classes with major roles in file I/O are:

| Purpose | Class |
|---------|-------|
| Sequential ASCII text file reading | FileInputStream |
| Sequential writing ASCII text to a file | FileOutputStream |
| Sequential UNICODE text file reading | BufferedReader |
| Sequential writing UNICODE text to a file | BufferedWriter |
| Sequential binary file reading | DataInputStream |
| Sequential binary file writing | DataOutputStream |
| Random access binary read/write | RandomAccessFile |
| Reading a URL over the network | InputStream |

# ASCII TEXT FILE I/O

ASCII text file I/O (for U.S. keyboard characters) is supported by the FileInputStream and FileOutputStream classes.

Data retrieved from files can be displayed in TextFields and TextAreas.

Some of the important I/O methods are:

## Constructors

**FileInputStream(String fileName)** - create object for input using filename or filename path.  Throws FileNotFound exception if file not found.

> Example:
> ```
> FileInputStream fin = new FileInputStream("c:\\mydir\\myfile");
> ```

**FileInputStream(File fobj)** - create FileInputStream object for input using File object.  Throws FileNotFound exception if file not found.

> Example:
> ```
> FileInputStream fin = new FileInputStream(myFileObj);
> ```

**FileOutputStream(String fileName)** - create object for output using filename or filename path. Throws IOException if file not found.

> Example:
> ```
> FileOutputStream fout = new FileOutputStream("c:\\mydir\\myfile");
> ```

**FileOutputStream(File fobj)** - create FileOutputStream object for output using File object. Throws IOException if file not found.

> Example:
> ```
> FileOutputStream fout = new FileOutputStream(myFileObj);
> ```

## Read Methods

**int read()** - reads one byte of data from the file.  Returns -1 at the end of the file.  Throws IOException if I/O error occurs.

Example:
```
int cj;
while((cj = fin.read()) != -1) // ends automatically when end of file detected.
```

**int read(byte barr[])** - reads bytes placing them in the array up to the size of the array.  Returns the number of bytes actually read, or -1 at the end of the file.  Throws IOException if I/O error occurs.

Example:
```
byte barr[] = new byte[80];
while((num_read = fin.read(barr)) != -1) // ends when end of file detected.
```

**int read(byte barr[], int b_offset, int max_num)** - reads bytes placing them in the array up to max_num bytes.  Places the bytes in array starting at barr[b_offset].  Returns the number of bytes actually read, or -1 at the end of the file.  Throws IOException if I/O error occurs.

Example:
```
byte barr[] = new byte[80];
while((num_read = fin.read(barr,3,10)) != -1) // ends when end of file detected.
```

**long skip(long num_bytes)** - skips num_bytes of input from file.  Returns the number of bytes actually skipped.

Example:
```
fin.skip(80);
```

## Write Methods

**void write(int c)** - writes one byte of data to the file. Throws IOException if I/O error occurs.

> Example:
> ```
> int cj;
> ...
> fout.write(cj);    // only byte containing character written
> ```

**void write(byte barr[])** - writes the entire array to the file. Throws IOException if I/O error occurs.

> Example:
> ```
> byte barr[] = new byte[80];
> ...
> fout.write(barr);
> ```

**void write(byte barr[], int b_offset, int num)** - writes num bytes from array to file starting from barr[b_offset]. Throws IOException if I/O error occurs.

> Example:
> ```
> byte barr[] = new byte[80];
> ...
> fout.write(barr, 3, 10);
> ```

## Closing a File

**void close()** - closes file input stream.

> Examples:
> ```
>         fin.close();
>         fout.close();
> ```

## Program Illustrating FileInputStream and FileOutputStream

**File: c15_3.java**

```java
import java.io.*;

public class c15_3
{
        public static void main(String args[]) throws IOException // due to
                                                // potential throws from
                                                // constructor and write().
        {       // create file writing object.
                FileOutputStream fout = new FileOutputStream("myfile");

                byte barr[] = new byte[30];
                int x;
                x = (int)'A';
                barr[0] = (byte) 'B';
                barr[1] = (byte) 'C';
                barr[2] = (byte) 'D';
                barr[3] = (byte) 'E';
                barr[4] = (byte) 'F';
                fout.write(x);
                fout.write(barr);
                fout.close();
                readIt();
        }

        static void readIt() throws IOException  // due to potential throw
                                                 // from constructor and read().
        {       // create file reading object.
                File f = new File("myfile");
                FileInputStream fin = new FileInputStream(f);
                byte barr[] = new byte[30];
                int x;
                if((x = fin.read()) == -1)
                        System.exit(1);
                fin.read(barr);
                fin.close();
                System.out.println("File: "      + f.getName());
                System.out.println("Path: "      + f.getPath());
                System.out.println("Size: "      + f.length());

                System.out.print("\nData: " + (char)x);
                System.out.write(barr);
                System.out.flush();
        }
}
```

**Output:**
```
File: myfile
Path: myfile
Size: 31

Data: ABCDEF
```

# UNICODE TEXT FILE I/O - BufferedReader & BufferedWriter

UNICODE text (two byte characters) file I/O is supported by the BufferedReader and BufferedWriter classes.

Data retrieved from files can be displayed in TextFields and TextAreas.

Some of the important I/O methods are:

## Constructors

### Input
An InputStreamReader maps byte streams to character streams. It reads bytes and translates them into characters.

```
BufferedReader fin  = new BufferedReader(new InputStreamReader(
                                new FileInputStream("myFile")));
```

A BufferedReader object also reads a byte stream and converts it to a char stream:

```
BufferedReader fin    = new BufferedReader(new FileReader("myFile"));
```

### Output
A FileWriter sends its output to the output stream.

```
BufferedWriter fout = new BufferedWriter(new FileWriter("myFile"));
```

## Read Methods

**int read()** - reads one char (two bytes) of data from the file. Returns -1 at the end of the file. Throws IOException if I/O error occurs.

Example:
```
int cj;
while((cj = fin.read()) != -1) // ends automatically when end of file detected.
```

**int read(char carr[], int c_offset, int max_num)** - reads chars placing them in the array up to max_num chars. Places the chars in array starting at carr[c_offset]. Returns the number of bytes actually read, or -1 at the end of the file. Throws IOException if I/O error occurs.

Example:
```
char carr[] = new char[80];
while((num_read = fin.read(carr, 3, 10)) != -1)
```

**String readLine()** - Reads a line of UNICODE text. A line ends with a '\n', '\r', or a \r\n. The returned String does not include the line termination character.

Example:
```
String s = fin.readLine();
```

**long skip(long num_chars)** - skips num_chars of input from file. Returns the number of chars actually skipped.

Example:
```
fin.skip(80);
```

## Write Methods

**void write(int c)** - writes one char of data to the file. Throws IOException if I/O error occurs.

> Example:
> ```
> int cj;
> ...
> fout.write(cj);    // only char containing character written
> ```

**void write(char carr[], int c_offset, int num)** - writes num chars from array to file starting from carr[c_offset]. Throws IOException if I/O error occurs.

> Example:
> ```
> char carr[] = new char[80];
> ...
> fout.write(carr, 3, 10);
> ```

**void write(String s, int off, int len)** - Writes len chars from s to file starting from offset off in s.

> Example:
> ```
> fout.write( myString, 3, 10);
> ```

**void newLine()** - Writes a line separator (usually a '\n') to file.

> Example:
> ```
> fout.newLine();
> ```

**void flush()** - Flushes output to file.

> Example:
> ```
> fout.flush();
> ```

## Closing a File

**void close()** - closes file input stream.

> Example:
> ```
>                   fout.close();
> ```

## Program Illustrating BufferedReader and BufferedWriter

**File: c15_4.java**

```java
import java.io.*;

public class c15_4
{
        public static void main(String args[]) throws IOException
        {       // potential throws from many methods below.
                BufferedWriter fout = new BufferedWriter(
                                        new FileWriter("myfile"));

                char carr[] = new char[5];
                int x;
                String s = "GHIJK";
                x = (int)'A';
                carr[0] = 'B';
                carr[1] = 'C';
                carr[2] = 'D';
                carr[3] = 'E';
                carr[4] = 'F';
                fout.write(x);
                fout.write(carr, 0, 5);
                fout.write(s, 1, 3);
                fout.close();
                readIt();
        }

        static void readIt() throws IOException
        {           // potential throws from many methods below.
                BufferedReader fin = new BufferedReader(
                                        new FileReader("myfile"));
                char carr[] = new char[5];
                int x;
                String s;

                if((x = fin.read()) == -1)
                        System.exit(1);
                fin.read(carr, 0, 5);
                s = fin.readLine();
                fin.close();
```

**15. Java Terminal and File I/O**

```
        System.out.print("\nData: " + (char)x);
        System.out.println(carr + s);
        System.out.flush();
    }
}
```

**Output:**
```
ABCDEFHIJ
```

# BINARY FILE I/O

- Binary (also called raw) file I/O is supported by the DataInputStream and DataOutputStream classes. Normal ASCII files can also be accessed by methods of these classes.

- Data retrieved from files can be used in processing or displayed in TextFields and TextAreas.

- Some of the important I/O methods are:

## Constructors

**DataInputStream(InputStream finobj)** - create DataInputStream object for input using InputStream object.

> Example:
> ```
>         FileInputStream fi = new FileInputStream("myFile");
>         DataInputStream fin = new DataInputStream(fi);
> ```

**DataOutputStream(OutputStream fobj)** - create DataOutputStream object for output using OutputStream object.

> Example:
> ```
>         FileOutputStream fo = new FileOutputStream("myfile");
>         DataOutputStream fout = new DataOutputStream(fo);
> ```

## Read Methods

**byte readByte()** - reads one byte of data from the file. Returns -1 at the end of the file. Throws IOException if I/O error occurs.

> Example:
> ```
> int cj;
> while((cj = fin.readByte()) != -1)
> ```

**int read(byte barr[])** - reads bytes placing them in the array up to the size of the array. Returns the number of bytes actually read, or -1 at the end of the file. Throws IOException if I/O error occurs. Blocks until some input is fetched.

> Example:
> ```
> byte barr[] = new byte[80];
> while((num_read = fin.read(barr)) != -1)
> ```

**int read(byte barr[], int b_offset, int max_num)** - reads bytes placing them in the array up to max_num bytes. Places the bytes in array starting at barr[b_offset]. Returns the number of bytes actually read, or -1 at the end of the file. Throws IOException if I/O error occurs. Blocks until some input is fetched.

> Example:
> ```
> byte barr[] = new byte[80];
> while((num_read = fin.read(barr, 3, 10)) != -1)
> ```

**void readFully(byte barr[])** - reads bytes placing them in the array up to the size of the array. Blocks until all bytes are read. Throws IOException if I/O error occurs. Throws EOFException if end of file occurs before all bytes are read.

> Example:
> ```
> byte barr[] = new byte[80];
> fin.readFully(barr));
> ```

**void readFully(byte barr[], int b_offset, int max_num)** - reads bytes placing them in the array up to max_num bytes. Waits until all bytes are read. Places the bytes in array starting at barr[b_offset]. Throws IOException if I/O error occurs. Throws EOFException if end of file occurs before all bytes are read.

> Example:
> ```
> byte barr[] = new byte[80];
> fin.readFully(barr, 3, 10);
> ```

## Methods For Reading Specific Types of Input

These DataInputStream methods throw an IOException if an I/O error occurs.

**String readLine()** - reads one line from a file returning it in a String object. Lines are terminated with a \n, \r, \n\r or the end of the file.

**byte readByte()** - reads and returns one byte from the file.

**int readUnsignedByte()** - reads one unsigned byte from the file. Returns value as an int.

**short readShort()** - reads and returns one short from the file.

**int readUnsignedShort()** - reads an unsigned short from the file.

**char readChar()** - reads and returns a 16-bit char from the file.

**int readInt()** - reads and returns an int from the file.

**long readLong()** - reads and returns one long from the file.

**float readFloat()** - reads and returns one float from the file.

**double readDouble()** - reads and returns one double from the file.

**boolean readBoolean()** - reads and returns one boolean from the file. (Reads in a byte from file.)

**int skipBytes(int num_bytes)** - skips num_bytes of input from file. Returns the number of bytes actually skipped. Throws IOException if I/O error occurs.

Example:
```
fin.skipBytes(80);
```

## Write Methods

These DataOutputStream methods throw IOException if an I/O error occurs.

**void write(int c)** - writes one byte of data to the file.

> Example:
> ```
> int cj;
> ...
> fout.write(cj);   // only byte containing character written
> ```

**void write(byte barr[])** - writes the entire array to the file.

> Example:
> ```
> byte barr[] = new byte[80];
> ...
> fout.write(barr);
> ```

**void write(byte barr[], int b_offset, int num)** - writes num bytes from array to file starting from barr[b_offset].

> Example:
> ```
> byte barr[] = new byte[80];
> ...
> fout.write(barr, 3, 10);
> ```

**void flush()** - causes the output buffer contents to be sent to the file.

**int size()** - returns number of bytes written in last write.

## Methods For Writing Specific Types of Output

**void writeBytes(String s)** - writes the characters in the string object to the file as bytes.

**void writeChars(String s)** - writes the characters in the string object to the file as chars.

**void writeByte(int j)** - writes one byte to the file.

**void writeShort(int j)** - writes one short to the file.

**void writeChar(int j)** - writes a 16-bit char to the file.

**void writeInt(int j)** - writes an int to the file.

**void writeLong(long j)** - writes one long to the file.

**void writeFloat(float f)** - writes one float to the file.

**void writeDouble(double d)** - writes one double to the file.

**void writeBoolean(boolean b)** - writes one boolean to the file. (Writes a byte to file.)
1 = true;   0 = false (<u>in the file only</u>).

## Closing a File

**void close()** - closes file input stream.

Examples:
```
fin.close();
fout.close();
```

## Program Illustrating Binary DataInputFile and DataOutputFile I/O

**File: c15_5.java**

```java
import java.io.*;

public class c15_5
{
        public static void main(String args[]) throws IOException
        {               // potential throws from many methods below.
                FileOutputStream fo = new FileOutputStream("myfile");
                DataOutputStream fout = new DataOutputStream(fo);

                byte barr[] = new byte[5];
                byte x;
                x = (byte) 'A';
                barr[0] = (byte) 'B';
                barr[1] = (byte) 'C';
                barr[2] = (byte) 'D';
                barr[3] = (byte) 'E';
                barr[4] = (byte) 'F';
                fout.writeByte(x);
                fout.write(barr);
                fout.writeDouble(77.88);
                fout.close();
                readIt();
        }

        static void readIt() throws IOException
        {
                File f = new File("myfile");
                FileInputStream fi = new FileInputStream(f);
                DataInputStream fin = new DataInputStream(fi);
                byte barr[] = new byte[5];
                int x;
                double y;
                x = fin.readByte();
                if(fin.read(barr) == -1)
                        System.exit(0);
                y = fin.readDouble();
                fin.close();
                System.out.println("File: "       + f.getName());
                System.out.println("Path: "       + f.getPath());
                System.out.println("Size: "       + f.length());
                System.out.print("\nData: " + (char)x);
                System.out.write(barr);
                System.out.print(" " + y);
                System.out.flush();
        }
}
```

**Output:**
```
File: myfile
Path: myfile
Size: 14
Data: ABCDEF 77.88
```

# READING URL INPUT STREAMS

- Java allows you to read URL's as input streams similar to file input streams.
- The procedure begins by defining an InputStream object and opening an InputStream for it.
- Then the InputStream can be read with the standard read() methods.

**File: c15_6.html**
```
<applet code="c15_6.class" width = 300 height = 170></applet>
```

**File: c15_6.java**
```java
import java.net.*;
import java.io.*;
import java.lang.*;
import java.applet.*;
import java.awt.*;

public class c15_6 extends Applet
{
        byte barr[] = new byte[52];// 52 bytes in top line of file.

        public void init()
        {
                setBackground(Color.white);
                try
                {
                        InputStream iurl = new URL(getDocumentBase(),
                                                "c14_1.html").openStream();
                        iurl.read(barr, 0, barr.length);
                        iurl.close();
                }
                catch(Exception e) { }
        }
        public void paint(Graphics g)
        {
                g.drawBytes(barr, 0, barr.length, 10, 70);
        }
}
```

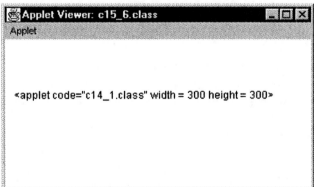

# RANDOM ACCESS FILE I/O

- The RandomAccessFile class supports random I/O with files.

- You can position the read/write point within a file, and read or write the file starting from the selected point. This allows you to leap to a record in a data file and read or modify it.

- All the following RandomAccessFile methods throw an IOException if an I/O error occurs.

- Some of the important methods in class RandomAccessFile are:

## Constructors

**RandomAccessFile(String fileName, String mode)** - creates a random access interface for the specified file. The mode can specify read-only with "r" or read/write with "rw". Throws an IOException if an I/O error occurs.

> Example:
> ```
> RandomAccessFile r = new RandomAccessFile("myfile", "rw");
> ```

**RandomAccessFile(File fileObj, String mode)** - creates a random access interface for the specified file. The mode can specify read-only with "r" or read/write with "rw". Throws an IOException if an I/O error occurs.

> Example:
> ```
> File f = new File("myfile");
> RandomAccessFile r = new RandomAccessFile(f, "rw");
> ```

## Random Access Methods

These important methods enable you to move around in a file and also to determine where you are relative to the end of the file.

**long getFilePointer()** - returns location in file as the number of bytes from the beginning of the file.

**void seek(long pos)** - moves read/write point to pos bytes from the beginning of the file.

**long length()** - returns length of the file.

## Read Methods (Same as Binary Read Methods)

**int read()** - reads one byte of data from the file. Returns -1 at the end of the file.

> Example:
> ```
> int cj;
> while((cj = r.read()) != -1)
> ```

**int read(byte barr[])** - reads bytes placing them in the array up to the size of the array. Returns the number of bytes actually read, or -1 at the end of the file.

> Example:
> ```
> byte barr[] = new byte[80];
> while((num_read = r.read(barr)) != -1)
> ```

**int read(byte barr[], int b_offset, int max_num)** - reads bytes placing them in the array up to max_num bytes. Places the bytes in array starting at barr[b_offset]. Returns the number of bytes actually read, or -1 at the end of the file.

> Example:
> ```
> byte barr[] = new byte[80];
> while((num_read = r.read(barr, 3, 10)) != -1)
> ```

**void readFully(byte barr[])** - reads bytes placing them in the array up to the size of the array. Waits until all bytes are read. Throws EOFException if end of file occurs before all bytes are read.

> Example:
> ```
> byte barr[] = new byte[80];
> r.readFully(barr));
> ```

**void readFully(byte barr[], int b_offset, int max_num)** - reads bytes placing them in the array up to max_num bytes. Waits until all bytes are read. Places the bytes in array starting at barr[b_offset]. Throws EOFException if end of file occurs before all bytes are read.

> Example:
> ```
> byte barr[] = new byte[80];
> r.readFully(barr, 3, 10);
> ```

**int skipBytes(int num_bytes)** - skips num_bytes of input from file. Returns the number of bytes actually skipped.

> Example:
> ```
> r.skipBytes(80);
> ```

## Methods For Reading Specific Types of Input

**String readLine()** - reads one line from a file returning it in a String object. Lines are terminated with a \n or the end of the file.

**byte readByte()** - reads and returns one byte from the file.

**int readUnsignedByte()** - reads one unsigned byte from the file. Returns value as an int.

**short readShort()** - reads and returns one short from the file.

**int readUnsignedShort()** - reads an unsigned short from the file.

**char readChar()** - reads and returns a 16-bit char from the file.

**int readInt()** - reads and returns an int from the file.

**long readLong()** - reads and returns one long from the file.

**float readFloat()** - reads and returns one float from the file.

**double readDouble()** - reads and returns one double from the file.

**boolean readBoolean()** - reads and returns one boolean from the file. (Reads in a byte from file.)

## Write Methods (Same as Binary Write Methods)

**void write(int c)** - writes one byte of data to the file.

> Example:
> ```
> int cj;
> ...
> r.write(cj);    // only byte containing character written
> ```

**void write(byte barr[])** - writes the entire array to the file.

> Example:
> ```
> byte barr[] = new byte[80];
> ...
> r.write(barr);
> ```

**void write(byte barr[], int b_offset, int num)** - writes num bytes from array to file starting from barr[b_offset].

> Example:
> ```
> byte barr[] = new byte[80];
> ...
> r.write(barr, 3, 10);
> ```

## Methods For Writing Specific Types of Output

**void writeBytes(String s)** - writes the characters in the string object to the file as bytes.

**void writeChars(String s)** - writes the characters in the string object to the file as chars.

**void writeByte()** - writes one byte to the file.

**void writeShort()** - writes one short to the file.

**void writeChar()** - writes a 16-bit char to the file.

**void writeInt()** - writes an int to the file.

**void writeLong()** - writes one long to the file.

**void writeFloat()** - writes one float to the file.

**void writeDouble()** - writes one double to the file.

**void writeBoolean()** - writes one boolean to the file. (Writes an int to file.)

## Closing a File

**void close()** - closes file.

Example:
```
r.close();
```

## Program Illustrating Random Access

**File: c15_7.java**

```java
import java.io.*;

public class c15_7
{
        public static void main(String args[]) throws IOException
        {
                FileOutputStream fo = new FileOutputStream("myfile");
                DataOutputStream fout = new DataOutputStream(fo);

                byte barr[] = new byte[50];
                for(int j = 0; j < 50; j++)
                        barr[j] = (byte) (65 + j);
                fout.write(barr); // puts ABC… in file.
                fout.close();
                readIt();
        }

        static void readIt() throws IOException
        {
                RandomAccessFile r = new RandomAccessFile("myfile", "rw");

                byte barr[] = new byte[10];

                r.seek(10);
                if(r.read(barr) == -1) // reads KLM… from file
                        System.exit(0);
                System.out.print("\nData: ");
                System.out.write(barr);
                System.out.flush();

                for(int j = 0; j < 10; j++)
                        barr[j] = (byte) (97 + j);
                r.seek(10);
                r.write(barr); // puts abc … in file.

                r.seek(11);
                if(r.read(barr) == -1) // reads bcd … from file.
                        System.exit(0);
                r.close();

                System.out.print("\nData: ");
                System.out.write(barr);
                System.out.flush();
        }
}
```

**Output:**

```
Data: KLMNOPQRST
Data: bcdefghijU
```

# SUMMARY

This module has described terminal and file I/O in the Java programming environment. The kinds of file handling we examined are:

- File information methods

- Text file I/O

- Binary file I/O

- Buffered file I/O

- Inputting URL streams

- Random access files

**15. Java Terminal and File I/O**

468

# EXERCISES

1.  Using binary I/O develop a program which creates a file containing an int 5, a double 9.87, and a long 123456L. Then have the program read the data in the file and display it on screen.

2.  Using BufferedReader and BufferedWriter develop a program which creates a file containing an int 5, a double 9.87, and a long 123456L. Then have the program read the data in the file and display it on screen.

3.  Change the program of exercise 1 to do random access when it reads the created file. Seek to the location of the double in the file, fetch its value and display it on screen.

# *Appendix A. Java Networking With Sockets*

## OBJECTIVES

At the end of this module you should be able to:

- Describe and perform local and network interprocess communication with Java sockets.

# CLIENT-SERVER INTERPROCESS COMMUNICATION

Sockets are a means of communicating between processes—usually over a network.

- TCP sockets called Stream sockets are sockets which transmit messages of variable length.

- UDP sockets called Datagram sockets are sockets which transmit messages in packets. The packets can arrive out of order and may be lost.

The typical model for socket communications (with some socket-related methods displayed) is the client-server model:

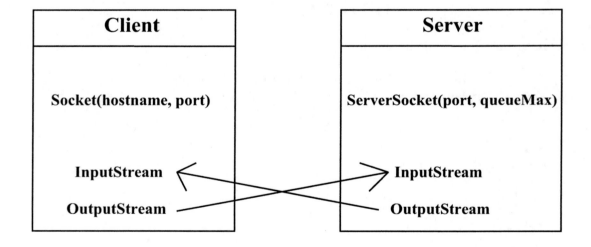

# SERVER SOCKETS

The ServerSocket class supports TCP/IP network sockets on the server side. Some of the important methods used in TCP/IP socket communications are:

## Constructors

These constructors throw IOExceptions if an I/O error takes place.

**ServerSocket(int port)** - This constructor creates a server socket on the port.

**ServerSocket(int port, int queueMax)** - This constructor creates a server socket on the port and specifies the maximum number of connect requests which can be queued until an accept() is made.

## Server Socket Methods

**Socket accept()** - accepts a connection from another socket. Blocks until connection made. Throws IOException if an I/O error occurs while waiting.

**void close()** - closes the server socket. Throws Ioexception if an I/O error occurs.

# SOCKET CLASS

The Socket class supports TCP/IP network sockets on the client side. Some of the important methods used in TCP/IP socket communications are:

## Constructors

These constructors throw IOExceptions if an I/O error takes place.

**Socket(String host, int port)** - This constructor creates a socket for the specified host computer at the specified port.

**Socket(InetAddress address, int port)** - This constructor creates a socket for the host computer at the specified address at the specified port.

**InetAddress InetAddress.getByName(String computerName)** – This static method creates an InetAddress object containing the Internet address of the computer named as the argument of the method call. On each platform it looks up the address in the relevant system file containing computer name – internet address pairs. If *null* is the argument it fetches the Internet address of the computer on which it is executed.

# METHODS FOR SETTING UP COMMUNICATIONS

These methods create objects for the input and output of data through sockets. These objects can be used with file I/O methods to send and receive data. The methods throw IOExceptions if an I/O error takes place.

**InputStream getInputStream()** - gets an InputStream for the current Socket object which can be used with file input methods.

**OutputStream getOutputStream()** - gets an OutputStream for the current Socket object which can be used with file output methods.

**void close()** - closes the server socket. Throws IOException if an I/O error occurs.

# NETWORK SOCKET PROGRAMS

The following examples are prototypes illustrating server and client Java programs. To test run these programs:

1. Open up an MS-DOS prompt window (a command window in UNIX or LINUX).
2. Compile and run the below standalone Java server program. It will block (wait).
3. Open up another MS-DOS prompt window (a command window in UNIX or LINUX).
4. Compile and run the standalone Java client program on the next page.
5. The client program will automatically connect to the server program by looping back through your computer's socket interface. Data will be exchanged and displayed in each window.

**Server Program:**
**File: cA_1.java**

```java
import java.net.*;
import java.io.*;
import java.awt.*;

public class cA_1
{
        public static void main(String args[]) throws IOException
        {
                ServerSocket ss = new ServerSocket(2001, 5);// port 2001
                Socket s;
                DataOutputStream os;
                DataInputStream is;
                byte barr [] = new byte[20];

                System.out.println("Server:");

                s = ss.accept(); // blocks until client connects
                        // sets up communication channels
                os = new DataOutputStream(s.getOutputStream());
                is = new DataInputStream(s.getInputStream());

                for(int j = 0; j < 20; j++)
                        barr[j] = (byte) (j + 97);

                        // reads and writes client.
                os.write(barr);
                is.read(barr);

                s.close();

                System.out.write(barr);
                System.out.flush();
        }
}
```

**Client Program:**
**File: cA_2.java**

```java
import java.net.*;
import java.io.*;
import java.awt.*;

public class cA_2
{
        public static void main(String args[]) throws IOException
        {                   // access server on port 2001 of this computer.
                Socket s = new Socket(InetAddress.getByName(null),
                                                        2001);
                DataInputStream is;
                DataOutputStream os;
                byte barr [] = new byte[20];

                        // establish communication channels.
                is = new DataInputStream(s.getInputStream());
                os = new DataOutputStream(s.getOutputStream());

                System.out.println("Client:");

                        // read socket.
                is.read(barr);
                System.out.write(barr);
                System.out.flush();

                for(int j = 0; j < 20; j++)
                        barr[j] = (byte) (j + 65);

                        // write socket.
                os.write(barr);
                s.close();
        }
}
```

# *Appendix B.  Supplemental Material*

## OBJECTIVES

At the end of this module you should be able to:

- Implement more advanced Java language features.

# TEXTFIELD DESIGN

TextFields have a number of features which make them an effective way of obtaining keyboard input with basic editing capabilities from end users. These features include:

- support for editing keys to insert, delete, and overwrite text.

- automatic tabbing between TextFields.

- support for highlighting text using select() and selectAll(). Highlighted text "disappears" when ordinary keys are pressed. Using the arrow keys allows insertions to be made in highlighted text.

- support for passwords and hidden fields using the setEchoChar() method.

# METHODS SUPPORTING TEXTFIELD MANAGEMENT

Some of the important methods supporting TextField management and manipulation are:

**TextField(int cols)** - This constructor initializes a TextField object with cols columns of text displayed.

**TextField(String s, int cols)** - This constructor initializes a TextField object with the characters of s displayed in a TextField of cols columns.

**setBackground(Color c)** - This method can set the background color of a TextField object.

**setForeground(Color c )** - This method can set the foreground color of a TextField.

**setText(String s)** - This method places a string of characters inside a TextField object.

**setEditable(boolean b)** - This method specifies whether a TextField object is editable. A TextField object is editable by default unless setEditable(false) is applied to it.

**requestFocus()** - This method can be used to activate a TextField for input. The cursor is placed in the TextField display and the keyboard text entry is enabled. This method can be run from an actionPerformed() method to automatically switch between TextFields when the ENTER key is pressed.

**select(int begIndex, int endIndex)** - This method selects (reverse videos) the characters starting from the begIndex up to but not including the endIndex character and highlights the characters. The first character in a TextField has index number zero. If an arrow key is the first key pressed within a highlighted area the highlight is removed and the text can be normally edited. If a "normal" text key is pressed, then the highlighted text is replaced with the typed key character.

**selectAll()** - This method selects all of the characters in a TextField and highlights them. The effect of pressing keys is the same as in the above select() overload.

**getSelectedText()** - This method returns a String object containing the text selected with a selectAll() or a select().

**getSelectionStart()** - This method returns an int - the index number of the first character of selected text.

**getSelectionEnd()** - This method returns the index number of the character after the last character of selected text.

**getText()** - This method returns a String containing the text within a TextField object.

**setEchoChar(char c)** - This method sets the character displayed in a TextField on screen when a keyboard character is typed. This method can be used to create TextFields for passwords or other privileged data entries which should not be displayed on screen.

**setCaretPosition(int pos)** - sets cursor position to point before character of the specified index number.

An example which illustrates the use of these methods and moving between textfields using the tab key and the ENTER key is:

**File: cB_1.html**
```
<applet code="cB_1.class" width = 500 height = 350>
</applet>
```

**File: cB_1.java**
```java
import java.awt.*;
import java.awt.event.*;
import java.applet.Applet;

public class cB_1 extends Applet implements ActionListener
{
        private TextField t1, t2, t3 , t4;
        private String text = "";
        private Font f1 = new Font("SansSerif", Font.BOLD, 16);
        private Graphics g1;
        private int j = 0;

        public void init()
        {
                g1 = getGraphics();
                t1 = new TextField(10);
                t1.setFont(f1);
                t1.setText("ABCDEFGH");
                add(t1);
                t2 = new TextField(10);
                t2.setBackground(Color.yellow); // sets text field colors.
                t2.setForeground(Color.blue);
                t2.setText("ABCDEFGH");
                add(t2);

                t3 = new TextField(10);
                t3.setBackground(Color.blue);
                t3.setForeground(Color.white);
                t3.setText("ABCDEFGH");
                t3.setEchoChar('*'); // set the display character to *
                add(t3);
                t4 = new TextField(10);
                t4.setBackground(Color.yellow);
                t4.setForeground(Color.red);
```

```java
        t4.setText("ABCDEFGH");  // set the text in the text field.
        add(t4);
        t1.addActionListener(this);
        t2.addActionListener(this);
        t3.addActionListener(this);
        t4.addActionListener(this);
}
public void start()
{ // highlights all of t1, puts in focus, sets cursor position.
        t1.selectAll();
        t1.requestFocus();
        t1.setCaretPosition(3);
}
public void actionPerformed(ActionEvent e)
{
        g1.setFont(f1);
        g1.setColor(Color.black);
        if(e.getSource() instanceof TextField)
        {
                if(e.getSource().equals(t1))
                {
                        text = "Field 1: " + t1.getText()
                                + " Selecting 1-3 in t2";
                        g1.drawString(text, 40, 120 + 15 * j++);
                        t2.requestFocus();
                        t2.select(1,4);
                        text = "                Selected Text = "
                                + t2.getSelectedText();
                        text = text + " Start-End Select = "
                                + t2.getSelectionStart()
                                + " - "
                                + t2.getSelectionEnd();
                }
                else if(e.getSource().equals(t2))
                {
                        text = "Field 2: " + t2.getText();
                        t3.requestFocus();
                        t3.selectAll();
                }
                else if(e.getSource().equals(t3))
                {
                        text = "Field 3: " + t3.getText();
                        t4.requestFocus();
                        t4.selectAll();
                }
                else if(e.getSource().equals(t4))
                {
                        text = "Field 4: " + t4.getText();
                        t1.requestFocus();
                        t1.selectAll();
                }
```

```
if(j > 15)
{
        j = 0;
        g1.clearRect(0, 0, 500, 350);
}
g1.drawString(text, 40, 120 + 15 * j++);
        }
    }
}
```

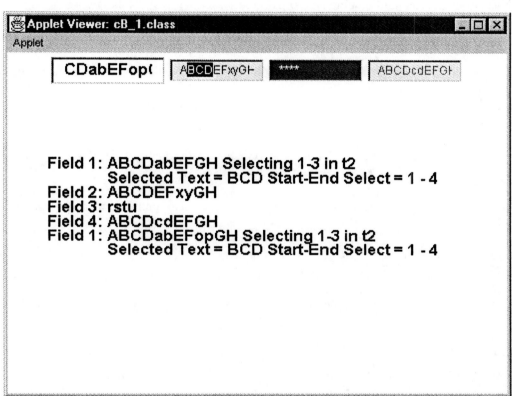

# COMPONENT POSITIONING AND LOCATION

Components can be positioned on an applet using default placement (centered FlowLayout), or using a layout such as BorderLayout and placing the component within a region of the layout.

Another way of placing a component on an applet is with the setLocation() or setBounds() methods.

Some of the methods which relate to the sizing of components, their placement and their location are:

**getScreenSize()** - This awt.Toolkit class method returns a Dimension object containing the overall screen size in pixels.

**getSize()** - This awt method returns a Dimension object containing the size of the recipient object in pixels.

**setLocation(int x, int y)** - This awt.Component method positions a component at the specified x and y coordinates.

**setBounds(int x, int y, int width, int height)** - This awt.Component method positions a component at the specified x and y coordinates, and with the specified width and height.

**setSize(int x, int y)** - This awt.Component method resizes a component with the specified width and height.

**getLocation()** - This awt.Component method returns a Point object containing the upper left hand pixel coordinates of a component. Point objects contain an x variable and y variable.

**getComponentAt(int x, int y)** - This awt.Component method returns the Component object at the specified coordinates.

Examples of the preceding methods:

**File: cB_2.html**
```
<applet code="cB_2.class" width = 520 height = 350>
</applet>
```

**File: cB_2.java**
```java
import java.awt.*;
import java.awt.event.*;
import java.applet.Applet;

public class cB_2 extends Applet implements MouseListener,
                                            ActionListener
{
        private Button b1, b2, b3, b4;
        private String text = "";
        private Graphics g1;
        private int j = 0, k = 0;
        private Dimension dScreen;

        public void init()
        {
                setLayout(null);
                g1 = getGraphics();
                dScreen = this.getToolkit().getScreenSize();
                b1 = new Button("B1");
                add(b1);
                b2 = new Button("B2");
                add(b2);
                b3 = new Button("B3");
                add(b3);
                b4 = new Button("B4");
                add(b4);
                b1.setBounds(50,50, b1.getPreferredSize().width,
                                    b1.getPreferredSize().height);
                b2.setBounds(100,100, b2.getPreferredSize().width,
                                    b2.getPreferredSize().height);
                b3.setBounds(150, 150, 50, 50);
                b4.setBounds(200,250, b4.getPreferredSize().width,
                                    b4.getPreferredSize().height);

                b1.requestFocus(); // pressing spacebar executes button
                                   // in Windows 95.  RETURN may execute
                                   // button on other platforms.
                addMouseListener(this);
                b1.addActionListener(this);
                b2.addActionListener(this);
                b3.addActionListener(this);
                b4.addActionListener(this);
        }
```

```java
public void paint(Graphics g)
{
        text = "Screen: Width: " + dScreen.width +
                                " Height: " + dScreen.height;
        g1.drawString(text, 200, 10);
}
public void actionPerformed(ActionEvent e)
{
        if(e.getSource() instanceof Button)
        {
                text = ((Button)e.getSource()).getLabel();
                g1.drawString(text, 40, 120 + 15 * j++);

                Point p = ((Button)e.getSource()).getLocation();

                text = "Location: x = " + p.x + " y = " + p.y;
                g1.drawString(text, 200, 25 + 15*k);

                text = "Comp = " + getComponentAt(p.x+10,
                                        p.y+10).toString();
                g1.drawString(text, 200, 40 + 15*k);
                k += 2;
                if(j > 15 || k > 15)
                {
                        j = k = 0;
                        repaint();
                }
        }
}
public void mousePressed(MouseEvent e)
{
        text = "Location: x = " + e.getX() + " y = "
                                        + e.getY();
        g1.drawString(text, 200, 25 + 15*k);

        text = "Comp = " + getComponentAt(e.getX(),
                                e.getY()).toString();
        g1.drawString(text, 200, 40 + 15*k);
        k += 2;
        if(j > 15 || k > 15)
        {
                j = k = 0;
                repaint();
        }
}
public void mouseClicked(MouseEvent e) {}
public void mouseReleased(MouseEvent e) {}
public void mouseEntered(MouseEvent e)  {}
public void mouseExited(MouseEvent e)  {}
}
```

The output applet is:

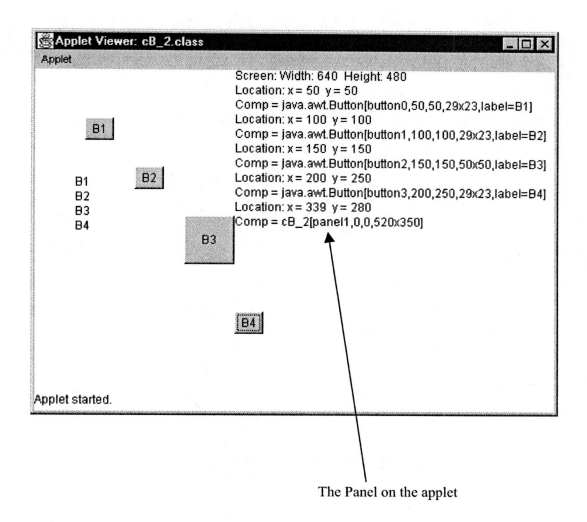

The Panel on the applet

# FOCUS - SELECTION OF COMPONENTS

Often when we start an applet or open a window we would like a component, such as a button, to be activated so pressing ENTER or spacebar automatically causes the component event to be generated. Or we may wish a textField to be automatically activated when an applet starts. Activating a component is called putting it in focus.

The requestFocus() method places a component in focus. Clicking with a mouse on a component also usually places a component in focus. For example,

```
obj.requestFocus();
```

puts the focus on the component obj.

The transferFocus() method places the focus on the next component following the recipient object component. For example,

```
obj.transferFocus();
```

puts the focus on the next component in the layout after obj.

When a component loses focus a lost focus event is generated which is handled by the FocusLost() event handler. When a component gains focus a "got" focus event is generated which is handled by the FocusGained() event handler.

The order of events when one component loses focus and another gains focus is:

1. FocusLost event
2. FocusGained event
3. component event

For example, clicking on a button can result in three events: previous component in focus loses focus, button gets focus, and Button event is generated.

Some focus-related methods are:

**requestFocus()** - This method can be used to activate a component such as a TextField for input.

**transferFocus()** - This method places the focus on the next component after the recipient object component.

**focusGained(FocusEvent e)** - This event handler method which you define executes when a component gets the focus. The programmer provides this method.

**focusLost(FocusEvent e)** - This event handler method which you define executes when a component loses the focus. The programmer provides this method.

**File: cB_3.html**
```
<applet code="cB_3.class" width = 520 height = 350></applet>
```

**File: cB_3.java**
```java
import java.awt.*;
import java.awt.event.*;
import java.applet.Applet;

public class cB_3 extends Applet implements FocusListener,
                                            ActionListener
{
        private Button b1, b2, b3, b4;
        private String text = "";
        private Graphics g1;
        private int j = 0, k = 0;

        public void init()
        {
                g1 = getGraphics();
                setBackground(Color.white);
                b1 = new Button("B1");
                add(b1);
                b2 = new Button("B2");
                add(b2);
                b3 = new Button("B3");
                add(b3);
                b4 = new Button("B4");
                add(b4);
                b1.requestFocus(); // pressing spacebar executes button
                                   // in Windows 95.  RETURN may execute
                                   // button on other platforms.
                b1.addFocusListener(this);
                b2.addFocusListener(this);
                b3.addFocusListener(this);
                b4.addFocusListener(this);

                b1.addActionListener(this);
                b2.addActionListener(this);
                b3.addActionListener(this);
                b4.addActionListener(this);
        }
        public void focusGained(FocusEvent e)
        {
                // code for focusGained events.
                if(e.getSource() instanceof Button)
                        g1.drawString("Got Focus: "
                                + ((Button)e.getSource()).getLabel(),
                                40, 120 + 15 * j++);
        }
```

```java
public void focusLost(FocusEvent e)
{
        // code for LostFocus events.
        if(e.getSource() instanceof Button)
                g1.drawString("Lost Focus: "
                + ((Button)e.getSource()).getLabel(),
                40, 120 + 15 * j++);
}

public void actionPerformed(ActionEvent e)
{
        if(e.getSource() instanceof Button)
        {
                text = ((Button)e.getSource()).getLabel();
                g1.drawString(text, 40, 120 + 15 * j++);

                Point p = ((Button)e.getSource()).getLocation();

                text = "Location: x = " + p.x + "  y = " + p.y;
                g1.drawString(text, 200, 50 + 15*k++);
                if(j > 15 || k > 15)
                {
                        j = k = 0;
                        repaint();
                }
                if(e.getSource().equals(b3))
                {
                        ((Button)e.getSource()).transferFocus();
                        g1.drawString("nextFocus ran.", 40,
                                        120 + 15 * j++);
                }
        }
}
}
```

## Output Applet

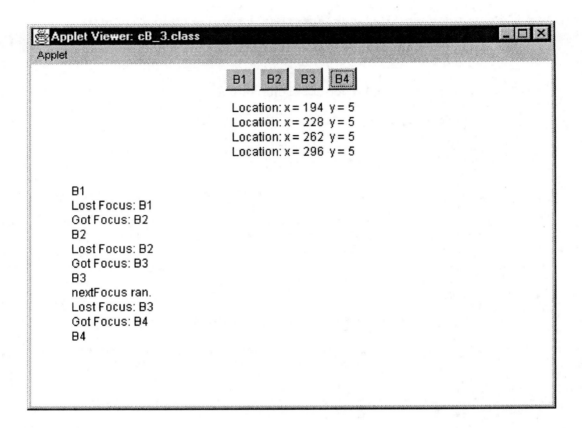

# CARDLAYOUT

The awt.CardLayout class implements a layout scheme based on a stack of cards paradigm. It is analogous to tab card layouts (without the tabs) in windows environments. Some of the important methods for CardLayouts are:

**CardLayout(int horizontalGap, int verticalGap)** - constructor for a CardLayout specifying the horizontal and vertical borders.

**add(String label, Component c)** - adds a card to a CardLayout. The component is placed on the card. The label becomes the name of the card.

**cardLayoutObj.show(Component c, String label)** - shows the card of the component c with the corresponding label. c is often a panel with a CardLayout on it.

An example of an applet with a CardLayout. The applet simulates tab cards using a canvas for the tabs and a set of cards as the tab cards. This approach can be used practically. However it is far easier to use the tab cards provided by the Swing package. See the Appendix on the Swing package.

**File: cB_4.html**
```
<applet code="cB_4.class" width = 450 height = 350>
</applet>
```

**File: cB_4.java**
```
import java.awt.*;
import java.awt.event.*;
import java.applet.Applet;

public class cB_4 extends Applet implements ActionListener,
                                            MouseListener
{
        private CardLayout c;
        private Button b1, b2, b3v, b3h, b4, b5, b6, b7, b8;
        private List cards = new List(4, false);
        private Panel p1, p2, pc, pc1, pc2, pc3, pc4;
        private String text = "";
        private int j = 0, index = 0;
        private String labels[] = {"Circle", "Square", "Oval",
                                                "Triangle"};
        private String selection;
        private cardCanvas cc;

        public void init()
        {
                setBackground(Color.white);
```

```java
setLayout(new GridLayout(1,2));
pc = new Panel();
pc1 = new Panel();
pc2 = new Panel();
pc3 = new Panel();
pc4 = new Panel();
p1 = new Panel();
p2 = new Panel();

p1.setLayout(new BorderLayout());
cc = new cardCanvas(labels); // canvas for the tabs.
p1.add("North", cc);

c = new CardLayout(0, 0); // sets 0 pixel borders.
pc.setLayout(c);   // holds the cards.

b1 = new Button("Circle");
pc1.add(b1);
pc1.setBackground(Color.lightGray);
pc.add("Circle", pc1);

b2 = new Button("Square");
pc2.add(b2);
pc2.setBackground(Color.lightGray);
pc.add("Square", pc2);

b3v = new Button("Vertical Oval");
b3h = new Button("Horizontal Oval");
pc3.add(b3v);
pc3.add(b3h);
pc3.setBackground(Color.lightGray);
pc.add("Oval", pc3);

b4 = new Button("Triangle");
pc4.add(b4);
pc4.setBackground(Color.lightGray);
pc.add("Triangle", pc4);

p1.add("Center", pc);

b5 = new Button("First");
p2.add(b5);
b6 = new Button("Previous");
p2.add(b6);
b7 = new Button("Next");
p2.add(b7);
b8 = new Button("Last");
p2.add(b8);

cards.add("Circle");
cards.add("Square");
```

```
              cards.add("Oval");
              cards.add("Triangle");
              p2.add(cards);

              add(p1);  add(p2);
              b7.requestFocus();
              b1.addActionListener(this);
              b2.addActionListener(this);
              b3v.addActionListener(this);
              b3h.addActionListener(this);
              b4.addActionListener(this);
              b5.addActionListener(this);
              b6.addActionListener(this);
              b7.addActionListener(this);
              b8.addActionListener(this);

              cards.addActionListener(this);

              cc.addMouseListener(this);
      }
   public void actionPerformed(ActionEvent e)
   {
              if(e.getSource() instanceof Button)
              {    // handles first, previous, next, and last buttons.
                     if(e.getSource().equals(b5))
                     {
                            c.first(pc);
                            index = 0;
                     }
                     else if(e.getSource().equals(b6))
                     {
                            c.previous(pc);
                            index--;
                            if(index < 0)
                                   index = labels.length - 1;
                     }
                     else if(e.getSource().equals(b7))
                     {
                            c.next(pc);
                            index++;
                            if(index >= labels.length)
                                   index = 0;
                     }
                     else if(e.getSource().equals(b8))
                     {
                            c.last(pc);
                            index = labels.length - 1;
                     }
              }
              else if(e.getSource() instanceof List)
              {    // handles events from list of cards.
```

```java
                        index = ((List)e.getSource())
                                          .getSelectedIndex();
                        c.show(pc, labels[index]);
                }
                cc.draw(index); // redraws tabs to front selected tab.

        }
        public void mousePressed(MouseEvent e)
        {  // handles clicks on tabs.
                index = e.getX()/50;

                if(index >= labels.length ) index--;
                selection = labels[index];
                c.show(pc, selection);  // shows card
                cc.draw(index);  // redraws tabs to front selected tab.
        }
        public void mouseClicked(MouseEvent e)
        { }
        public void mouseReleased(MouseEvent e)
        { }
        public void mouseEntered(MouseEvent e)
        { }
        public void mouseExited(MouseEvent e)
        { }
}

class cardCanvas extends Canvas
{
        private String labels[];
        private Graphics g1;

        cardCanvas(String labels[])
        {
                this.labels = labels;
                setBounds(25, 0, 200, 25);
                setBackground(Color.lightGray);
        }
        public void paint(Graphics g)
        {
                g1 = getGraphics();
                for(int j = labels.length - 1; j >= 0; j--)
                {
                        g.setColor(Color.lightGray);
                        g.fill3DRect(50*j-1, 5, 52, 23, true);
                        g.fill3DRect(50*j, 6, 50, 21, true);
                        g.setColor(Color.white);
                        g.drawString(labels[j], 50*j, 20);
                }
                g1.setColor(Color.white);
                g1.drawLine(50, 23, 250, 23);
        }
```

```
public void draw(int index)
{
        int x1, x2;
                // translates index numbers to pixels.
        x1 = 50*index;
        x2 = 50*(index + 1);
        paint(g1);
        g1.setColor(Color.lightGray);
        g1.fill3DRect(50*index-1, 5, 52, 23, true);
        g1.fill3DRect(50*index, 6, 50, 21, true);
        g1.drawLine(0, 23, 250, 23);

        g1.setColor(Color.white);
        g1.drawString(labels[index], 50*index, 20);

        g1.drawLine(0, 23, x1, 23);
        g1.drawLine(x2, 23, 250, 23);
}
}
```

**Cards**                    **canvas for tabs**

# GRIDBAGLAYOUT

The GridBagLayout superimposes a grid structure with rows and columns on a container.  Each row is as high as the highest component it contains.  Each column is as wide as the widest component it contains.

A component is placed in a container with a GridBagLayout using the setConstraints() method of class awt.GridBagLayout.  The setConstraints() method has the format

```
setConstraints(Component com, GridBagConstraints g)
```

The GridBagConstraints argument g must have the following parameters set prior to the setConstraints() call:

int gridx - horizontal grid cell location - starts with 0.
int gridy - vertical grid cell location - starts with 0.
int gridwidth - width of space for component - measured in cells.
int gridheight - height of space for component - measured in cells.
int fill - specifies whether component should grow to fill width and/or height.  Allowed values are:
> GridBagConstraints.HORIZONTAL - grow to fill horizontally.
> GridBagConstraints.VERTICAL - grow to fill vertically.
> GridBagConstraints.BOTH - grow to fill in both ways.
> GridBagConstraints.NONE - no growth.
int anchor - specifies how component is positioned within grid cells if space available.  The choices are:
> GridBagConstraints.CENTER
> GridBagConstraints.NORTH
> GridBagConstraints.SOUTH
> GridBagConstraints.EAST
> GridBagConstraints.WEST
> GridBagConstraints.NORTHWEST
> GridBagConstraints.NORTHEAST
> GridBagConstraints.SOUTHEAST
> GridBagConstraints.SOUTHWEST

double weightx - horizontal resize proportionality factor when container resized.  0.0 = no change - centered within allotted area.  1.0 is the maximum.
double weighty - vertical resize proportionality factor when container resized.  0.0 = no change - no change - centered within allotted area.  1.0 is the maximum.
int ipadx - horizontal padding of component (increases component's horizontal "size" by 2*ipadx).
int ipady - vertical padding of component (increases component's vertical "size" by 2*ipadx).
Insets insets - specifies margins on the sides of a component in pixels using the constructor:

```
Insets(int top, int left, int bottom, int right)
```

**An example of a GridBagLayout**

**File: cB_5.html**
```
<applet code="C_5.class" width = 400 height = 350>
</applet>
```

**File: cB_5.java**
```java
import java.awt.*;
import java.awt.event.*;
import java.applet.Applet;

public class cB_5 extends Applet implements ActionListener
{
        private GridBagLayout gb = new GridBagLayout();
        private Button b1, b2, b3, b4, b5, b6, b7, b8;
        private Panel p1;

        public void init()
        {
                setBackground(Color.white);
                p1 = new Panel();

                p1.setLayout(gb);
                b1 = new Button("B1");
                b2 = new Button("B2");
                b3 = new Button("B3");
                b4 = new Button("B4");
                b5 = new Button("B5");
                b6 = new Button("B6");
                b7 = new Button("B7");
                b8 = new Button("B8");
                b1.addActionListener(this);
                b2.addActionListener(this);
                b3.addActionListener(this);
                b4.addActionListener(this);
                b5.addActionListener(this);
                b6.addActionListener(this);
                b7.addActionListener(this);
                b8.addActionListener(this);
// The bagIt() method (defined on next page) places a component in the layout.
                bagIt(p1, new Label("Button 1"), 0, 0, 1, 1);
                bagIt(p1, b1, 0, 1, 1, 1);
                bagIt(p1, new Label("Button 2"), 0, 2, 1, 1);
                bagIt(p1, b2, 0, 3, 1, 1);
                bagIt(p1, new Label("Button 3"), 0, 4, 1, 1);
                bagIt(p1, b3, 0, 5, 1, 1);
                bagIt(p1, new Label("Button 4"), 1, 0, 1, 1);
                bagIt(p1, b4, 1, 1, 1, 1);
                bagIt(p1, new Label("Button 5"), 1, 2, 1, 1);
```

```
                bagIt(p1, b5, 1, 3, 1, 1);
                bagIt(p1, new Label("Button 6"), 1, 4, 1, 1);
                bagIt(p1, b6, 1, 5, 1, 1);
                bagIt(p1, new Label("Button 7"), 2, 0, 1, 1);
                bagIt(p1, b7, 2, 1, 1, 1);
                bagIt(p1, new Label("Button 8"), 2, 2, 1, 1);
                bagIt(p1, b8, 2, 3, 1, 1);

                this.setLayout(gb);
                bagIt(this, p1, 0, 0, 1, 1);
        }
        public void bagIt(Container con, Component com, int x,
                int y, int width, int height, int fill, int anchor,
                double xweight, double yweight, int ipadx, int ipady,
                int top, int left, int bottom, int right)
        {

                GridBagConstraints g = new GridBagConstraints();
                g.gridx = x;
                g.gridy = y;
                g.gridwidth = width;
                g.gridheight = height;
                g.fill = fill;
                g.anchor = anchor;
                g.weightx = xweight;
                g.weighty = yweight;
                g.ipadx = ipadx;
                g.ipady = ipady;
                if(top+right+bottom+left > 0)
                        g.insets = new Insets(top, left, bottom, right);
                ((GridBagLayout)con.getLayout()).setConstraints(com, g);
                con.add(com);
        }
        public void bagIt(Container con, Component com, int x,
                int y, int width, int height)
        {

                bagIt(con, com, x, y, width, height,
                        GridBagConstraints.HORIZONTAL,
                        GridBagConstraints.NORTHWEST,
                        0.0, 0.0, 0, 0, 0, 0, 0, 0);
        }
        public void actionPerformed(ActionEvent e)
        {
                // code for Buttons
        }
}
```

**Output applet:**

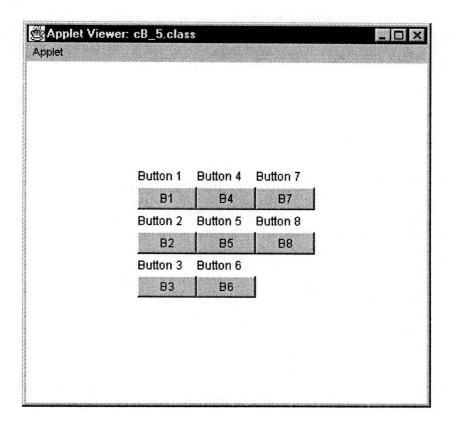

**501**

# FRAMES, DIALOGS AND WINDOWS

This section describes features of Frames, Dialogs and Windows. Some new Frame features are:

**setTitle(String s)** - This awt.Frame method sets a title for a frame.

**setIconImage(Image I)** - This awt.Frame method sets an icon image for the frame.

## Setting the Mouse Cursor in a Frame

**setCursor(new Cursor( int cursor_type))** - This awt.Frame method sets the cursor type. The types are:
> Frame.DEFAULT_CURSOR - platform-dependent cursor.
> Frame.CROSSHAIR_CURSOR - crosshair.
> Frame.HAND_CURSOR - hand cursor.
> Frame.MOVE_CURSOR - indicates something is being moved.
> Frame.TEXT_CURSOR - indicates text being edited.  Usually an I bar.
> Frame.WAIT_CURSOR - program is doing something.  Often an hourglass.
> Frame.E_RESIZE_CURSOR - cursor which indicates right edge being dragged.
> Frame.NE_RESIZE_CURSOR - upper right corner being dragged.
> Frame.NW_RESIZE_CURSOR - upper left corner being dragged.
> Frame.N_RESIZE_CURSOR - top edge being dragged.
> Frame.SE_RESIZE_CURSOR - lower right corner being dragged.
> Frame.SW_RESIZE_CURSOR - lower left corner being dragged.
> Frame.S_RESIZE_CURSOR - bottom edge being dragged.
> Frame.W_RESIZE_CURSOR - left edge being dragged.

- Dialog classes and window classes are created in a way which is similar to frame classes although there are differences in detail.

- A window class subclasses from class Window and displays as a window with a bar at the top and simple borders.  It is not modal - it cannot "capture the screen".

- A dialog class subclasses from class Dialog and displays a window with a title (possibly) and an "x" box to close the window.  Dialog windows will "capture the screen" if the modality is set to true or will not "capture the screen" if the modality is set to false.

- The following program illustrates the key features of Dialog and Window classes.

**File: cB_6.html**

```
<applet code="cB_6.class" width = 200 height =200></applet>
```

**File: cB_6.java**

```java
import java.awt.*;
import java.awt.event.*;
import java.awt.image.*;
import java.applet.Applet;

public class cB_6 extends Applet implements ActionListener
{   // defines applet.
        private myFrame f;
        private Button b;
        static boolean win = true;
        private Image img;

        public void init()
        {
                setSize(200, 150);
                b = new Button("myFrame?");
                add(b);
                img = getImage(getDocumentBase(), "myimage.gif");
                f = new myFrame("MYFRAME",img);
                b.addActionListener(this);
        }
        public void actionPerformed(ActionEvent e)
        {
                if(e.getSource() instanceof Button)
                {
                        if(win)
                        {
                                f.start();
                                win = false;
                        }
                        else
                        {
                                f.setVisible(false);
                                win = true;
                        }
                }
        }
}

class myFrame extends Frame implements ActionListener, WindowListener
{
        private Button b1, b2;
        private myDialog d;
        private myWindow w;
        public myFrame(String s, Image img)
        {
```

```
            super(s);
            setLayout(null);
            setBounds(300, 50, 200, 150);
            setBackground(Color.white);
            b1 = new Button("myDialog");
            b2 = new Button("myWindow");
            w = new myWindow(this);
            add(b1);
            add(b2);
            b1.setBounds(30, 50, 60, 27);
            b2.setBounds(120, 50, 65, 27);
            b1.addActionListener(this);
            b2.addActionListener(this);
            addWindowListener(this);
            setIconImage(img);
            setCursor(new Cursor(Frame.HAND_CURSOR));
    }
    public void start()
    {
            setVisible(true);
    }
    public void actionPerformed(ActionEvent e)
    {
            if( e.getSource().equals(b1)) // generates dialog
            {                             // modal!!
                    d = new myDialog(this, "MYDIALOG", true);
                    d.start();
            }
            else if(e.getSource().equals(b2))
            {
                    w.start();  // generates window.
            }
    }
    public void windowClosing(WindowEvent e)
    {
            cB_6.win = true;
            setVisible(false);
    }
    public void windowOpened(WindowEvent e) {}
    public void windowClosed(WindowEvent e){}
    public void windowIconified(WindowEvent e){}
    public void windowDeiconified(WindowEvent e){}
    public void windowActivated(WindowEvent e){}
    public void windowDeactivated(WindowEvent e){}
}
```

```java
class myDialog extends Dialog implements ActionListener, WindowListener
{
        private Button b;

        public myDialog(Frame f, String s, boolean mode)
        {
                super(f, s, mode); // runs Dialog constructor.
                setLayout(null);
                setBounds(150, 250, 200, 200);
                b = new Button("OK");
                add(b);
                b.setBounds(80, 100, 40, 27);
                b.addActionListener(this);
                addWindowListener(this);
        }
        public void paint(Graphics g)
        {
                setBackground(Color.white);
        }
        public void start()
        {
                setVisible(true);
        }
        public void actionPerformed(ActionEvent e)
        {
                if( e.getSource().equals(b))
                {
                        dispose();
                }
        }
        public void windowClosing(WindowEvent e)
        {
                dispose();
        }
        public void windowOpened(WindowEvent e) {}
        public void windowClosed(WindowEvent e){}
        public void windowIconified(WindowEvent e){}
        public void windowDeiconified(WindowEvent e){}
        public void windowActivated(WindowEvent e){}
        public void windowDeactivated(WindowEvent e){}
}
```

```
class myWindow extends Window implements ActionListener
{
        private Button b;

        public myWindow(Frame f)
        {
                super(f);      // a Window subclass requires a Frame object
                               // to be created.
                setBackground(Color.white);
                setLayout(null);
                setBounds(400, 250, 200, 200);
                b = new Button("OK");
                add(b);
                b.setBounds(80, 100, 40, 27);
                b.addActionListener(this);
        }
        public void start()
        {
                setVisible(true);
        }
        public void actionPerformed(ActionEvent e)
        {
                if( e.getSource().equals(b))
                {
                        setVisible(false);
                }
        }
}
```

## Output Windows

Window-type window

myimage.gif icon

Dialog-type window

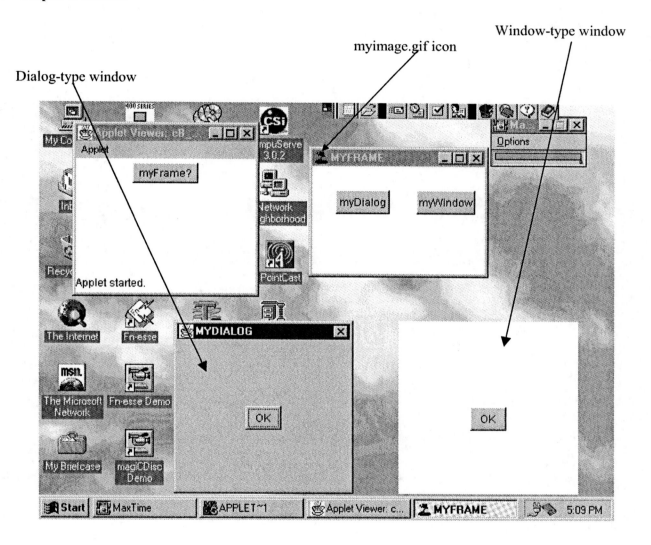

# Appendix C.  Java 1.1 Changes of Java 1.02 Features

## OBJECTIVES

At the end of this Appendix you should be able to:

- Understand the changes of Java 1.02 features embodied in Java 1.1.

- Replace deprecated features of Java 1.02 with Java 1.1 constructs.

# NEW WAYS TO IMPLEMENT JAVA 1.02 FEATURES

- Many standard features of Java 1.02 have been placed in the "deprecated" category suggesting they will be discontinued in forthcoming Java versions.

- However some deprecated features such as the setLocation() method appear to be worth keeping so SUN may change its mind. Keep in mind SunOS which was deprecated and survived.

- A trend toward increased support for data privacy is evident with "getXXXX()" and "setXXXX()" methods replacing methods with simple common names.

- Several methods of Java 1.02 which threw exceptions no longer throw the same exceptions. A noteworthy example is the clone() method of java.lang.Object.

- A new approach to event handling was introduced in Java 1.1 called Delegation Event handling.

- New constructs have been added to the language such as inner classes.

- The evident trend is towards a more complex, full-featured language with a complexity level which may approach C++.

# CHANGE IN ACCESS CATEGORIES

The access categories of variables and methods in Java 1.1 are:

**public** - can be referenced by any other class method without limitation.

**"package"** - can be referenced by any methods in any class in the same package.

**protected** - can be referenced only by methods in its own class, in a subclass of its class, or in another class in its own package.

**private** - can be referenced only by methods in the same class.

- The **private protected** access category has been eliminated.

# SOME POPULAR DEPRECATED 1.02 METHODS

| Java1.02 Methods | Java 1.1 Method Replacement |
|---|---|

**AWT Package**

*Component class:*

| Java1.02 Methods | Java 1.1 Method Replacement |
|---|---|
| enable(), enable(boolean), disable() | setEnabled(boolean) |
| show(), show(boolean), hide() | setVisible(boolean) |
| location() | getLocation() |
| move(int, int) | setLocation(int, int) |
| size() | getSize() |
| resize(width, height) | setSize(width,height) |
| resize(Dimension) | setSize(Dimension) |
| bounds() | getBounds() |
| reshape(x,y,width,height) | setBounds(x,y,width,height) |
| preferredSize() | getPreferredSize() |
| inside(x,y) | contains(x,y) |
| locate(x,y) | getComponentAt(x,y) |
| All Event handlers | Delegation Event Handling |

*Container class:*

| | |
|---|---|
| preferredSize() | getPreferredSize() |
| locate(x,y) | getComponentAt(x,y) |

*Frame class:*

| | |
|---|---|
| setCursor(int) | Component.setCursor(Cursor) |
| getCursorType() | Component.getCursor() |

*MenuItem class:*

| | |
|---|---|
| enable(), enable(boolean), disable() | setEnabled(boolean) |

*Scrollbar class:*

| | |
|---|---|
| setLineIncrement(int) | setUnitIncrement(int) // sets increment for up/down gadgets |
| setPageIncrement(int) | setBlockIncrement(int) // sets "paging" |

*TextArea Class:*

| | |
|---|---|
| insertText(String,int) | insert(String, int) |
| appendText(String) | append(String) |

*TextField class:*

| | |
|---|---|
| setEchoCharacter(char) | setEchoChar(char) |

<u>lang Package</u>
One minor deprecate

<u>applet Package</u>
no deprecates

<u>net Package</u>
one minor deprecate

<u>util Package</u>
some deprecates in Date class

<u>io Package</u>
changed approach to file I/O

# FONT CHANGES IN JAVA 1.1

| | | |
|---|---|---|
| TimesRoman | $\rightarrow$ | Serif |
| Helvetica | $\rightarrow$ | SansSerif |
| Courier | $\rightarrow$ | Monospaced |
| | | |
| ZapfDingbats | $\rightarrow$ | \u2700 set in UNICODE |

# *Appendix D. Delegation Event Handling*

Objective: To illustrate Java 1.1 Delegation Event Handling.

# OVERALL APPROACH

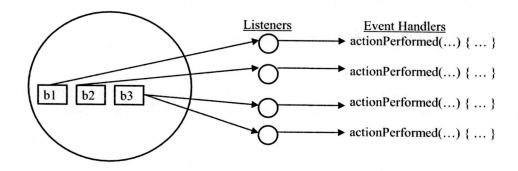

## Event Classes

- Delegation Event Handling has many kinds of event objects: MouseEvent objects, ActionEvent objects, ItemEvent objects, WindowEvent objects, and so on. The various event object classes are in a class hierarchy rooted at java.util.EventObject.

## Event Sources

- An *Event Source* is an object which generates events. The source's class contains add<EventType>Listener(…) calls which register specific listeners for those events.

- An event is *delivered from a "Source" object to a "Listener" object* by invoking a handler method in the listener class. The handler method argument is an object of the event class corresponding to the event.

**Event Listeners**

- A *Listener* is an object whose class implements the <Event Type>Listener interface corresponding to the type of event for which it listens.

- An <Event Type>Listener interface defines one or more abstract event handler methods.

- The class of a listener object must provide a definition of each abstract event handler method specified in the interface. The appropriate event handler method runs when the listener object receives an event.

- An event handler can fetch information about the event using:

  eventObj.getSource() - fetch component that generated the event.

  eventObj.getX() - fetch x coordinate of the event.

  eventObj.getY() - fetch y coordinate of the event.

  eventObj.getID() - fetch ID number of the event. Some event objects such as MouseEvent objects contain an ID number to distinguish between the various types of events the event object could represent.

## A Compact Event Handler Example

**File: simpEvt.html**

```
<applet code="simpEvt.class" width = 200 height =200></applet>
```

**File: simpEvt.java**

```java
import java.awt.*;
import java.awt.event.*;
import java.applet.*;

public class simpEvt extends Applet implements ActionListener, ItemListener
{
        Button b1;
        Button b2;
        Choice c = new Choice();

        public void init()
        {
                add(b1 = new Button("Prog1"));
                b1.addActionListener(this);

                add(b2 = new Button("Prog2"));
                b2.addActionListener(this);

                c.addItem("Prog3a");
                c.addItem("Prog3b");
                c.addItemListener(this);
                add(c);
        }
        public void actionPerformed(ActionEvent e)
        {
                System.out.println("Action:");
                String s = ((Button)e.getSource()).getLabel();
                System.out.println("    Running " + s + " ... ");
        }
        public void itemStateChanged(ItemEvent e)
        {
                System.out.println("Item:");
                String s = ((Choice)e.getSource()).getSelectedItem();
                System.out.println("    Running " + s + " ...");
        }
}
```

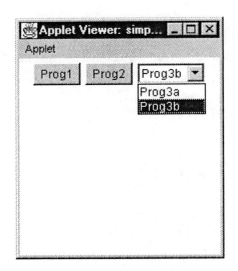

MS-DOS Prompt Window
Action:
    Running Prog1 ...
Action:
    Running Prog2 ...
Item:
    Running Prog3a ...
Item:
    Running Prog3b ...

## A More Complex Example of Delegation Event Handling

```java
File: delEvt.java
import java.awt.*;
import java.awt.event.*;

public class delEvt
{
        static public void main(String args[])
        {
                myFrame m = new myFrame();
        }
}


class myFrame
{
        public myFrame()   // Creating a frame directly.
        {
                Frame f = new Frame();
                f.setLayout(new FlowLayout());
                myProg p1 = new myProg(myProg.PROG1);
                myProg p2 = new myProg(myProg.PROG2);
                myProg p3 = new myProg(myProg.PROG3);
                myProg p4 = new myProg(myProg.PROG4);

                Button b1;
                f.add(b1 = new Button("Run Prog1"));
                b1.addActionListener(p1);
                b1.addActionListener(p2);

                Button b2;
                f.add(b2 = new Button("Run Prog2"));
                b2.addActionListener(p3);

                Choice c = new Choice();
                f.add(c);
                c.addItem("ProgA");
                c.addItem("ProgB");
                c.addItemListener(p4);

                f.setSize(200, 200);
                f.show();
        }
}
```

```java
class myProg implements ActionListener,ItemListener // listener object's class
{
        static final int PROG1 = 1;
        static final int PROG2 = 2;
        static final int PROG3 = 3;
        static final int PROG4 = 4;
        int id;

        public myProg(int id)
        {
                this.id = id;
        }
        public void actionPerformed(ActionEvent e)
        {
                System.out.println("Action: Button - "
                        + ((Button)e.getSource()).getLabel());
                switch(id)
                {
                        case PROG1:
                                System.out.println("    Listener: p1");
                                prog1();
                                break;
                        case PROG2:
                                System.out.println("    Listener: p2");
                                prog1();
                                break;
                        case PROG3:
                                System.out.println("    Listener: p3");
                                prog2();
                                break;
                }
        }
        public void itemStateChanged(ItemEvent e)
        {
                System.out.println("Item: " + "Choice Button");
                System.out.println("    Listener: p4");
                prog(((Choice)e.getSource()).getSelectedItem());
        }
        public void prog1()
        {
                System.out.println("    Running prog1 ... ");
        }
        public void prog2()
        {
                System.out.println("    Running prog2 ... ");
        }
        public void prog(String prog)
        {
                System.out.println("    Running " + prog + " ...");
        }
}
```

**Frame created**

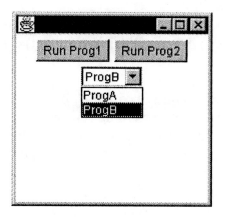

<u>MS-DOS Prompt Window</u>
```
class\delEvt> java delEvt
Action: Button - Run Prog1
     Listener: p1
     Running prog1 ...
Action: Button - Run Prog1
     Listener: p2
     Running prog1 ...
Action: Button - Run Prog2
     Listener: p3
     Running prog2 ...
Item: Choice Button
     Listener: p4
     Running ProgA ...
Item: Choice Button
     Listener: p4
     Running ProgB ...
```

# LIMITING & VALIDATING DATA ENTERED IN TEXTFIELDS

- Often a programmer wishes to limit the number of characters which a person types in a TextField.

- Or a programmer may wish to validate (check out) each character as they are typed into a text field.

The following example shows how to limit the number of characters that are typed into a text field. If the end user exceeds the number a warning screen might be generated and the user automatically moved to the next TextField. It also shows how to examine each character as it is typed. Two approaches are shown: one using Text Listening and the other using Key Listening.

Example:

**File: cD_1.html**
```
<applet code="cD_1.class" width = 500 height = 350>
</applet>
```

**File: cD_1.java**
```java
import java.awt.*;
import java.awt.event.*;
import java.applet.Applet;

public class cD_1 extends Applet implements ActionListener, KeyListener
{
        private myTextField t1, t2, t3 , t4;
        private String text = "";
        private Font f1 = new Font("SansSerif", Font.BOLD, 16);
        private Graphics g1;
        private int j = 0;

        public void init()
        {
                g1 = getGraphics();
                        // class myTextField defined on next page.
                t1 = new myTextField("ABCDE", 10, 8, this);
                t1.setFont(f1);
                add(t1);
                t2 = new myTextField("ABCDE", 10, 7, this);
                t2.setBackground(Color.yellow);
                t2.setForeground(Color.blue);
                add(t2);
                t3 = new myTextField("ABC", 6, 4, this);
```

```java
        t3.setBackground(Color.blue);
        t3.setForeground(Color.white);
        t3.setEchoChar('*');
        add(t3);
        t4 = new myTextField("ABCDE", 10, 8, this);
        t4.setBackground(Color.yellow);
        t4.setForeground(Color.red);
        add(t4);
        t1.addActionListener(this);
        t2.addActionListener(this);
        t3.addActionListener(this);
        t4.addActionListener(this);
        t1.addKeyListener(this);
        t2.addKeyListener(this);
        t3.addKeyListener(this);
        t4.addKeyListener(this);
    }
public void start()
{
        t1.selectAll();
        t1.requestFocus();
}
public void keyReleased(KeyEvent e) // handler for Key events typed in
                                    // myTextField object.
{
        char c = (char)e.getKeyCode(); // fetches character typed.
        if(c == '\t')
                myAction(e, false); // responds to pressing tab key.
}
public void actionPerformed(ActionEvent e)
{
        myAction(e, true);  // responds to pressing ENTER key in
                            // text field.
}
public void myAction(AWTEvent e, boolean doIt)
{
        g1.setFont(f1);
        g1.setColor(Color.black);

        if(e.getSource() instanceof myTextField)
        {
                if(e.getSource().equals(t1))
                {
                        if(doIt)
                        {
                                text = "Field 1: " +
                                        t1.getText() +
                                        " Selecting 1-3 in t2";
                                g1.drawString(text, 40, 120
                                                    + 15 * j++);
                                t2.requestFocus();
                        }
```

```java
                t2.select(1,4);
                if(doIt)
                {
                        text = "                Selected Text = "
                                    + t2.getSelectedText();
                        text = text + " Start-End Select = "
                                    + t2.getSelectionStart() +
                                " - " + t2.getSelectionEnd();
                }
        }
        else if(e.getSource().equals(t2))
        {
                if(doIt)
                {
                        text = "Field 2: "
                                    + t2.getText();
                        t3.requestFocus();
                }
                t3.selectAll();
        }
        else if(e.getSource().equals(t3))
        {
                if(doIt)
                {
                        text = "Field 3: " +
                                    t3.getText();
                        t4.requestFocus();
                }
                t4.selectAll();
        }
        else if(e.getSource().equals(t4))
        {
                if(doIt)
                {
                        text = "Field 4: " +
                                    t4.getText();
                        t1.requestFocus();
                }
                t1.selectAll();
        }
        if(j > 15)
        {
                j = 0;
                g1.clearRect(0, 0, 500, 350);
        }
        if(doIt)
        {
                g1.drawString(text, 40, 120 + 15 * j++);
        }
    }
}
```

```java
        public void keyPressed(KeyEvent e)
        { }
        public void keyTyped(KeyEvent e)
        { }
}

class myTextField extends TextField implements KeyListener,
                              ActionListener, TextListener
{
        private int size, maxChar, j = 0;
        private boolean begin = true;
        private static int k = 0;
        private Applet a;
        private Graphics g1;
        private String oldString;

        public myTextField(String s, int size, int maxChar, Applet a)
        {
                super(size); // sets up TextField superclass part.
                this.size = size;
                this.maxChar = maxChar;
                this.a = a;
                oldString = s;
                setText(s);
                j = s.length();
                g1 = a.getGraphics();
                addKeyListener(this); // listen for each key event.
                addActionListener(this); // listen for action events
                            // generated by pressing ENTER or RETURN.
                addTextListener(this); // listen for text key pressed on
                                    // keyboard. (ignore other keys)
        }
        public void textValueChanged(TextEvent e) // handles text key events:
        {    // limits number of chars typed to maxChar.
                String label = getText();
                if(label.length() > maxChar)
                {
                        Frame f;
                            // Dialog window for error message.
                        myDialog d = new myDialog(f = new Frame(),
                            "Character Limit Exceeded", true,
                                                maxChar, label);
                        d.start();
                        begin = true;
                        setText(oldString);
                        requestFocus();
                }
                else
                        oldString = getText();
        }
```

```
        public void keyReleased(KeyEvent e)   // Alternate approach to
        { // using text key listening. Much more complex. Therefore it is
            // commented out. Needs more detail to complete.
//                char c = (char)e.getKeyCode();
//                if(begin && (c == ' ' ||
//                            Character.isUnicodeIdentifierPart(c)))
//                      begin = false;
//                else if(c != '\n')
//                      begin = false;
//                j = getText().length();
//                if(!begin && j > maxChar && (c == ' ' ||
//                Character.isUnicodeIdentifierPart(c)))
//                {
//                      Frame f;
//                      setText(oldString);
//                      myDialog d = new myDialog(f = new Frame(),
//                                "Character Limit Exceeded", true,
//                                 maxChar, getText());
//                      d.start();
//                      begin = true;
//                      requestFocus();
//                      j = getText().length();
//                }
//              oldString = getText();
        }
        public void actionPerformed(ActionEvent e)
        {
                begin = true;
        }
        public void keyPressed(KeyEvent e)
        { }
        public void keyTyped(KeyEvent e)
        { }
}

class myDialog extends Dialog implements ActionListener, WindowListener
{   // Dialog window for error messages.
        private Button b;
        private String s;
        private int maxChar;

        public myDialog(Frame f, String title, boolean mode,
                                                int maxChar, String s)
        {
                super(f, title, mode);
                this.s = s;
                this.maxChar = maxChar;
                setLayout(null);
                setBounds(250, 200, 350, 250);
                b = new Button("OK");
                add(b);
```

```
            b.setBounds(155, 140, 40, 27);
            b.requestFocus();
            b.addActionListener(this);
            addWindowListener(this);
    }
    public void paint(Graphics g)
    {
            setBackground(Color.white);
            g.drawString("Maximum Number of " + maxChar +
                                    " Characters exceeded: ",
                        20, 80);
            g.drawString("Current Text: " + s, 20, 110);
    }
    public void start()
    {
            setVisible(true);
    }
    public void actionPerformed(ActionEvent e)
    {
            if( e.getSource().equals(b))
                    dispose();
    }
    public void windowClosing(WindowEvent e)
    {
            dispose();
    }
    public void windowOpened(WindowEvent e) {}
    public void windowClosed(WindowEvent e){}
    public void windowIconified(WindowEvent e){}
    public void windowDeiconified(WindowEvent e){}
    public void windowActivated(WindowEvent e){}
    public void windowDeactivated(WindowEvent e){}
}
```

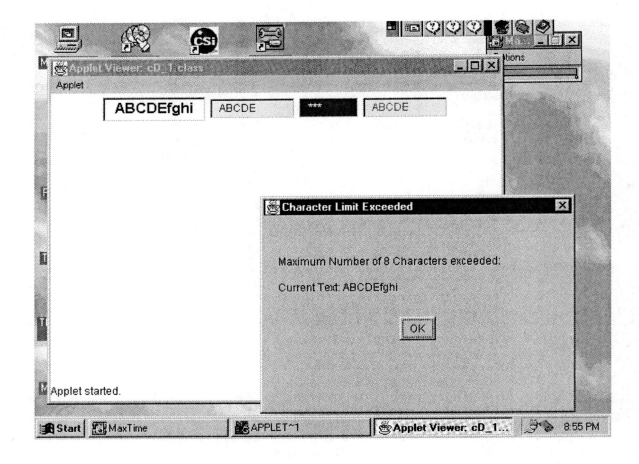

# *Appendix E. Java Foundation Classes (JFC) Swing Package*

Objective: To describe the Java Swing package.

# NEW SWING COMPONENTS AND FEATURES

The Swing packages add many new features to Java:

> JPanel
> Icons
> JLabel
> JButton
> AbstractButton
> JCheckBox
> JRadioButton
> JToggleButton
> JTextComponents
> > JTextField & JTextArea
> > JTextPane
> > JPasswordField
> JScrollBar
> JSlider
> JProgressBar
> JComboBox
> JList
> Borders
> JScrollPane
> ViewPorts
> Menus
> JSeparator
> JFrame and Windows
> > JRootPane
> > JLayeredPane
> JPopupMenu
> Tooltips
> Toolbars
> JTabbedPane
> JSplitPane
> Swing Layouts
> > BoxLayout
> > Box
> > ScrollPaneLayout
> > ViewportLayout
> Swing Event Features
> > Swing Event Objects
> > Swing Event Listeners
> > Swing Event Sources

- Sun Microsystems used the technology of Netscape, IBM, and Lighthouse Design to create a set of Graphical User Interface (GUI) classes.

- This collection of APIs is called the Java Foundation Classes (JFC). The JFC consists of five APIs:

  > AWT
  > Java 2D
  > Accessibility
  > Drag and Drop
  > Swing

- The AWT 1.1 widgets and event model are supported in Java 1.2 and 1.3.

- Swing adds a set of components, the JComponents, and a group of related support classes.

- Swing components are all JavaBeans and support in the JavaBeans event model.

- Some Swing widgets are similar to the basic AWT widgets.

- Some Swing widgets are lightweight components, rather than peer-based components. The lightweight component architecture was introduced in AWT 1.1.

- Lightweight components can exist without native operating system widgets.

- Lightweight components support the Model-View-Controller (MVC) architecture described later.

- In AWT, subclasses of java.awt.Container can contain java.awt.Components. Since Containers are themselves Components, nesting is supported.

- Swing goes one step further. All JComponents are subclasses of java.awt.Container. This allows Swing widgets, such as JLabel, to contain other components (either AWT or Swing). We will see an example of placing a JButton on a JButton.

# JAVA SWING PACKAGE AND SUBPACKAGES

javax.swing
   Consists of components, adapters, default component models and interfaces.

javax.swing.basic
   Contains the User Interface (UI) classes (delegates) which implement the default look-and-feel for Swing components.

javax.swing.beaninfo
   Contains BeanInfo support classes for use in bean builders: BeanBox, Sun's Java Workshop, IBM's VisualAge for Java, Borland's JBuilder, and Visual Café.

javax.swing.border
   Contains the Border interface and classes, which define specific border rendering styles.

javax.swing.event
   Supports Swing-specific event types and listeners.

javax.swing.multi
   Contains the Multiplexing UI classes (delegates) which permit the creation of components from different UI factories.

javax.swing.plaf
   Contains the Pluggable Look-and-Feel API for developers interested in defining custom interfaces.

javax.swing.table
   Contains the interfaces and classes, which support the Swing table component.

javax.swing.target
   Contains the support classes for Action target management.

javax.swing.text
   Contains the support classes for the Swing document framework.

javax.swing.text.html
   Contains the support classes for a basic HTML renderer.

javax.swing.undo
   Supports classes implementing undo/redo capabilities in a GUI.

# SURVEY OF SWING COMPONENTS AND CONTAINERS

### Icons

An icon is not a component. An Icon is used to describe fixed-size pictures, or glyphs. Icons can be placed on labels, buttons, lists and many other Swing components.

The classes of objects that act as icons implement the Icon interface. The Icon interface contains a paintIcon() method that defines a graphic drawing. The picture specified in the paintIcon method is in a rectangle with an origin (x, y), a width given by getIconWidth(), and a height given by getIconHeight().

```
public interface Icon
{
        void paintIcon(Component c, Graphics g, int x,
                                                int y);
        int getIconWidth();
        int getIconHeight();
}
```

The ImageIcon class implements Icon. An ImageIcon object can be created from an input graphics file:

```
Icon aPicture = new ImageIcon("myimage.gif");
```

or from an Image or a URL object.

If the Image is an animated GIF89 file, you must specify an ImageObserver object with the ImageIcon. The observer is the component upon which the image is to be displayed:

```
ImageIcon myIm = new ImageIcon("myimage.gif");
JButton b = new JButton(myIm);
myIm.setImageObserver(b);
```

An alternative approach to using an ImageIcon is to define a class implementing Icon:

```java
public class RedOval implements Icon
{
        public void paintIcon(Component c, Graphics g,
                                        int x, int y)
        {
                g.setColor(Color.red);
                g.drawOval (x, y, getIconWidth(),
                                getIconHeight());
        }
        public int getIconWidth()
        {
                return 15;
        }
        public int getIconHeight()
        {
                return 30;
        }
}
```

## JLabel Component

A JLabel is similar to a java.awt.Label. A JLabel has extra – primarily graphical – features:

1. Add an Icon

2. Set the vertical and horizontal position of text relative to Icon

3. Set the relative position of contents within component

Example:

```java
public class LabelPanel extends JPanel
{
    public LabelPanel()
    {
        JLabel myLabel = new JLabel("A Label");
        add(myLabel);

        JLabel yourLabel = new JLabel("Your Label");

        Font yourFont = new Font("SansSerif", Font.BOLD |
                                        Font.ITALIC, 16);

        yourLabel.setFont(yourFont);

        Icon dogIcon = new ImageIcon("dog.gif");

        yourLabel.setIcon(dogIcon);

        yourLabel.setHorizontalAlignment(JLabel.RIGHT);

        add(yourLabel);
    }
}
```

## JButton

A JButton is like a java.awt.Button. It notifies specified ActionListener objects when pushed. JButtons have additional features:

setMnemonic - Add a keyboard accelerator char to a text label

doClick - Programmatically, select the button

setDisabledIcon, setDisabledSelectedIcon,

setPressedIcon, setRolloverIcon,

setRolloverSelectedIcon, setSelectedIcon - Change the displayed Icon, based on the button state (in addition to setIcon)

setVerticalAlignment, setHorizontalAlignment - Anchors icon/text on button

setVerticalTextPosition, setHorizontalTextPosition - Positions text around icon

Some examples are:

```
public class ButtonPanel extends JPanel
{
      public ButtonPanel()
      {
            JButton myButton = new JButton("My Label");
            myButton.setBackground(SystemColor.control);
            add(myButton);
      }
}
public class ButtonPanel extends JPanel
{
      public ButtonPanel()
      {
            Icon myIcon = new ImageIcon("myimage.gif");

            JButton myButton = new JButton("My Label", myIcon);

            myButton.setBackground(SystemColor.control);

            add(myButton);
      }
}
```

## JPanel

JPanel is a lightweight Panel object that offers built-in support for double buffering. When buffering is enabled, either through the constructor or the setBuffered method, all the drawing of components within the panel are sent to an offscreen drawing area before being drawn to the screen.

## JFrame

The JFrame class is an alternative for the Frame class. In addition to being able to add a java.awt.MenuBar via setMenuBar to a JFrame, you can add a JMenuBar to a JFrame via setJMenuBar.

In addition, for both JFrame, JWindow and JDialog classes you do not add components to each directly or directly do a setLayout to change the LayoutManager. Instead you fetch a content pane and add components to it or set its layout.

```
public class FrameTester
{
        public static void main (String args[])
        {
                JFrame f = new JFrame("JFrame Example");

                Container c = f.getContentPane();

                c.setLayout(new FlowLayout());

                for (int i = 0; i < 5; i++)
                {
                        c.add (new JButton("No")).setBackground(
                                        SystemColor.control);
                        c.add (new Button("Batter"));
                }
                c.add (new JLabel("Swing"));
                f.setSize (300, 200);
                f.show();
        }
}
```

The reason for getting a content pane is because the inside of a JFrame window is now composed of a JRootPane.

## JRootPane

A JRootPane is a Container that consists of two objects, a glass pane and a layered pane.

The glass pane is initially invisible, so all you "see" is the layered pane. The layered pane also consists of two objects, an optional menu bar and a content pane. You interact with the content pane just like you would with a Window, Dialog, or Frame.

If you place a component in a glass pane, it will appear above the content pane. This enables popup menus, tool tip text, and so on to work properly. The layering effect is the result of using the JLayeredPane component.

Normal code such as:

```
aFrame.setLayout(new FlowLayout());
aFrame.add(aComponent);
```

is replaced with "J" code accessing the content pane:

```
aFrame.getContentPane().setLayout (new FlowLayout());
aFrame.getContentPane().add(aComponent);
```

The other panes are accessed with the methods:

```
Container getContentPane();
setContentPane(Container);
Component getGlassPane();
setGlassPane(Component);
JLayeredPane getLayeredPane();
setLayeredPane(JLayeredPane);
JMenuBar getMenuBar();
setMenuBar(JMenuBar);
```

**Standalone Program with JLabels and JButtons:**

**File: MyJLBFrame.java**

```java
import java.awt.*;
import java.awt.event.*;

import javax.swing.*;
import javax.swing.event.*;
import javax.swing.plaf.*;
import javax.swing.border.*;
import javax.swing.text.*;

class MyJLBFrame extends JFrame implements ActionListener
{
        private int j = 0;

        MyJLBFrame()
        {
                super("Buttons and Labels");
                Icon i = new ImageIcon("cow.gif");
                Icon press = new ImageIcon("b2.gif");
                Icon roll = new ImageIcon("b3.gif");
                Icon disab = new ImageIcon("dbut.gif");

                JButton b1 = new JButton("Tea", i); // graphical button
                b1.setBackground(Color.green);
                b1.setVerticalTextPosition(JButton.TOP); // positioning
                b1.setHorizontalTextPosition(JButton.LEFT);
                b1.setMnemonic('t'); // accelerator key is alt-t

                                // set matte border 5 pixels thick.
                b1.setBorder(new MatteBorder(5,5,5,5, Color.darkGray));

                JLabel labela=new JLabel("The true story"); // graphical label
                labela.setToolTipText("Big help");
                labela.setForeground(Color.red);
                labela.setVerticalTextPosition(JLabel.CENTER);
                labela.setHorizontalTextPosition(JLabel.LEFT);
                labela.setIcon(i);
                labela.setHorizontalAlignment(JLabel.RIGHT);
                labela.setBorder(new EtchedBorder());

                JButton b2 = new JButton("Coffee", i);
                b2.setDisabledIcon(disab); // set disabled look.
//                b2.setEnabled(false);
                        // set look as mouse rolls over button.
                b2.setRolloverIcon(roll);
                b2.setPressedIcon(press);
```

```java
        b2.setBackground(Color.lightGray);
        b2.setVerticalTextPosition(JButton.BOTTOM);
        b2.setHorizontalTextPosition(JButton.RIGHT);
        b2.setMnemonic('c');

        JLabel labelb = new JLabel("The other story");
        labelb.setToolTipText("Little help");
        labelb.setForeground(Color.black);
        labelb.setVerticalTextPosition(JLabel.BOTTOM);
        labelb.setHorizontalTextPosition(JLabel.CENTER);
        labelb.setIcon(i);
        labelb.setHorizontalAlignment(JLabel.CENTER);
        labelb.setBorder(new LineBorder(Color.black, 5));

        b1.addActionListener(this); // same listening as Buttons
        b2.addActionListener(this);
        b1.requestFocus();
                // MUST add everything to ContentPane!
        Container c = getContentPane();
// BoxLayout creates a layout consisting of a vertical or
// horizontal pile of boxes.
    c.setLayout(new BoxLayout(c, BoxLayout.Y_AXIS)); // vertical

// Strut - Insert box 10 pixels high - empty - top box.
        c.add(Box.createVerticalStrut(10));
        c.add(b1);
// Strut - Insert box 10 pixels high - empty. More Struts below.
        c.add(Box.createVerticalStrut(10));
        c.add(labela);
        c.add(Box.createVerticalStrut(10));
        c.add(b2);
        c.add(Box.createVerticalStrut(10));
        c.add(labelb);
        c.add(Box.createHorizontalStrut(10));
}
public void paint(Graphics g)
{
    // If a paint() method is placed in the class then the inherited
    // paint() method is overridden. Since the inherited paint()
    // method draws the Swing components on the screen it MUST
    // execute or we will see no components. Therefore we must
    // explicitly call the superclass paint() method in this case
    // since this paint() method overrides the inherited paint().

    super.paint(g);
}
```

```java
public void actionPerformed(ActionEvent e)
{ // handles JButton events.
        getGraphics().drawString(
                ((JButton)e.getSource()).getText(),
                        250, 100 + 15*j++);
}
public static void main(String args[])
{
        MyJLBFrame f = new MyJLBFrame();

    // The next statement adds a listener object for Window events
    // using a definition called anonymous inner classes. The argument
    // of addWindowListener() is an object created by the new operator
    // of a class that has no name but has the structure that it has
    // WindowAdapter as its superclass and the method windowClosing()
    // as its only other contents. This no-name class inherits all the
    // window event handlers from its superclass and overrides the
    // inherited windowClosing() method. After the object is created
    // the anonymous (no-name) class definition is discarded.

        f.addWindowListener(new WindowAdapter() {
                public void windowClosing(WindowEvent e)
                {System.exit(0);}
        });
        f.setSize(300, 400);
        f.setVisible(true);
}
}
```

"Normal" Coffee Button look

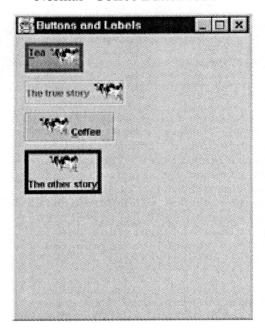

"Rollover" Coffee Button look

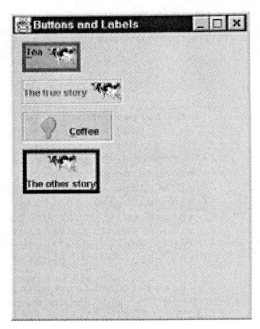

"Pressed" Coffee Button Look

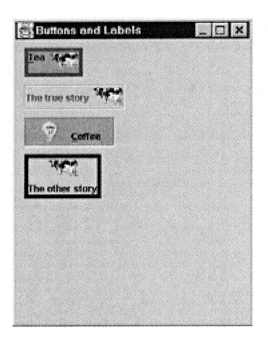

"Disabled" Coffee Button Look

## Applet with a Jbuttons on a JButton

### File: MyJLabBut.html

```
<applet code="MyJLabBut.class" width = 300 height = 400></applet>
```

### File: MyJLabBut.java

```java
import java.awt.*;
import java.awt.event.*;
import java.applet.*;

import javax.swing.*;
import javax.swing.event.*;
import javax.swing.plaf.*;
import javax.swing.border.*;
import javax.swing.text.*;

public class MyJLabBut extends JApplet implements ActionListener
{
        private JPanel p;
        private JButton b1, b2, b2a;
        private JLabel labela, labelb;
        private Graphics g1;
        private int j = 0;

        public void init()
        {
                Icon i = new ImageIcon("cow.gif");
                p = new JPanel();
                p.setLayout(new BoxLayout(p, BoxLayout.Y_AXIS));
                p.add(Box.createVerticalStrut(10));

                b1 = new JButton("Tea", i);
                b1.setBackground(Color.green);
                b1.setVerticalTextPosition(JButton.TOP);
                b1.setHorizontalTextPosition(JButton.LEFT);
                b1.setMnemonic('t');
                b1.setBorder(new MatteBorder(5,5,5,5, Color.darkGray));
                p.add(b1);
                p.add(Box.createVerticalStrut(10));

                labela = new JLabel("The true story");
                labela.setToolTipText("Big help");
                labela.setForeground(Color.red);
                labela.setVerticalTextPosition(JLabel.CENTER);
                labela.setHorizontalTextPosition(JLabel.LEFT);
                labela.setIcon(i);
                labela.setHorizontalAlignment(JLabel.RIGHT);
                labela.setBorder(new EtchedBorder());
                p.add(labela);
```

```
                p.add(Box.createVerticalStrut(10));

                b2 = new JButton("Coffee", i);
                b2.setBackground(Color.red);
                b2.setVerticalTextPosition(JButton.BOTTOM);
                b2.setHorizontalTextPosition(JButton.RIGHT);
                b2.setMnemonic('c');
                p.add(b2);
                b2.setLayout(null);
// Add a Jbutton on top of a Jbutton. We set the layout to null on b2
// so we can position b2a on it with setBounds().
                b2a = new JButton("Caffe");
                b2a.setBackground(Color.green);
                b2a.setMnemonic('a');
                b2.add(b2a);
                b2a.setBounds(10, 10, 80, 50);
                p.add(Box.createVerticalStrut(10));

                labelb = new JLabel("The other story");
                labelb.setToolTipText("Little help"); // Help string.
                labelb.setForeground(Color.black);
                labelb.setVerticalTextPosition(JLabel.BOTTOM);
                labelb.setHorizontalTextPosition(JLabel.CENTER);
                labelb.setIcon(i);
                labelb.setHorizontalAlignment(JLabel.CENTER);
                labelb.setBorder(new LineBorder(Color.black, 5));
                p.add(labelb);
                p.add(Box.createVerticalStrut(10));

                ImageIcon upBut    = new ImageIcon("ubut.gif");
                ImageIcon downBut  = new ImageIcon("dbut.gif");
                JButton b3 = new JButton("HotButton", upBut);
                b3.setToolTipText("This Button changes when pressed");
                b3.setPressedIcon(downBut);
                b3.setBorder(new EtchedBorder());
                b3.setMnemonic('h');
                p.add(b3);

                p.add(Box.createHorizontalStrut(10));
                getContentPane().add(p);
                b1.addActionListener(this);
                b2.addActionListener(this);
                b2a.addActionListener(this);
                b3.addActionListener(this);
                g1 = getGraphics();
                b1.requestFocus();
        }
    public void paint(Graphics g)
    {
                super.paint(g);
    }
```

```
public void actionPerformed(ActionEvent e)
{
        g1.drawString(((JButton)e.getSource()).getText(), 200,
                                            220 + 15*j++);
    }
}
```

"Unpressed" Hot Button                    "Pressed" Hot Button

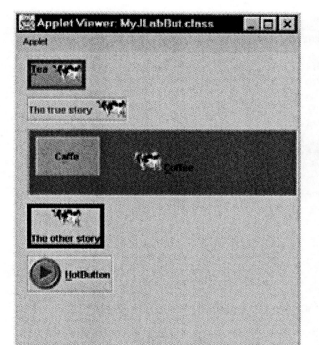
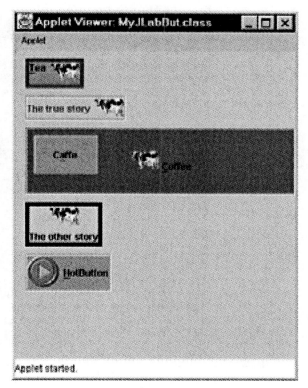

## JCheckBox

- A JCheckBox is like an AWT Checkbox except you can choose the graphics.
- Specify your own Icon objects for both the checked and unchecked state.

```java
public class CheckboxPanel extends JPanel
{
    class ToggleIcon implements Icon   // inner member class: a class within
    {// a class. This local class can only be used inside CheckboxPanel.

        boolean state;           // Specifies checked and unchecked icons
        public ToggleIcon (boolean s)
        {
            state = s;
        }
        public void paintIcon(Component c, Graphics g, int x, int y)
        {
            int width = getIconWidth();
            int height = getIconHeight();
            g.setColor (Color.darkGray);
            if(state)
                    g.fillOval(x, y, width, height); // checked icon
            else
                    g.drawOval(x, y, width, height); // unchecked icon
        }
        public int getIconWidth()
        {
            return 15;
        }
        public int getIconHeight()
        {
            return 15;
        }
    }
        // create icons from inner class definition.
    Icon unchecked = new ToggleIcon(false);
    Icon checked = new ToggleIcon(true);

    public CheckboxPanel()
    {
        setLayout(new GridLayout(2, 1));
        JCheckBox c1 = new JCheckBox("Checkbox1", true);
        c1.setIcon(unchecked);
        c1.setSelectedIcon(checked);
        JCheckBox c2 = new JCheckBox("Checkbox2", false);
        c2.setIcon(unchecked);
        c2.setSelectedIcon(checked);
```

```java
            add(c1);
            add(c2);
        }
}
```

## JCheckbox Example

## File: CheckboxEx.java

```java
import java.awt.*;
import java.awt.event.*;

import javax.swing.*;
import javax.swing.event.*;
import javax.swing.plaf.*;
import javax.swing.border.*;
import javax.swing.text.*;

class CheckboxEx extends JFrame
{
        private int j = 0;
        private CheckboxPanel p = new CheckboxPanel();

        CheckboxEx()
        {
                super("Checkbox");

                Container c = getContentPane();
                c.add(p);
        }
        public static void main(String args[])
        {
                CheckboxEx f = new CheckboxEx();
                f.addWindowListener(new WindowAdapter() {
                        public void windowClosing(WindowEvent e)
                        {System.exit(0);}
                });
                f.setSize(300, 300);
                f.setVisible(true);
        }
}

class CheckboxPanel extends JPanel
{
        private Icon unchecked = new ToggleIcon (false);
        private Icon checked = new ToggleIcon (true);
        private Icon b1 = new ImageIcon("b1.gif");
        private Icon b2 = new ImageIcon("b2.gif");
        private Icon b3 = new ImageIcon("b3.gif");
        private Icon b4 = new ImageIcon("cow.gif");
        private JCheckBox c3, c4, c5;
```

```java
class ToggleIcon implements Icon
{
        boolean state;
        public ToggleIcon (boolean s)
        {
                state = s;
        }
        public void paintIcon(Component c, Graphics g, int x,
                                                        int y)
        {
                int width = getIconWidth();
                int height = getIconHeight();
                g.setColor (Color.darkGray);
                if (state)
                        g.fillRect(x, y, width, height);
                else
                        g.drawOval(x, y, width, height);
        }
        public int getIconWidth()
        {
                return 15;
        }
        public int getIconHeight()
        {
                return 15;
        }
}

public CheckboxPanel()
{
    setLayout(new GridLayout(5, 1));
    JCheckBox c1 = new JCheckBox("Checkbox1", true);
    c1.setIcon(unchecked);
    c1.setSelectedIcon(checked);
    c1.setToolTipText("This is Checkbox 1");
    c1.setMnemonic('1'); // set accelerator key alt-1

    JCheckBox c2 = new JCheckBox("Checkbox2", false);
    c2.setIcon(unchecked);
    c2.setToolTipText("This is Checkbox 2");
    c2.setMnemonic('2'); // Set accelerator key alt-2
    c2.setSelectedIcon(checked);

    c3 = new JCheckBox("Checkbox3", b1);
    c3.setSelectedIcon(b2);
    c3.setDisabledIcon(b3);
    c3.setMnemonic('3');
```

```
        c4 = new JCheckBox("Checkbox4", b1);
        c4.setSelectedIcon(b4);
        c4.setDisabledIcon(b3);
        c4.setMnemonic('4');

        c5 = new JCheckBox("Checkbox5", b1);
        c5.setSelectedIcon(b2);
        c5.setDisabledIcon(b3);
        c5.setMnemonic('5');

        add(c1);
        add(c2);
        add(c3);
        add(c4);
        add(c5);
    }
}
```

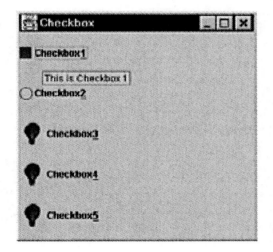
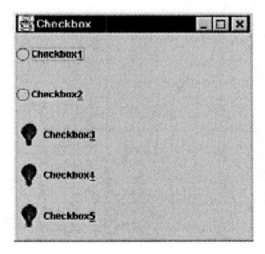

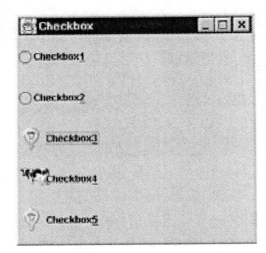

## JRadioButton

The Swing equivalent of a CheckBoxGroup of CheckBoxes is a ButtonGroup of JRadioButtons.

```
public class RadioButtonPanel extends JPanel
{
        public RadioButtonPanel()
        {
                setLayout(new GridLayout(4,1));
                JRadioButton rb1, rb2;
                // create ButtonGroup object.
                ButtonGroup rbg = new ButtonGroup();

                JLabel jb = new JLabel("Dogs: ");
                jb.setFont(new Font("SansSerif", Font.BOLD,14));
                add(jb);
                        // create JradioButton object
                rb1 = new JRadioButton("Fido");
                add(rb1);   // add rb1 to JPanel
                rb1.setMnemonic('f'); // set accelerator key

                rbg.add (rb1); // add rb1 to button group.

                rb1.setSelected(true); // set rb1 as selected.

                rb2 = new JRadioButton("Lassie");
                rb2.setMnemonic ('l');
                add (rb2);
                rbg.add (rb2);

                rb3 = new JRadioButton("Shep");
                rb3.setMnemonic ('s');
                add (rb3);
                rbg.add(rb3);
        }
}
```

## JRadio Button Example

### File: RadioButtonEx.java

```java
import java.awt.*;
import java.awt.event.*;

import javax.swing.*;
import javax.swing.event.*;
import javax.swing.plaf.*;
import javax.swing.border.*;
import javax.swing.text.*;

class RadioButtonEx extends JFrame  // define a JFrame
{
        private int j = 0;
        private RadioButtonPanel p = new RadioButtonPanel();

        RadioButtonEx()
        {
                super("RadioButtons");

                Container c = getContentPane();
                c.add(p);
        }
        public static void main(String args[]) // creates Jframe window
        {
                RadioButtonEx f = new RadioButtonEx();
                f.addWindowListener(new WindowAdapter() {
                        public void windowClosing(WindowEvent e)
                        {System.exit(0);}
                });
                f.setSize(250, 300);
                f.setVisible(true);
        }
}

class RadioButtonPanel extends Jpanel // creates a Jpanel
{
        private JRadioButton rb1, rb2, rb3;
        private ButtonGroup rbg1 = new ButtonGroup();
        private ButtonGroup rbg2 = new ButtonGroup();
        private ButtonGroup rbg3 = new ButtonGroup();
        private JPanel p1, p2, p3;

        public RadioButtonPanel()
        {
                Icon d2 = new ImageIcon("b1.gif");
                Icon dw  = new ImageIcon("b2.gif");
                Icon dwr = new ImageIcon("b3.gif");
```

```java
Icon r = new ImageIcon("r.gif");
Icon rs  = new ImageIcon("rs.gif");
Icon rp = new ImageIcon("rp.gif");
        // 3 subpanels for 3 groups of buttons.
p1 = new JPanel();
p2 = new JPanel();
p3 = new JPanel();

setLayout(new GridLayout(3,1));
p1.setLayout(new GridLayout(1, 4));
p1.setBorder(new EtchedBorder()); // etched border for JPanel.

JLabel jb = new JLabel("Dogs: ");
jb.setFont(new Font("SansSerif", Font.BOLD,14));
p1.add(jb);

rb1 = new JRadioButton("Fido");
rb1.setMnemonic('f');
rb1.setToolTipText("We like Fido");
p1.add(rb1);
rbg1.add(rb1);
rb1.setSelected(true);

rb2 = new JRadioButton("Lassie");
rb2.setMnemonic ('l');
rb2.setToolTipText("We like Lassie");
p1.add(rb2);
rbg1.add(rb2);

rb3 = new JRadioButton("Shep");
rb3.setMnemonic ('s');
rb3.setToolTipText("We like Shep");
p1.add(rb3);
rbg1.add(rb3);

p2.setLayout(new GridLayout(1, 3));
p2.setBorder(new EtchedBorder());

rb1 = new JRadioButton(d2);
rb1.setSelectedIcon(dw);
rb1.setPressedIcon(dwr);
rb1.setSelected(true);
rb1.setToolTipText("RadioButton with a Icon");
p2.add(rb1);
rbg2.add(rb1);

rb1 = new JRadioButton(d2);
rb1.setSelectedIcon(dw);
rb1.setPressedIcon(dwr);
rb1.setSelected(true);
rb1.setToolTipText("RadioButton with a Icon");
```

```
        p2.add(rb1); // must add button to panel
        rbg2.add(rb1); // must add button to group.

        rb1 = new JRadioButton(d2);
        rb1.setSelectedIcon(dw);
        rb1.setPressedIcon(dwr);
        rb1.setSelected(true);
        rb1.setToolTipText("RadioButton with a Icon");
        p2.add(rb1);
        rbg2.add(rb1);

        p3.setLayout(new GridLayout(1, 3));
        p3.setBorder(new EtchedBorder());

        rb1 = new JRadioButton("Yes", r);
        rbg3.add(rb1);
        rb1.setToolTipText("RadioButton with a Icon and Text");
        rb1.setSelected(true);
        rb1.setSelectedIcon(rs);
        rb1.setPressedIcon(rp);
        rb1.setMnemonic('y');
        p3.add(rb1);

        rb1 = new JRadioButton("Maybe", r);
        rbg3.add(rb1);
        rb1.setToolTipText("RadioButton with a Icon and Text");
        rb1.setSelected(true);
        rb1.setSelectedIcon(rs);
        rb1.setPressedIcon(rp);
        rb1.setMnemonic('m');
        p3.add(rb1);

        rb1 = new JRadioButton("No", r);
        rbg3.add(rb1);
        rb1.setToolTipText("RadioButton with a Icon and Text");
        rb1.setSelected(true);
        rb1.setSelectedIcon(rs);
        rb1.setPressedIcon(rp);
        rb1.setMnemonic('n');
        p3.add(rb1);
           // add subpanels to panel
        add(p1);
        add(p2);
        add(p3);
    }
    public void paint(Graphics g)
    {
        super.paint(g); // required to see Swing components.
    }
}
```

## Borders

The java.awt.swing.border package consists of classes enabling you to draw various borders around components. They all implement the Border interface, which consists of three methods:

**`public Insets getBorderInsets(Component c)`**
Defines the drawable area necessary to draw the border

**`public boolean isBorderOpaque()`**
Defines if the border area is opaque or transparent

**`public void paintBorder (Component c, Graphics g,
                    int x, int y, int width, int height)`**
Defines how to draw the border within the specified area. This method should only draw into the area requested with getBorderInsets.

The Border interface is implemented by JComponent, so all subclasses inherit bordering.

The nine built-in borders provided by Swing are:

BevelBorder - A 3D border that may be raised or lowered

CompoundBorder - A border that can nest multiple borders

DefaultBorder - A class that implements the Border interface, but does nothing

EmptyBorder - A border where you specify the reserved space for an undrawn border

EtchedBorder - A border that appears as a groove, instead of raised or lowered

LineBorder - A border for single color borders, with arbitrary thickness

MatteBorder - A border that permits tiling of an icon or color

SoftBevelBorder - A 3D border with softened corners

TitledBorder - A border that permits title strings in arbitrary locations

## JLayeredPane

A JLayeredPane container allows you to overlap or superimpose components. It places its children in numbered layers that define the order in which its components are painted. When adding a component to the pane, you specify a layer in which to place it:

```
myLayeredPane.add(myComponent, new Integer(3));
```

The default layer has the value JLayeredPane.DEFAULT_LAYER.

You can add or subtract values from this value to have things appear in layers above or below it.

The LayoutManager of each pane determines what happens with the layers.

A FlowLayout or GridLayout places the components as they are added. They are not drawn on top of each other.

## Layered Pane Example

**LayeredPaneEx.java**
```java
import java.awt.*;
import java.awt.event.*;

import javax.swing.*;
import javax.swing.event.*;
import javax.swing.plaf.*;
import javax.swing.border.*;
import javax.swing.text.*;

class LayeredPaneEx extends JFrame
{
        private int j = 0;
        private LayeredPane p = new LayeredPane();

        LayeredPaneEx()
        {
                super("LayeredPanes");

                Container c = getContentPane();
                c.add(p);
        }
```

```
        public static void main(String args[])
        {
                LayeredPaneEx f = new LayeredPaneEx();
                f.addWindowListener(new WindowAdapter() {
                        public void windowClosing(WindowEvent e)
                  {System.exit(0);}
                });
                f.setSize(350, 450);
                f.setVisible(true);

        }
}

class LayeredPane extends JLayeredPane
{
        JButton b1, b2, b3, b4, b5;
        public LayeredPane()
        {
                add(b1=new JButton("zero"), new Integer(0));
                add(b2=new JButton("one"), new Integer(1));
                add(b3=new JButton("two"), new Integer(2));
                add(b4=new JButton("three"), new Integer(3));

                b1.setBounds(100, 100, 90, 50);
                b2.setBounds(140, 130, 90, 50);
                b3.setBounds(180, 160, 90, 50);
                b4.setBounds(220, 190, 90, 50);
        }
}
```

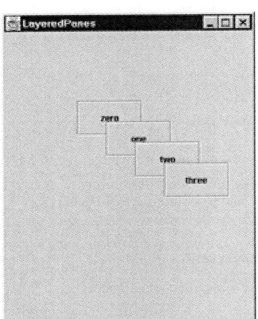

## JTabbedPane

The JTabbedPane component creates a "tab card" look.for easy access to multiple panels. After creating a JTabbedPane object, add "tab cards" to it with the addTab method.

There are three forms for the addTab method. The simplest one offers a quick way to associate a JToolTip to a tab, while the others supportl text, an Icon, or both. Any Component subclass object can be added to a card.

```
addTab(String title, Component c)
```
- Create a new tab with specified title as tab label and specified component on the tab.

```
addTab(String title, Icon icon, Component c)
```
- Creates tab with an icon and title. Either may be null.

```
addTab(String title, Icon icon, Component c, String tip)
```
– Creates tab with an icon, title and tip.

Sample Code:

```java
public class TabbedPanel extends JPanel
{
        String tabs[] = {"One", "Two", "Three", "Four"};
        public JTabbedPane tabbedPane = new JTabbedPane();
        public TabbedPanel()
        {
                setLayout(new BorderLayout());

                for(int i=0;i<tabs.length;i++)
                        tabbedPane.addTab(tabs[i], null, // does tabbing
                                        createPane(tabs[i]));

                tabbedPane.setSelectedIndex(0);
                add(tabbedPane, BorderLayout.CENTER);
        }
        JPanel createPane(String s)
        {
                JPanel p = new JPanel();
                p.setBackground(SystemColor.control);
                p.add(new JLabel(s));
                return p;
        }
}
```

## Tabbed Pane Example

## File: TabbedPaneEx.java

```java
import java.awt.*;
import java.awt.event.*;

import javax.swing.*;
import javax.swing.event.*;
import javax.swing.plaf.*;
import javax.swing.border.*;
import javax.swing.text.*;

class TabbedPaneEx extends JFrame
{
        private int j = 0;
        private TabbedPanel p = new TabbedPanel();

        TabbedPaneEx()
        {
                super("TabbedPanes");

                Container c = getContentPane();
                c.add(p);
        }
        public static void main(String args[])
        {
                TabbedPaneEx f = new TabbedPaneEx();
                f.addWindowListener(new WindowAdapter() {
                        public void windowClosing(WindowEvent e)
                        {System.exit(0);}
                });
                f.setSize(350, 450);
                f.setVisible(true);
        }
}

class TabbedPanel extends JPanel
{
        private String tabs[] = {"Labels and Buttons","Checkboxes",
                                "RadioButtons"};
        private JTabbedPane tabbedPane = new JTabbedPane();
        private MyJLBPanel p1 = new MyJLBPanel();
        private CheckboxPanel p2 = new CheckboxPanel();
        private RadioButtonPanel p3 = new RadioButtonPanel();
```

```java
        public TabbedPanel()
        {
                setLayout(new BorderLayout());
                tabbedPane.addTab(tabs[0], null, p1); // Sets up tab panes.
                tabbedPane.addTab(tabs[1], null, p2);
                tabbedPane.addTab(tabs[2], null, p3);

                tabbedPane.setSelectedIndex(0);
                add(tabbedPane, BorderLayout.CENTER);
        }
}


        // The definition of the panels on each tab pane. Each panel was defined
        // in previous examples.

class MyJLBPanel extends JPanel implements ActionListener
{
        private int j = 0;

        MyJLBPanel()
        {
                Icon i = new ImageIcon("cow.gif");

                JButton b1 = new JButton("Tea", i);
                b1.setBackground(Color.green);
                b1.setVerticalTextPosition(JButton.TOP);
                b1.setHorizontalTextPosition(JButton.LEFT);
                b1.setMnemonic('t');
                b1.setBorder(new MatteBorder(5,5,5,5, Color.darkGray));

                JLabel labela = new JLabel("The true story");
                labela.setToolTipText("Big help");
                labela.setForeground(Color.red);
                labela.setVerticalTextPosition(JLabel.CENTER);
                labela.setHorizontalTextPosition(JLabel.LEFT);
                labela.setIcon(i);
                labela.setHorizontalAlignment(JLabel.RIGHT);
                labela.setBorder(new EtchedBorder());

                JButton b2 = new JButton("Coffee", i);
                b2.setBackground(Color.lightGray);
                b2.setVerticalTextPosition(JButton.BOTTOM);
                b2.setHorizontalTextPosition(JButton.RIGHT);
                b2.setMnemonic('c');

                JLabel labelb = new JLabel("The other story");
                labelb.setToolTipText("Little help");
                labelb.setForeground(Color.black);
                labelb.setVerticalTextPosition(JLabel.BOTTOM);
                labelb.setHorizontalTextPosition(JLabel.CENTER);
```

```java
                    labelb.setIcon(i);
                    labelb.setHorizontalAlignment(JLabel.CENTER);
                    labelb.setBorder(new LineBorder(Color.black, 5));

                    b1.addActionListener(this);
                    b2.addActionListener(this);
                    b1.requestFocus();
                    setLayout(new BoxLayout(this, BoxLayout.Y_AXIS));
                    add(Box.createVerticalStrut(10));
                    add(b1);
                    add(Box.createVerticalStrut(10));
                    add(labela);
                    add(Box.createVerticalStrut(10));
                    add(b2);
                    add(Box.createVerticalStrut(10));
                    add(labelb);
                    add(Box.createHorizontalStrut(10));
            }
            public void paint(Graphics g)
            {
                    super.paint(g);
            }
            public void actionPerformed(ActionEvent e)
            {
                    getGraphics().drawString(
                                    ((JButton)e.getSource()).getText(),
                                    250, 100 + 15*j++);
            }
}

class CheckboxPanel extends JPanel
{
        private Icon unchecked = new ToggleIcon (false);
        private Icon checked = new ToggleIcon (true);
        private Icon b1 = new ImageIcon("b1.gif");
        private Icon b2 = new ImageIcon("b2.gif");
        private Icon b3 = new ImageIcon("b3.gif");
        private Icon b4 = new ImageIcon("cow.gif");
        private JCheckBox c3, c4, c5;

        public CheckboxPanel()
        {
            setLayout(new GridLayout(5, 1));
            JCheckBox c1 = new JCheckBox("Checkbox1", true);
            c1.setIcon(unchecked);
            c1.setSelectedIcon(checked);
            c1.setToolTipText("This is Checkbox 1");
            c1.setMnemonic('1');
```

```java
        JCheckBox c2 = new JCheckBox("Checkbox2", false);
        c2.setIcon(unchecked);
        c2.setToolTipText("This is Checkbox 2");
        c2.setMnemonic('2');
        c2.setSelectedIcon(checked);
        c3 = new JCheckBox("Checkbox3", b1);
        c3.setSelectedIcon(b2);
        c3.setDisabledIcon(b3);
        c3.setMnemonic('3');

        c4 = new JCheckBox("Checkbox4", b1);
        c4.setSelectedIcon(b4);
        c4.setDisabledIcon(b3);
        c4.setMnemonic('4');
        c5 = new JCheckBox("Checkbox5", b1);
        c5.setSelectedIcon(b2);
        c5.setDisabledIcon(b3);
        c5.setMnemonic('5');

        add(c1);
        add(c2);
        add(c3);
        add(c4);
        add(c5);
}
class ToggleIcon implements Icon
{
        boolean state;

        public ToggleIcon (boolean s)
        {
                state = s;
        }
        public void paintIcon(Component c, Graphics g, int x,
                                                       int y)
        {
                int width = getIconWidth();
                int height = getIconHeight();
                g.setColor (Color.darkGray);
                if (state)
                        g.fillRect(x, y, width, height);
                else
                        g.drawOval(x, y, width, height);
        }
        public int getIconWidth()
        {
                return 15;
        }
```

```java
        public int getIconHeight()
        {
                return 15;
        }
    }
}


class RadioButtonPanel extends JPanel
{
        private JRadioButton rb1, rb2, rb3;
        private ButtonGroup rbg1 = new ButtonGroup();
        private ButtonGroup rbg2 = new ButtonGroup();
        private ButtonGroup rbg3 = new ButtonGroup();
        private JPanel p1, p2, p3;

        public RadioButtonPanel()
        {
                Icon d2 = new ImageIcon("b1.gif");
                Icon dw  = new ImageIcon("b2.gif");
                Icon dwr = new ImageIcon("b3.gif");
                Icon r = new ImageIcon("r.gif");
                Icon rs  = new ImageIcon("rs.gif");
                Icon rp = new ImageIcon("rp.gif");

                p1 = new JPanel();
                p2 = new JPanel();
                p3 = new JPanel();

                setLayout(new GridLayout(3,1));
                p1.setLayout(new GridLayout(1, 4));
                p1.setBorder(new EtchedBorder());

                JLabel jb = new JLabel("Dogs: ");
                jb.setFont(new Font("SansSerif", Font.BOLD,14));
                p1.add(jb);

                rb1 = new JRadioButton("Fido");
                rb1.setMnemonic('f');
                rb1.setToolTipText("We like Fido");
                p1.add(rb1);
                rbg1.add(rb1);
                rb1.setSelected(true);

                rb2 = new JRadioButton("Lassie");
                rb2.setMnemonic ('l');
                rb2.setToolTipText("We like Lassie");
                p1.add(rb2);
                rbg1.add(rb2);
```

```java
rb3 = new JRadioButton("Shep");
rb3.setMnemonic ('s');
rb3.setToolTipText("We like Shep");
p1.add(rb3);
rbg1.add(rb3);

p2.setLayout(new GridLayout(1, 3));
p2.setBorder(new EtchedBorder());

rb1 = new JRadioButton(d2);
rb1.setSelectedIcon(dw);
rb1.setPressedIcon(dwr);
rb1.setSelected(true);
rb1.setToolTipText("RadioButton with a Icon");
p2.add(rb1);
rbg2.add(rb1);

rb1 = new JRadioButton(d2);
rb1.setSelectedIcon(dw);
rb1.setPressedIcon(dwr);
rb1.setSelected(true);
rb1.setToolTipText("RadioButton with a Icon");
p2.add(rb1);
rbg2.add(rb1);

rb1 = new JRadioButton(d2);
rb1.setSelectedIcon(dw);
rb1.setPressedIcon(dwr);
rb1.setSelected(true);
rb1.setToolTipText("RadioButton with a Icon");
p2.add(rb1);
rbg2.add(rb1);

p3.setLayout(new GridLayout(1, 3));
p3.setBorder(new EtchedBorder());

rb1 = new JRadioButton("Yes", r);
rbg3.add(rb1);
rb1.setToolTipText("RadioButton with a Icon and Text");
rb1.setSelected(true);
rb1.setSelectedIcon(rs);
rb1.setPressedIcon(rp);
rb1.setMnemonic('y');
p3.add(rb1);

rb1 = new JRadioButton("Maybe", r);
rbg3.add(rb1);
rb1.setToolTipText("RadioButton with a Icon and Text");
rb1.setSelected(true);
rb1.setSelectedIcon(rs);
rb1.setPressedIcon(rp);
rb1.setMnemonic('m');
```

```
            p3.add(rb1);

            rb1 = new JRadioButton("No", r);
            rbg3.add(rb1);
            rb1.setToolTipText("RadioButton with a Icon and Text");
            rb1.setSelected(true);
            rb1.setSelectedIcon(rs);
            rb1.setPressedIcon(rp);
            rb1.setMnemonic('n');
            p3.add(rb1);

            add(p1);
            add(p2);
            add(p3);
        }

public void paint(Graphics g)
        {
            super.paint(g);
        }
}
```

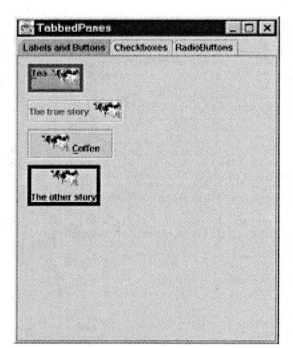
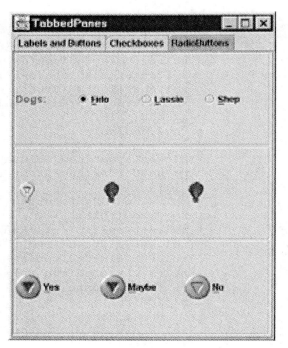

## JSplitPane

JSplitPane supports user controlled resizing of two components within a container.

You can place a JSplitPane within a JSplitPane if there are more than two components, and you can specify whether splitting is vertical or horizontal.

The setContinuousLayout(true) method causes each pane to be updated continuously as the splitter is dragged.

## SplitPane Example

### File: SplitPaneEx2.java

```java
import java.awt.*;
import java.awt.event.*;

import javax.swing.*;
import javax.swing.event.*;
import javax.swing.plaf.*;
import javax.swing.border.*;
import javax.swing.text.*;

class SplitPaneEx2 extends JFrame
{
        private int j = 0;
        private SplitPanel2 p = new SplitPanel2();

        SplitPaneEx2()
        {
                super("Split Panes 2");

                Container c = getContentPane();
                c.add(p);
        }
        public static void main(String args[])
        {
                SplitPaneEx2 f = new SplitPaneEx2();
                f.addWindowListener(new WindowAdapter() {
                        public void windowClosing(WindowEvent e)
                        {System.exit(0);}
                });
                f.setSize(520, 450);
                f.setVisible(true);
        }
}
```

```java
class SplitPanel2 extends JPanel
{
        public SplitPanel2()
        {
                CheckboxPanel pcheck = new CheckboxPanel();
                RadioButtonPanel pradio = new RadioButtonPanel();

                        // sets up split pane.
                add(new JSplitPane(JSplitPane.HORIZONTAL_SPLIT, pcheck,
                                                                pradio));
        }
}


        // Defines JPanels in split pane. These panels were used in
        // earlier examples.

class CheckboxPanel extends JPanel
{
        private Icon unchecked = new ToggleIcon (false);
        private Icon checked = new ToggleIcon (true);
        private Icon b1 = new ImageIcon("b1.gif");
        private Icon b2 = new ImageIcon("b2.gif");
        private Icon b3 = new ImageIcon("b3.gif");
        private Icon b4 = new ImageIcon("cow.gif");
        private JCheckBox c3, c4, c5;

        public CheckboxPanel()
        {
// crucial: must set these sizes or split pane doesn't work.
        setPreferredSize(new Dimension(250, 300));
        setMinimumSize(new Dimension(200, 300));

        setLayout(new GridLayout(5, 1));
        JCheckBox c1 = new JCheckBox("Checkbox1", true);
        c1.setIcon(unchecked);
        c1.setSelectedIcon(checked);
        c1.setToolTipText("This is Checkbox 1");
        c1.setMnemonic('1');

        JCheckBox c2 = new JCheckBox("Checkbox2", false);
        c2.setIcon(unchecked);
        c2.setToolTipText("This is Checkbox 2");
        c2.setMnemonic('2');
        c2.setSelectedIcon(checked);

        c3 = new JCheckBox("Checkbox3", b1);
        c3.setSelectedIcon(b2);
        c3.setDisabledIcon(b3);
        c3.setMnemonic('3');
```

```java
        c4 = new JCheckBox("Checkbox4", b1);
        c4.setSelectedIcon(b4);
        c4.setDisabledIcon(b3);
        c4.setMnemonic('4');

        c5 = new JCheckBox("Checkbox5", b1);
        c5.setSelectedIcon(b2);
        c5.setDisabledIcon(b3);
        c5.setMnemonic('5');

        add(c1);
        add(c2);
        add(c3);
        add(c4);
        add(c5);
    }
class ToggleIcon implements Icon
{
        boolean state;

        public ToggleIcon (boolean s)
        {
                state = s;
        }

        public void paintIcon(Component c, Graphics g, int x,
                                                        int y)
        {
                int width = getIconWidth();
                int height = getIconHeight();
                g.setColor (Color.darkGray);
                if (state)
                        g.fillRect(x, y, width, height);
                else
                        g.drawOval(x, y, width, height);
        }
        public int getIconWidth()
        {
                return 15;
        }
        public int getIconHeight()
        {
                return 15;
        }
    }
  }
}
```

```
class RadioButtonPanel extends JPanel
{
        private JRadioButton rb1, rb2, rb3;
        private ButtonGroup rbg1 = new ButtonGroup();
        private ButtonGroup rbg2 = new ButtonGroup();
        private ButtonGroup rbg3 = new ButtonGroup();
        private JPanel p1, p2, p3;

        public RadioButtonPanel()
        {
                Icon d2 = new ImageIcon("b1.gif");
                Icon dw  = new ImageIcon("b2.gif");
                Icon dwr = new ImageIcon("b3.gif");
                Icon r = new ImageIcon("r.gif");
                Icon rs  = new ImageIcon("rs.gif");
                Icon rp = new ImageIcon("rp.gif");

                p1 = new JPanel();
                p2 = new JPanel();
                p3 = new JPanel();

// crucial: must set these sizes or split pane doesn't work.
                setPreferredSize(new Dimension(250, 300));
                setMinimumSize(new Dimension(200, 300));

                setLayout(new GridLayout(3,1));
                p1.setLayout(new GridLayout(1, 4));
                p1.setBorder(new EtchedBorder());

                JLabel jb = new JLabel("Dogs: ");
                jb.setFont(new Font("SansSerif", Font.BOLD,14));
                p1.add(jb);

                rb1 = new JRadioButton("Fido");
                rb1.setMnemonic('f');
                rb1.setToolTipText("We like Fido");
                p1.add(rb1);
                rbg1.add(rb1);
                rb1.setSelected(true);

                rb2 = new JRadioButton("Lassie");
                rb2.setMnemonic ('l');
                rb2.setToolTipText("We like Lassie");
                p1.add(rb2);
                rbg1.add(rb2);

                rb3 = new JRadioButton("Shep");
                rb3.setMnemonic ('s');
                rb3.setToolTipText("We like Shep");
                p1.add(rb3);
                rbg1.add(rb3);
```

```java
p2.setLayout(new GridLayout(1, 3));
p2.setBorder(new EtchedBorder());

rb1 = new JRadioButton(d2);
rb1.setSelectedIcon(dw);
rb1.setPressedIcon(dwr);
rb1.setSelected(true);
rb1.setToolTipText("RadioButton with a Icon");
p2.add(rb1);
rbg2.add(rb1);

rb1 = new JRadioButton(d2);
rb1.setSelectedIcon(dw);
rb1.setPressedIcon(dwr);
rb1.setSelected(true);
rb1.setToolTipText("RadioButton with a Icon");
p2.add(rb1);
rbg2.add(rb1);

rb1 = new JRadioButton(d2);
rb1.setSelectedIcon(dw);
rb1.setPressedIcon(dwr);
rb1.setSelected(true);
rb1.setToolTipText("RadioButton with a Icon");
p2.add(rb1);
rbg2.add(rb1);

p3.setLayout(new GridLayout(1, 3));
p3.setBorder(new EtchedBorder());

rb1 = new JRadioButton("Yes", r);
rbg3.add(rb1);
rb1.setToolTipText("RadioButton with a Icon and Text");
rb1.setSelected(true);
rb1.setSelectedIcon(rs);
rb1.setPressedIcon(rp);
rb1.setMnemonic('y');
p3.add(rb1);

rb1 = new JRadioButton("Maybe", r);
rbg3.add(rb1);
rb1.setToolTipText("RadioButton with a Icon and Text");
rb1.setSelected(true);
rb1.setSelectedIcon(rs);
rb1.setPressedIcon(rp);
rb1.setMnemonic('m');
p3.add(rb1);
```

```
        rb1 = new JRadioButton("No", r);
        rbg3.add(rb1);
        rb1.setToolTipText("RadioButton with a Icon and Text");
        rb1.setSelected(true);
        rb1.setSelectedIcon(rs);
        rb1.setPressedIcon(rp);
        rb1.setMnemonic('n');
        p3.add(rb1);

        add(p1);
        add(p2);
        add(p3);
    }
    public void paint(Graphics g)
    {
        super.paint(g);
    }
}
```

Normal starting view using preferred size.

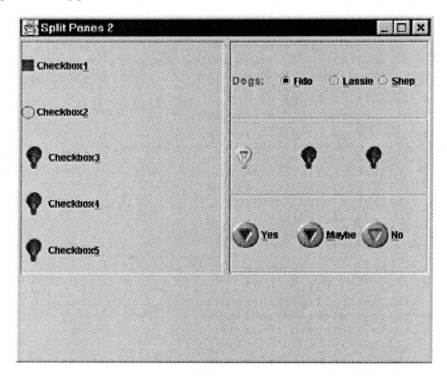

Adjustable border dragged to the right as much as possible.

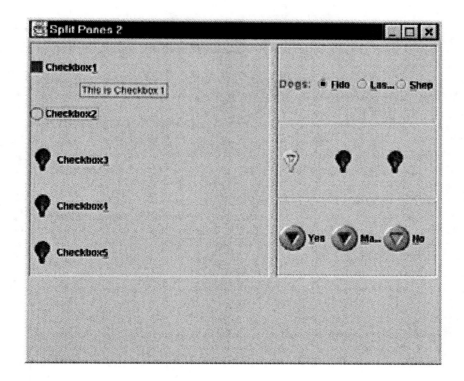

Adjustable border dragged to the left as much as possible.

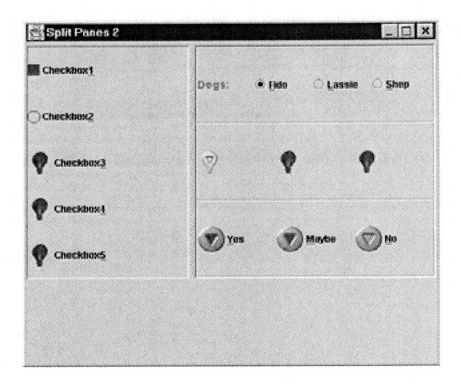

# SUMMARY

Java provides many exciting new capabilities in the JFC and its Swing components.

# *Appendix F.  JDBC and the JDBC-ODBC Bridge*

## OBJECTIVES

At the end of this module you should be able to:

- Understand features of JDBC and the JDBC-ODBC bridge.

# JDBC (Java DataBase Connectivity)

- Direct Connection to a Database

- Data Management and Retrieval Using SQL

- Supported by Oracle, Sybase and other Databases.

# JDBC-ODBC BRIDGE

- Connects Java JDBC to standard ODBC Database interface

- General solution until all DB vendors support JDBC API.

- Used with databases not supporting JDBC directly.

# Sample JDBC-ODBC Program

This program illustrates many of the features of JDBC. For more information see some of the many excellent books on the subject.

**File: JdbcEx.java**

```java
import java.net.URL;
import java.sql.*;

class JdbcEx
{
    public static void main (String args[])
    {
        String url   = "jdbc:odbc:myDatabase";
        String query = "SELECT * FROM emp"; // Standard query.

        try
        {
            // Load the jdbc-odbc bridge driver. Provided by vendor.

            Class.forName ("jdbc.odbc.JdbcOdbcDriver");

            // Attempt to connect to a driver.  Each one
            // of the registered drivers will be loaded until
            // one is found that can process this URL

            Connection myCon = DriverManager.getConnection (
                        url, "myUserName", "myPassword");

            // If unable to connect, an exception would be thrown.
            // If no throw, then successfully connected to the URL

            // Check for, and display and warnings generated
            // by the connect.

            checkWarnings (myCon.getWarnings ());

            // Get the DatabaseMetaData object and display
            // information about the connection.

            DatabaseMetaData dbma = myCon.getMetaData ();

            System.out.println("\nConnected to " + dbma.getURL());
            System.out.println("Driver         " + dbma.getDriverName());
            System.out.println("Version        "+dbma.getDriverVersion());
            System.out.println("");
```

```java
        // Create a Statement object so we can submit SQL statements
        // to the driver.

        Statement stmt = myCon.createStatement ();

        // Submit a query, creating a ResultSet object.
        // A result set contains a "table" of rows and columns of
        // retrieved records.

        ResultSet myResults = stmt.executeQuery (query);

        // Display all columns and rows from the result set

        showResultSet (myResults);

        // Close the result set

        myResults.close();

        // Close the statement

        stmt.close();

        // Close the connection

        myCon.close();
    }
    catch (SQLException ex)
    {

        // If a SQLException was generated.  Catch it and
        // display the error information.  Note that there
        // could be multiple error objects chained together.

        System.out.println("\n*** SQLException caught ***\n");

        while (ex != null) {
            System.out.println ("SQLState: " +
                ex.getSQLState ());

            System.out.println ("Message:  " +
                ex.getMessage ());

            System.out.println ("Vendor:   " +

            ex.getErrorCode ());
            ex = ex.getNextException ();

            System.out.println ("");
        }
    }
```

```
        catch (java.lang.Exception ex)
        {

            // Got some other type of exception.  Dump it.

            ex.printStackTrace ();
        }
}




//----------------------------------------------------------------
// checkWarnings - Checks for and displays warnings.  Returns true if a
// warning is found.
//----------------------------------------------------------------

private static boolean checkWarnings (SQLWarning warn)
            throws SQLException
{
        boolean rc = false;

        // If a SQLWarning object was given, display the warning messages.
        // There could be multiple warnings chained together

        if (warn != null)
        {
            System.out.println ("\n *** Warning ***\n");
            rc = true;
            while (warn != null)
            {
                System.out.println ("SQLState: "+warn.getSQLState ());
                System.out.println ("Message:  "+warn.getMessage ());
                System.out.println ("Vendor:   "+warn.getErrorCode());
                System.out.println ("");

                warn = warn.getNextWarning ();
            }
        }
        return rc;
}
```

```java
//----------------------------------------------------------------
// showResultSet
// Displays all columns and rows in the given result set
//----------------------------------------------------------------

private static void showResultSet (ResultSet rs) throws SQLException
{
      int i;

      // Get the ResultSetMetaData - provides the column headings

      ResultSetMetaData rsmd = rs.getMetaData ();

      // Get the number of columns in the result set

      int numCols = rsmd.getColumnCount ();

      // Display column headings

      for (i=1; i<=numCols; i++)
      {
            if (i > 1) System.out.print(",");
            System.out.print(rsmd.getColumnLabel(i));
      }
      System.out.println("");

      // Display data, fetching until end of the result set

      boolean more = rs.next ();
      while (more)
      {
            // Loop through each column, getting the
            // column data and displaying

            for (i=1; i<=numCols; i++)
            {
                  if (i > 1) System.out.print(",");
                  System.out.print(rs.getString(i));
            }
            System.out.println("");

            // Fetch the next result set row

            more = rs.next ();
      }
}
}
```

# *INDEX*

| |
|---|

-- operator, 34

| ! |
|---|

!= operator, 43

| & |
|---|

&&, 42
&& operator, 43

| * |
|---|

*= operator, 33

| | |
|---|

||, 42
|| operator, 43

| + |
|---|

+ overload, 177
++ operator, 34
+= operator, 33
+= overload, 177

| < |
|---|

< operator, 43
<= operator, 43

| = |
|---|

== operator, 43, 159

| > |
|---|

> operator, 43
>= operator, 43

| A |
|---|

abstract, 22, 103, 130, 132, 133, 135, 137, 138, 155
abstract class, 130, 132, 133, 135
abstract method, 132
accept(), 523
action(Event e, Object o), 337
**ActionEvent**, 272, 273, 278, 290, 291, 295, 299, 306, 348, 351, 354, 360, 365, 370, 380, 393, 430, 451, 453, 460, 461, 466, 471, 532, 538, 545, 555, 559, 561, 563, 564, 573, 575, 578
**ActionListener**, 275, 276, 290, 291, 293, 298, 299, 306, 346, 347, 350, 353, 360, 364, 368, 380, 402, 419, 428, 430, 450, 452, 459, 461, 465, 470, 531, 532, 536, 537, 543, 553, 559, 561, 563, 564, 575, 577, 578
**actionPerformed()**, 272, 278, 290, 291, 295, 299, 306, 345, 348, 351, 354, 359, 360, 365, 370, 380, 430, 451, 453, 460, 461, 466, 471, 530, 532, 538, 545, 555, 559, 561, 563, 564, 573, 575, 578
ActionPerformed(), 419
activeCount(), 231
add(), 301, 547
add() methods, 377
**addActionListener()**, 276, 290, 291, 293, 299, 306, 347, 350, 353, 360, 364, 368, 380, 419, 430, 450, 452, 459, 461, 465, 470, 532, 536, 537, 543, 553, 559, 561, 563, 564, 575, 577
**addAdjustmentListener()**, 276, 368, 369
addElement(), 161, 296, 298
addImage(), 468
addItem(), 337
**addItemListener()**, 276, 337, 338, 341, 342, 343, 345, 350, 353, 419, 430, 575, 577
**addMouseListener()**, 276, 280, 283, 287, 319, 389, 391, 434, 536
**addMouseMotionListener()**, 276, 287
address, 4
addTab method, 617
align attribute
    Applet parameter, 264
and operator, 43
Animations, 458
**anonymous inner class**, 599
append( datatype d), 185
append(char [] carr, int offset, int length), 185
applet, 248
Applet, 152
Applet class, 316

# ABOUT THE AUTHOR

Dr. Stephen Blaha is a nationally known lecturer on programming languages. Dr. Blaha has taught literally thousands of students Java, C and C++. His book, *ANSI C++ for Professional Programmers*, is a standard work in the C++ language with a 5 star rating on Amazon.com. His course materials have been licensed by the largest computer companies to teach to their employees and by major U. S. government agencies. Dr. Blaha is noted for his clear, precise, authoritative style. His books are a joy to read (for the interested programmer) if only because they are short and to the point.